D0984191

CLASS AWARENESS
IN THE UNITED STATES

CLASS AWARENESS
IN THE UNITED STATES

Mary R. Jackman
and Robert W. Jackman

UNIVERSITY OF CALIFORNIA PRESS
Berkeley   Los Angeles   London

Portions of chapter 2 appeared previously under the
title "The subjective meaning of social class
identification in the United States," in the *Public
Opinion Quarterly*, 43 (Winter 1979), pp. 443-462.

UNIVERSITY OF CALIFORNIA PRESS
Berkeley and Los Angeles, California

UNIVERSITY OF CALIFORNIA PRESS, LTD.
London, England

Library of Congress Cataloging in Publication Data

Jackman, Mary R., 1948-
    Class Awareness in the United States.

    Bibliography: p.
    1. Social classes—United States. I. Jackman,
Robert W., 1946-   . II. Title.
HN90.S6J3   305.5'0973   82-2766
ISBN 0-520-04674-9   AACR2

Printed in the United States of America

1 2 3 4 5 6 7 8 9

In loving memory of
Betty and Roy

Contents

Acknowledgments

Some years ago, we wrote a paper on class identification in the United States. For a variety of reasons—most notably, the constraints imposed by secondary analysis of data collected by others—the focus of that paper was relatively narrow, and did not fully represent our concerns. Hence this book.

The data for this book were gathered as part of a larger project by Mary Jackman on intergroup attitudes and group consciousness. This larger project was funded by the National Institute of Mental Health (MH-26433) and the National Science Foundation (SOC 75-00405 and SOC 78-16857). Several people provided critical support and encouragement at the initial stages, which ensured that the project got off the ground. We are especially grateful to Joyce Lazar (of the National Institute of Mental Health), Gerald Gurin and Patricia Gurin (of the University of Michigan), Donald R. Ploch (then of the National Science Foundation), Sheldon Stryker (of Indiana University), and William J. Wilson (of the University of Chicago).

Our analyses are based on a sample survey of the United States, conducted by the Survey Research Center of the University of Michigan. We thank the staff of the Center for their excellent fieldwork and coding of the data. In particular, Jeanne Castro expertly managed the fieldwork, and made sure that deadlines were met as the data were collected. Jeanne and other members of the Field Office (including people from the interviewing staff) and the Coding Section also provided invaluable advice during the pretesting of the questionnaire. In a similar way, we are indebted to Mary Scheuer Senter for her resourceful suggestions and tireless assistance in all phases of the data collection process (including the construction of the questionnaire) and in the initial phases of the data analysis.

Since the data were collected, many others have been instrumental in helping us to complete this book. Among these are Anne Adams, Marie Crane, Leslie Eveland, Maria Kousis, Michael Muha, Suzanne Purcell, Arlene Sanderson, and Margalit Tal. Each of these individuals has been involved in different aspects of the analysis, ranging from the construction of complicated measures to the tedious chore of checking for errors.

We would also like to thank the anonymous referees for their helpful comments and criticisms on the original manuscript, and the people at the University of California Press for the professional way they produced this book. We are especially grateful to Stanley Holwitz for his patience and encouragement, and for his prompt handling of the manuscript.

Completion of the manuscript was materially aided by the National Institute of Mental Health, in the form of a Research Scientist Development Award to Mary Jackman (MH-00252). It was also facilitated by a fellowship to Robert Jackman from the John Simon Guggenheim Memorial Foundation, by the political science department at Michigan State University (which provided released time from teaching), and by the College Scholar program at Michigan State University. We thank these organizations for their support.

We would like to emphasize that this book is in every sense a joint effort, so that we share any blame for what follows. Mary Jackman drafted the first version of chapter 2, while Robert Jackman wrote the first draft of chapter 4. The drafting of the remaining chapters and the revisions to all chapters were done jointly. The dining room table may be a little the worse for wear, but we enjoyed writing this book.

Finally, we would like to thank our parents for their support and encouragement over the years, and for their understanding (if not appreciation) of the fact that we have been incorrigibly bad correspondents. Our daughter Rachael has mercifully remained oblivious to our efforts—we wish her well as she strives to perfect her game of Chutes and Ladders.

February, 1982

1

The Issues

Is class meaningful in the United States? The imperfection of the pure Marxist model of class has spawned a variety of answers to this question, answers that range from neo-Marxist modifications of the original model to arguments denying the contemporary relevance of class. The debate triggered by these analyses has been marked by two broad features. To begin with, class has been regarded by both its proponents and its detractors as something that must be simple and clear-cut. Along with this, most attention has centered on the structural aspects of class, while its subjective elements have been relatively neglected.

This book is an attempt to reorient the analysis of social class. First, we seek to break away from the restrictive assumptions on which much of the debate about class has been predicated. Second, we redirect attention to the subjective interpretation of social class: the meaning and reality of class cannot be evaluated without attention to its place in the public consciousness.

The lines of debate about class were set by the nature of the disagreement between Karl Marx and Max Weber. It hardly needs mentioning here that for Marx, classes were fundamentally and simply determined by relationship to the means of production, with the defining distinction being between owners and nonowners of capital. From this distinction arose clearly bounded groups with mutually opposed economic interests. These groups gradually evolved into distinctive social and political communities locked in conflict.

Weber (1946) disputed the simplicity of this model and introduced a series of supplementary considerations with which he sought to undercut the import of class. These modifications took two main forms. First, he argued that relationship to the means of production was not the only source of economic differentiation, and instead pointed less deterministically to a variety of market relations that can produce classes. Second, he relegated class narrowly to the economic sphere and questioned the inevitability of any relationship between economic and social standing, stressing instead the multiple bases or dimensions of stratification. Weber conceived of authority hierarchies as a formidable stratifying force, and he introduced the concept of status groups as something quite distinct from economic classes. Whereas class represents a group of people with similar economic life chances, status groups are social communities with which people identify. Weber argued that status groups frequently have a cultural base, and, indeed, he went so far as to assert that they "hinder the strict carrying through of the sheer market principle. *In the present context, they are of interest to us only from this one point of view* [italics added]" (Weber 1946:185). The legacy of Weber's general challenge to Marx has been that complications are typically treated as factors that undermine, rather than elaborate on, the idea of class.

The most prevalent expression of this legacy is that those who have found any single differentiating characteristic to be unsatisfactory have eschewed any conception of social class as too simplistic. At the same time, advocates of social class have generally felt it necessary to identify social classes according to a single defining characteristic: relationship to the means of production, authority relations, type of work. Thus, the legacy of Weber's dispute with Marx is a false distinction between class as something simple and clearly defined and social stratification as a multidimensional and complicated phenomenon.

This difference has been further widened by the pronounced preference of class theorists for portraying class systems as dichotomous: owners versus workers (Marx), those with authority and those without it (Dahrendorf 1959:165-73), or manual versus nonmanual labor (Goldthorpe et al. 1969; Vanneman and Pampel 1977; Gagliani 1981). At times, the desire to create a two-class system based on a single differentiating characteristic has become somewhat strained. For example, Wright identifies the main rift between the bourgeoisie and the proletariat; after naming the petty bourgeoisie as a distinct group that does not exhibit the full characteristics of either side, he proceeds to identify three "contradictory class locations" that by his own estimates account for between 41 and 53 percent of the population (1979:42). It is ironic that approximately half of the population is thus forced to inhabit what Parkin (1979:22) has called "the Marxist no-man's-land between bourgeoisie and proletariat." A similar predicament has been identified, by Robinson and Kelley (1979), in the authority/no-authority dichotomy. While it may be intuitively pleasing to divide the world into "command" and "obey" classes, closer inspection reveals important differences in degree of authority that make the demarcation of the boundary between those who command and those who obey somewhat arbitrary. Finally, the manual/nonmanual dichotomy has been subject to the criticism that it is an insensitive indicator of occupational differences in educational level, skill, autonomy, income, or feelings of social distance between occupations (Duncan 1966:83-90; Laumann 1966:59).

On the other side of the debate, those who are dissatisfied with the single-criterion, dichotomous class model have moved to the opposite extreme and conceived of social inequality in terms of multiple hierarchies. These hierarchies are not regarded as forming any clear clusters, but instead are taken to identify unbroken continua. For example, degrees of occupational status or prestige replace the idea of discrete classes. In addition, the sensitivity of analysts in this school to the idea of multiple criteria for stratification has often led them to emphasize the nonequivalence of various criteria. This, of course, leads directly to the common view that social life is organized around a plurality of crosscutting status hierarchies. The intersecting nature of these hierarchies works to discourage further the formation of clear-cut social groups or the emergence of group conflict.

Some analysts have pointed to the multiple dimensions of stratification—educational attainment, occupational prestige, earnings, capital assets—and argued that their intersecting nature and the lack of popular consensus about how to "count" these various factors results in popular confusion about social class (e.g., Hartmann and Newcomb 1939; Hodge and Treiman 1968; Nisbet 1970). Because there is no single economic criterion to which people attach overwhelming significance, so it is argued, class cannot become a stimulus around which people's identities are formed. The salience of class is pushed farther toward oblivion by the presence of other bases of affiliation—race, ethnicity, religion, voluntary associations, and so on. These factors are added to the multiple economic dimensions to form a giant web of crosscutting axes that divide and redivide the population into a constantly shifting series of specialized interest groups (see, e.g., Coser 1956:77; Lipset and Bendix 1959:64 ff.; Nisbet 1970; Parsons 1970; Polsby 1980:chap. 6). According to this pluralist view of industrial society, the multiple group memberships of all individuals inhibit the emergence of any single profound line of cleavage. In this fluid context, economic differentiation is seen as an especially improbable candidate for such a role.

The idea that economic distinctions have only passing significance has commonly been reinforced by allusion to other factors, especially in the United States. Among these, de Tocqueville's (1969) emphasis on civic equality, the lack of a landed aristocracy, and the opportunities for mobility is well known and has had considerable influence (see also Bryce 1899:vol. 2). In this spirit, some have argued more recently that the increased affluence and mobility associated with advanced industrial society weakens class awareness (e.g., Lipset 1960:253; Wilensky 1966). Others have even suggested that the tendency toward greater affluence represents a movement toward a "post-industrial" society where traditional class distinctions are of dwindling relevance (e.g., Bell 1973).

Thus, students of social stratification are presented with a choice. On the one hand is a society that is divided according to one powerful criterion into discrete class categories that are conceptually zero-sum and that form the basis for conflict. On the other hand is a pluralist society that arranges individuals harmoniously along a series of intersecting hierarchies. The ideas on both sides of the debate are premised on the assumption that economic differentiation must create a single clear-cut distinction in order to become the basis for the formation of meaningful social groups. This assumption is a false one.

There is nothing intrinsic to the notion of social groups that requires a single identifying criterion for membership. To be sure, the existence of such a criterion would increase the clarity of differentiation, but it is hardly essential. In this respect, it is helpful to compare groups based on race with those based on ethnicity. Racial groups are based on ascriptive physical characteristics that are readily visible. Even here, people must assemble a configuration of characteristics (e.g., skin color, facial features, hair type) to define group membership, but since all the characteristics are physical, their configuration becomes so routine that they are processed as a single criterion (e.g., "black" versus "white"). The definition of ethnic groups is somewhat more complex, since it involves a configuration of different kinds of criteria. These include physical characteristics, language, religious affiliation, cultural values, and (not least) subjective identification. People usually assemble these criteria almost as effortlessly as racial criteria to form an image of what distinguishes, say, Italians from Irish. At the same time, the fact that multiple criteria are involved introduces a little more ambiguity around the edges of group membership. In most cases, assignment to groups is straightforward, but group boundaries are less sharply defined because the various relevant factors are not equally visible or equally weighted by all observers.

The difference between racial and ethnic groups is one of degree rather than one of kind. Even assignment to racial groups is sometimes ambiguous, but less often than with ethnicity because the criteria are fewer and more straightforward. The physical criteria for racial group membership are sufficiently delineated so that in most cases individuals can be readily assigned to groups whether or not they personally identify with a group. On the other hand, neither race nor ethnicity can become the basis for meaningful social communities (Weberian "status groups") unless the relevant criteria assume subjective significance for substantial portions of the population. In this regard, it is important to remember that Weber did not view the haziness or clarity of group boundaries as problematic to the formation of status groups. On the contrary, he argued that status groups are "often of an amorphous kind" (1946:186), and he directed attention to variation in the permeability of status group boundaries in his comparison of caste relations with looser, more informal patterns of differentiation. Ultimately, it is the subjective interpretation of the relevant criteria for group membership (regardless of the number of criteria involved) that lends the resulting groups their character and social significance.

How do these considerations bear on our conception of social classes? They indicate that classes do not have to be based on a single criterion, such as production or authority relations, in order to acquire social significance. Nor do the boundaries between classes have to be precisely drawn or impermeable before people can recognize these classes as meaningful social groups.

If the assumption that classes must be based on a single criterion is a false one, so too is the common view that classes are of necessity based on a zero-sum dichotomy. The preference for dichotomous conceptions of class doubtless stems from the conflict view of society that class theorists have generally espoused (see the discussion on this point in Ossowski 1963:chap. 2). Violent revolutionary conflict is intuitively more comprehensible when considered in terms of two contending parties. Few revolutionary situations, however, actually do involve only two parties. The frequent appearance of only two sides does not reflect the underlying structure of relationships, but rather results from the formation of transitory coalitions among multiple contenders for power. Furthermore, it is important to remember that violent revolutionary conflict is hardly the sole (or even principal) form that class conflict may take, and current patterns in Western societies do not suggest that violent revolution is imminent.

Ironically, although the fascination with a dichotomous conception of class clearly stems from the Marxist link between class and revolution, few contemporary class theorists explicitly build revolution into their models. Even among neo-Marxists, the modifications introduced into Marx's class model are such as to minimize the potential for revolutionary change. Mandel's (1973) conception of the welfare state as a tool of the bourgeoisie that turns crises of overproduction into mere recessions envisions a greatly reduced opportunity for the revolutionary overthrow of capitalism. Wright's (1979) class scheme, which tacitly recognizes the managerial role and places about half of the population in a class position that knows not which side it is on, undercuts the clear and forceful notion of mutual conflict between two opposed camps found in Marx's model. Among non-Marxists, of course, the most popular dichotomy is the manual/nonmanual distinction, and this is often taken to have conflict implications (for example, the "us versus them" view suggested by Goldthorpe et al. [1969] and Vanneman and Pampel [1977]). There is nothing inherent, however, in the blue-collar/white-collar distinction that implies the kind of dominance/subordination relationship productive of zero-sum conflict (Parkin 1979:11-15). In fact, the theoretical underpinnings of the manual/nonmanual scheme run no deeper than a crude representation of occupational standing. Users of the authority dichotomy have also implicitly abandoned revolution as a pivotal idea. The command versus obey distinction (Dahrendorf 1959) may be found in any economic order, and is thus impervious to revolutionary change. Weber (who introduced the concept of authority) was at great pains to point this out, and, indeed, he conceived of bureaucratic authority in hierarchical rather than dichotomous terms.

More fundamentally, any conflict between classes implies the existence of a relationship between them. Some class theorists (e.g., Wright 1979:6-8) have assumed that dichotomous class models correspond exclusively with a relational portrayal of classes, and that gradational schemes preclude the idea that classes are related to one another. But while analyses using dichotomous class schemes have usually been more sensitive to the relational aspects of class, they are not immune from the portrayal of classes as neutrally ordered (see especially many analyses using the blue-collar/white-collar split). Nor are relational models the exclusive prerogative of dichotomous schemes. It needs to be emphasized that *no* system of inequality can neutrally order people according to their position. Inequality, by definition, implies a relationship between the parties involved: one person's privilege rests inevitably on another's loss. Consider inequalities of income and wealth: the standard of living of those at the top depends on the availability of people lower down to provide labor for goods and services at a rate that is cheaper than the rate received by the wealthy (Jencks et al. 1972:chap. 1; Gans 1974:chap. 4). The same principle holds for concepts like status and power. The high status of one group automatically implies the withdrawal of privilege from lower-status groups. Similarly, one group's power depends intrinsically on the subordination of others (Weber 1946:180). In other words, one group cannot be at a relative advantage without taking something from another group.

In light of these considerations, the theoretical imperative for a two-class model is not compelling. First, those who have persevered with the two-class format seem to have backed away from the idea of inevitable revolutionary change, which was the most persuasive (if flawed) rationale for the original two-class model. Second, while it might be easier to conceive of conflict as involving only two sides, it is clear that intergroup conflict can and does occur in situations involving more than two groups. While this argument may seem novel in the class context (but see Westergaard and Resler 1975:368), it has long been clear to students of comparative ethnic relations. Thus, while we readily concede that the conception of social stratification purely in terms of unbroken continua virtually rules out focused conflict,[1] a dichotomous class scheme is not the sole logical alternative.

How then are classes best conceived? Our discussion to this point allows us to eliminate two false leads. Classes do not have to be based on a single criterion in order to become meaningful social groups, and a dichotomous division of groups is not required for conflict to take place. Once we break free of these restrictive assumptions, we can begin to view social classes in a way that is not dictated by the terms of debate originally set by Marx and Weber.

If ethnic groups can be status groups, so too can classes. Notwithstanding Weber's determined effort to separate the concept of status groups from that of classes, there is nothing in his definition of status groups that logically precludes considering classes as social communities. Indeed, rather than undercutting the social significance of class, the substance (as opposed to the spirit) of Weber's discussion of status groups would seem to suggest classes as perfect candidates for social communities.

Like ethnic groups, these communities are loosely bounded and are based on multiple interrelated criteria. For classes, these involve configurations of economic and derivative cultural factors. Economic factors that enter the configuration include level of education, occupational prestige, job skill, security, autonomy and authority, earned income, and capital assets. These interrelated economic factors, in turn, produce variations in life styles that are expressed in patterns of consumption and cultural

---

[1]A recent example of such a conception can be found in Coleman and Rainwater (1978:119), who treat the terms *social position, social status, social standing,* and *social class* as synonymous.

values. Because the definition of classes involves multiple criteria, many of which fall on continua, complete consensus about the position of group boundaries is unlikely. Nonetheless, configurations of characteristics are assembled to form coherent social groups.

That classes are based on economic distinctions gives them a more powerful impetus for the formation of social identities than groups relying more exclusively on cultural factors for their definition (for example, ethnic groups). Economic distinctions routinely produce social differences that are readily visible and keenly experienced. Even Weber conceded that "of course, material monopolies provide the most effective motives for the exclusiveness of a status group; although in themselves they are rarely sufficient, almost always they come into play to some extent" (1946:191). Any social system that involves economic inequality will generate social classes. In social systems that exacerbate economic inequality, classes will be defined with greater sharpness and clarity, but economic distinctions are a sufficiently sensitive matter to produce social classes even when those distinctions are relatively attenuated.[2]

If classes are social groups, then they must exist in the public consciousness. The subjective definition and interpretation of social class is an empirical problem that is critical to any theoretical approach to class. Indeed, it is this issue, more than any other, that points to the inherent limitations of traditional conceptions of class. While those conceptions have provided abstract analyses that illuminate particular features of the social structure, even casual observation of social life reveals that the population has not divided itself up neatly into owners and workers, or into those who have authority and those who do not, and so on. On the other hand, we believe that the portrayal of society as lacking altogether in class awareness represents a distortion of reality that contributes little to our understanding of the dynamics of social inequality.

Observation of social life indicates that class labels are frequently used in popular discourse. These labels–poor, working class, middle class, upper-middle class, and upper class–bear no direct correspondence to traditional conceptions of class, and yet their widespread popular use suggests that they do have an empirical basis. We believe that the empirical referents for these terms are a graded series of status groups linked to one another in a relationship of inequality.

As we have already argued, this relationship is not manifested as a zero-sum dichotomy between those who have and those who do not have

---

[2]Thus, we are emphasizing inequality as the source of class formation, regardless of the absolute level of affluence. This, of course, runs counter to the assumption implicit in the embourgeoisement thesis (e.g., Lipset 1960:253; Wilensky 1966).

any single attribute. Instead, we believe that people are sensitive to the distribution of a variety of economic attributes that affect their overall socioeconomic position. Various economic characteristics cluster to form a graded series of social classes, each class with a unique set of interests bound up with its share of socioeconomic rewards. While the specific mix of ingredients that defines, say, working-class membership may vary across individuals, members of the working class do share an overall socioeconomic position that sets their interests apart from those of other classes. Insofar as classes are interest groups, relationships among them are inherently conflictual. It is for this reason that economic distinctions provide such a forceful basis for the development of social communities.

The identification of interest groups as a product of social inequality has been made in the past, especially in work dealing with social stratification and political attitudes. Yet the loose school of thought that we might term the interest-group approach to stratification has had only skeletal theoretical articulation. In general, this approach emerged as a response to the functionalist view that inequality is based on complementary rather than conflictual interests, and that inequality thus enjoys widespread consensual support. The principal purpose of the interest-group approach was to draw attention to inequality as a source of conflict. There has been little concern with trying to define explicitly the nature of the resulting interest groups. Instead, interest groups have been identified in a variety of empirical ways, and they have rarely been linked to the concept of social class. The only major exception is Centers's (1949) innovative study of subjective social class in the United States, in which he outlined an interest-group theory of classes:

> This theory implies that a person's status and role with respect to the economic process of society imposes upon him certain attitudes, values and interests relating to his role and status in the political and economic sphere. It holds, further, that the status and role of the individual in relation to the means of production and exchange of goods and services gives rise in him to a consciousness of membership in some social class which shares those attitudes, values and interests. [1949:28-29]

Our book is an attempt to build on Centers's approach to social class.

Our view of classes as a graded series of status groups defined by economic interests follows the same vein of thought as that outlined by Centers. Such an approach puts an explicit emphasis on *popular* conceptions of class. In order to explore and delineate the place of class in the popular consciousness, what issues do we need to address?

As a first and most fundamental step, we should identify class labels that are commonly used in popular discourse. For reasons that are elaborated in the next chapter, we believe that there are five class terms that meet this requirement: poor, working class, middle class, upper-middle class, and upper class. The next step is to assess the extent to which people personally identify with one of those labels, and the subjective significance of that identification. This involves examining the cognitive interpretation of class as well as the degree of emotional identification and sense of shared fate that class elicits. To what extent does class enter people's cognitive awareness and, beyond this, their sense of emotional identity? These are the issues we pursue in chapters 2 and 3.

The third step (and the one that has preoccupied most studies of subjective class) is to assess what factors determine people's identification with a particular class. The most fundamental issue here is the "accuracy" with which people translate their objective socioeconomic standing into an identification with a class. This bears directly on the extent to which classes do exist as cogent socioeconomic groups. Indeed, some observers have argued that there is a poor fit between objective standing and class identification, and have concluded that the salience of class is therefore minimal. Beyond this, there is the issue of how different components of socioeconomic standing influence class identification. This helps us to define more precisely the factors that give subjective class its character. Of course, these two issues are inseparable, since the question of "accuracy" presupposes that important explanatory factors have not been overlooked. These issues are addressed in chapters 4 through 8.

In chapter 4, we present a basic model of the effects of education, occupational status, and earned income on class identification, a model that corresponds to the one generally used. Subsequently, we elaborate this model in a variety of ways. This involves consideration of other elements of individual socioeconomic standing: the manual/nonmanual distinction, capital ownership, and work-related characteristics such as job authority and union membership. Chapter 6 addresses the way that different personal conceptions of class influence the conversion of social standing into a class identification. In chapters 7 and 8 we move beyond personal social standing to consider the role of other people in the individual's social environment. Here we focus on the influence of family members (from the family of origin and from the current family), work associates, and friends on the individual's class identification. These analyses bear directly on the extent to which social life should be viewed as an open network of crosscutting affiliations or as a more constrained reflection of socioeconomic distinctions. These analyses also help us evaluate the extent to which people's interpretations of their own experience are modified in the light of the experiences of other family members and associates.

Finally, we assess the implications of class identity for people's social predispositions and political orientations. The issue here is whether socioeconomic distinctions, and class in particular, condition people's social and political perspectives. Do people use class as a salient cue in their social lives? and to what extent does class produce conflicting political goals?

At various points in our analysis, we isolate different ascriptive groups whose socioeconomic experience has been sufficiently distinct to warrant special attention - namely, men and women, and whites and blacks. The traditional male dominance in family relationships combined with women's relative seclusion from the labor market suggests that women may have been one step removed from the economic forces producing classes. This has led to the common assumption that married women derive their class identification from their husbands' socioeconomic standing. It also raises the possibility that women in general may have a less sharply defined awareness of class. These issues are of particular interest given the recent increase in women seeking employment outside the home and entering the labor market.

Separate analysis of the class identity of blacks is essential given the long-standing debate about the relative significance of race and class. As we have already observed, Weber (1946) regarded racial groups as an important source of group identity that could undercut the development of class loyalties. This point was also recognized by Marx, although he viewed such cultural divisions as relatively superficial and transitory in comparison with the structurally based divisions represented by social class (Marx and Engels 1961). More recently, it has been suggested that the apparent division between blacks and whites in the United States is confounded substantially with socioeconomic differences between these two groups (Blalock 1967; Wilson 1980). In general, however, racial divisions have been treated as more central than class divisions to social and political life in the United States. Given this debate, one thing is clear: class identity cannot be assessed without also taking racial identity into account.

The data for our analyses are drawn from a national survey of people residing in the United States. This survey was conducted by the Survey Research Center at the University of Michigan in the fall of 1975, and was part of a larger study of intergroup attitudes and group consciousness among class, race, and gender groups. Face-to-face interviews were conducted with respondents from a random, multistage, probability sample of noninstitutionalized adults aged eighteen and over residing in the forty-eight contiguous states. Following standard Survey Research Center procedures, interviewers and respondents were matched by race. The response rate was just under 70 percent, which is in the normal range for national surveys conducted by the Survey Research Center in recent years. In all, 1,914 respondents were interviewed. The average duration of interviews was about one hour and twenty minutes. Interviews consisted mainly of verbally administered material, but, as will become clear in the text, some sections of the questionnaire were self administered by the respondent.

The data from this survey incorporate a variety of novel measures, and are designed to address unresolved issues about subjective social class in the United States. Is class a foreign concept to Americans, or is it a phenomenon with which they are familiar? Beyond this, what shape and meaning does class assume in the public consciousness? The analyses in this book address a broad variety of issues that bear directly on these questions. Taken as a whole, they will allow us to evaluate the degree to which classes should be characterized as a graded series of economically based status groups.

2

The Cognitive Interpretation of Social Class Identification

In this chapter we examine the subjective meaning of class identification in the United States. Our analysis hinges on two fundamental issues: is social class meaningful at all to Americans, and, if so, what *kind* of meaning does it assume? These two questions are at the heart of the debate about the interpretation and significance of social class in America.

Different answers to the first question are related to alternative strategies for the measurement of class identification. We address this issue in the presentation of our own measure and in our discussion of its properties. This leads directly into an analysis of how (if at all) Americans interpret standard class terms. Is there a relatively clear popular conception of class and, if so, what form does it take? Perhaps the most obvious place to start in addressing this problem is with an examination of the way people assign occupations to classes, given the traditional centrality of occupation in discussions of socioeconomic status and class. This in turn raises the broader issue of the kinds of criteria that people use to define membership in their own class—are these criteria purely economic, or do they include a social component as well? In addition, we examine whether one's own class membership influences one's perspective on class, or whether there is consensus on the meaning of class. Similarly, is the meaning attached to social class affected by membership in ascriptive groups, such as racial groups?

These interrelated issues raise a number of important empirical questions, to which we now turn.

THE MEASURE OF SOCIAL CLASS IDENTIFICATION

Our measure of social class identification is the following item, which introduced a series of questions about class in the interview schedule:

People talk about social classes such as the poor, the working class, the middle class, the upper-middle class, and the upper class. Which of these classes would you say you belong to?

Three aspects of the question's wording warrant discussion: our use of a closed-choice rather than an open-ended question, the general phrasing of the question, and our reasons for the five classes selected as response options. We discuss these issues in turn.

Those who believe that social class is peripheral argue that efforts to measure social class identification merely put the bewildered respondent through an irrelevant and mindless exercise. Such analysts have generally argued that closed-choice questions mask the respondent's confusion, and they have instead advocated open-ended questions as the only revealing way to measure class identification (see, e.g., Gross 1953; Haer 1957; Nisbet 1970). This argument has, in turn, received its strongest apparent support from data obtained from open-ended questions. The advantages of open-ended questions, however, are generally overstated and oversimplified. Confronting a respondent with a question such as, "What social class do you feel you belong to?" relies on the single cue "social class" to convey the referent of the question, making it more difficult for the respondent to interpret the question "correctly" (i.e., in socioeconomic terms). Many respondents may identify with a socioeconomic class but may not associate the sociological term "social class" with that identification, especially when other contextual information is absent. The provision of response options cues the respondent to what the investigator means by "social class."

For example, in response to the open-ended question used by Gross (1953), 20 percent said "don't know," 15 percent gave irrelevant responses, 5 percent gave no response, and 14 percent denied either the existence of classes or their belonging to one. Perhaps the critical figures here are the large proportions of "don't knows" and irrelevant responses to the open-ended question. Such responses suggest a failure to find the question meaningful in the former case, and an apparent misunderstanding of the question in the latter case. A closed-choice question later in the same survey ("Some authorities claim that there are four social classes: middle class, lower class, working class and upper class. To which of these social classes would you say you belonged?") elicited "don't know" from only 2 percent, no nonresponses, and denial of classes from just 1 percent of the sample (1953:402). If the class terms used in the closed-choice question did not have meaning for respondents, the provision of those terms would elicit not only as many "don't knows" and irrelevant responses as the open-ended question but also as many active rejections of the question. Thus, the failure of the open-ended question to elicit a positive class identification from 54 percent of Gross's respondents may not so much indicate the irrelevance of social class for those respondents as it reflects the inadequacy of the stimulus for directing the attention of many respondents to the appropriate information.

Indeed, this failure to direct respondents' attention to the appropriate information has been recognized as a problem with open-ended questions *generally* for some time (Rugg and Cantril 1944; Schuman and Presser 1979). For certain purposes, of course, this is not a "failure," as, for example, when an analyst is concerned with trying to identify what social problems people regard as important in a particular period. Here, however, we are concerned with the ways people react to terms often used in both scholarly and popular discourse, and thus the closed-choice format is more appropriate. Having made this decision, it becomes imperative that we probe respondents' interpretations of the response options we have provided in order to assess their validity and meaning (Schuman 1966). Indeed, that is the goal of this chapter and much of the remaining analysis in the book.

Many questions on class identification use a preamble that may load the question in favor of identifying with a class. One commonly used example (e.g., Vanneman and Pampel 1977) is the item developed in the American National Election Studies conducted by the Center for Political Studies at the University of Michigan, which is prefaced as follows:

> *There's been some talk these days about different social classes. Most people say* they belong either to the middle class or the working class. Do you ever think of yourself as belonging to one of these classes? [If yes] Which one? [If no or don't know] Well, if you had to make a choice, . . ? [emphasis added]

Another example is found in Gross's question cited earlier, with its mention of "some authorities. . ." Such wording may pressure the respondent by implying that social class is a current issue whose validity is acknowledged by "most people" or by "authorities" (although "authorities" is balanced off somewhat by the qualifier "some"). Since we wanted to ascertain how widespread class identification is, we avoided key words of this kind in order to keep any such pressures to a minimum. Additionally, respondents who answered that there are no social classes were not pressed any further but were instead asked, "Why do you say that?"

Beyond the general phrasing of the item, the nature and number of the response options is an important issue, since there is evidence that both factors affect the distribution of responses to class identification items (see, e.g., Centers 1949:30-33; 1950; Gross 1953; Hodge and Treiman 1968; Jackman and Jackman 1973). While some have implied that this is an issue peculiar to class-identification items, it is of course an issue in survey items generally (e.g., Rugg and Cantril 1944; Schuman and Presser 1981).[1] Our main concern was to use class terms that are the most commonly found in popular discourse; provision of less common terms would not only make the stimulus more ambiguous to respondents (and thus reduce the validity of their responses) but also would reduce the relevance of their responses. A class label frequently used in class identification questions but rarely, if ever, used in discussions of or references to social class in other contexts is "lower class." The most frequent popular usage of the term is as a pejorative adjective rather than as a label for a particular socioeconomic category of people (see also Miller 1964).[2] We therefore use the term *poor* rather than *lower class*, because the poor constitute a socioeconomic category that is frequently discussed in academic and popular literature and is also the object of long-standing policy concern. The other class terms we use need little comment. Their use in class-identification questions is fairly conventional, and they all meet the requirement of being commonly used in popular discourse. The latter point is least true of the term *upper class*. After considering and discarding terms such as *jet set* and *the rich* as being too narrow and too ambiguous, respectively (and both as too value-laden), it became clear that no satisfactory alternative was available to represent the topmost end of the class structure.

The use of five class categories means that the *middle class* is indeed in the middle of the categorization (a factor that should help clarify the stimulus), and that people can place themselves in the working class or upper-middle class without feeling that they are identifying with one of

---

[1]The literature is full of examples of this phenomenon. One of our favorites involves the items developed by McClosky (1958) to measure conservatism. Consider whether or not "we should respect the work of our forefathers and not think that we know better than they did": in one phrasing of this item, "our forefathers" are endorsed by 49 percent, but in another (superior) phrasing, they are endorsed by only 15 percent (Robinson et al. 1968:96-97). Another interesting instance of this phenomenon is discussed by Sullivan et al. (1978).

[2]This is also a problem with other terms that have "lower" as a prefix, most notably the label "lower-middle class" (more common in England than in the United States).

the extreme ends of the class categorization. Some class-identification questions present the various response options in jumbled order. We ordered them in a series from low to high, on the grounds that the respondent interprets each response option in the context of other response options available, and ordering the options aids quick comprehension of the context.

Distribution of Responses to the Class-Identification Question

Table 2.1 gives the distribution of responses to the class- identification question for the sample as a whole, and by race and by sex. The distribution for the total sample indicates that all but 3.5 percent of the respondents identified themselves with one of the five class categories provided.[3] The distribution among the five classes does not challenge intuition. One expects very few people in a cross-sectional sample to identify with the upper class, since this stimulus represents a socioeconomic elite, and the upper-middle class is an alternative available at the high end of the classification. Similarly, the figure of 7.6 percent identifying with the poor gives a considerably higher proportion at the extreme bottom end of the classification than has been obtained with class-identification questions that use "lower class" as the lowest of four or more alternatives. The latter type of question produces between 1 and 3 percent identifying with the "lower class" (see Centers 1949; Gross 1953; Hodge and Treiman 1968; Jackman and Jackman 1973). One presumes that the extra people identifying with the poor are drawn away from an identification with the working class by the availability of a nonodious alternative that is lower than the working class in the classification. Comparing the proportions identifying with the working through upper-middle classes in our survey with the corresponding figures in two 1964 National Opinion Research Center (NORC) surveys (Hodge and Treiman 1968; Jackman and Jackman 1973) also suggests that the creation of a nonodious alternative at the bottom end of the classification may encourage some other respondents to identify one class lower than they would otherwise. In the earlier surveys, similar proportions identified with the working and middle classes, but more people identified with the upper-middle class.[4]

The class-identification distributions in table 2.1 for racial groups conform to common expectations. Blacks are considerably more likely than

---

[3]Note that the level of "don't knows" and "missing data" compares favorably with survey items on other topics.

[4]The proportions identifying with the lower, working, middle, upper-middle, and upper classes are 2.3 percent, 34.3 percent, 44 percent, 16.6 percent, and 2.2 percent, respectively, in one 1964 NORC survey (Hodge and Treiman 1968); and 2.7 percent, 37.0 percent,

TABLE 2.1
DISTRIBUTION OF RESPONSES TO CLASS-IDENTIFICATION QUESTION
(FOR TOTAL SAMPLE, BY RACE AND SEX)

	Poor	Working	Middle	Upper-middle	Upper	Other[a]	No social classes	Don't know	Not ascertained	Total N
Total sample	7.6%	36.6	43.3	8.2	1.0	1.3	0.5	1.5	0.2	1,914
Whites	4.8%	35.8	46.4	9.0	1.0	1.1	0.5	1.3	0.2	1,648
Blacks	27.7%	41.5	22.1	1.5	1.5	2.6	0.5	2.6	0.0	195
Other[b]	14.1%	39.1	32.8	7.8	0.0	1.6	0.0	3.1	1.6	64
Men	5.4%	41.4	40.5	8.5	1.1	1.4	0.9	0.5	0.4	802
Women	9.2%	33.1	45.2	8.0	0.9	1.2	0.2	2.2	0.1	1,112

[a] This category includes identification with two classes (e.g., "poor and working," "working and middle") and irrelevant responses.
[b] This category includes Orientals, Spanish Americans, and American Indians.

whites to identify with the poor and less likely to identify with the middle class and upper-middle class. While it seems odd for blacks to be at least as likely as whites to identify with the upper class, it should be remembered that the total number of people identifying with the upper class (N = 19) is too small to provide reliable data. Comparing the overall distributions for blacks and whites, the overwhelming majority of blacks range between poor and middle class, while almost all whites are encompassed in the range between poor and upper-middle class. The third racial category, which includes Orientals, Spanish Americans, and American Indians, presents a subjective class range from poor to upper-middle class, with the proportion identifying with each class falling between that found for blacks and for whites. In contrast to these race differences, the distributions of class identification for men and women indicate no systematic between-group discrepancies.

In short, the distribution of responses to the class identification question lends support to the response options provided. The most notable deviation from distributions obtained in earlier studies is the higher proportion of respondents identifying with the lowest response option when it is labeled "poor" rather than "lower class." Having 8 percent rather than 1 to 3 percent of the sample identifying with the lowest social class in the classification is intuitively more plausible and is also more useful,

45.3 percent, 10.8 percent, and 2.3 percent, respectively, in another 1964 NORC survey (Jackman and Jackman 1973:582).

TABLE 2.2
MEAN SCORES FOR RESPONDENT'S EDUCATION, HEAD OF HOUSEHOLD'S SEI,
AND FAMILY INCOME (FOR EACH SUBJECTIVE CLASS)

	Respondent's education[a]	Head household's SEI[b]	Family income[c]
Poor	8.56 (3.49) [143]	20.95 (15.33) [129]	$ 5,081 (4,745) [123]
Working	10.89 (2.61) [697]	31.76 (18.99) [672]	$10,558 (7,171) [651]
Middle	12.52 (2.95) [824]	46.02 (23.44) [776]	$14,390 (10,747) [764]
Upper-middle	14.04 (2.93) [157]	60.82 (19.75) [148]	$24,302 (18,690) [144]
Upper	13.22 (3.66) [18]	45.13 (23.39) [14]	$22,300 (25,250) [15]
Total sample	11.68 (3.24) [1902]	39.74 (23.45) [1796]	$13,072 (11,209) [1749]

NOTE: Numbers in parentheses are standard deviations, and numbers in brackets are cell Ns.
[a] Respondent's education ranges from 1 to 20+ years of education.
[b] Head of household's SEI ranges from 4.1 to 96.0.
[c] Earned family income ranges from $0 to $97,500.

especially in view of the strong academic and policy concern with the poor.

Objective Status Composition of the Five Subjective Classes

The mean objective status characteristics of the poor, working class, middle class, and upper-middle class identifiers lend confidence to those categories of the class identification measure. The figures in table 2.2 indicate that mean scores for respondent's education, head of household's socioeconomic status (determined by the Duncan Socioeconomic Index, or SEI), and family income increase steadily from the poor to the upper-middle class. The objective status composition of the upper class, however, reverts to a middle-class level for socioeconomic status, and to a level between the middle and upper-middle classes for respondent's education and family income. Recall that only nineteen people identified with the upper class, too small a number to yield reliable data, since only a handful of respondents are required to affect the mean substantially. These data therefore underscore the fact that the responses of the upper class identifiers should be treated with caution. Perhaps it is unreasonable to expect any cross-sectional sample of the population as a whole to provide a fruitful vehicle for the analysis of such a small group as the upper class. In this study, the upper-class category is intended instead to mark the extreme top end of the class categorization, thus contributing to the validity of other class identifications as well as providing a stimulus for the analysis of images of the upper class held by the population at large.

Comprehension and Salience of Class Identification

Shortly after the class-identification item in the questionnaire, interviewers were asked "Was there any indication that R [the respondent] misunderstood or had problems understanding the class terms? Had problems; Didn't have problems." It should be remembered that interviewers were not trained as observers, but data from this item can give an approximate guide to the apparent comprehension of the class terms. Most respondents (86 percent) were judged by interviewers as having had no difficulty in understanding the class terms. With the exception of the upper class, the higher the subjective class, the smaller the proportion of respondents who had apparent difficulty in understanding the class terms.[5] It is possible that the predominantly middle-class interviewers were more likely to perceive that "poor" people had comprehension problems, but the proportions probably reflect the educational attainment (and presumably general knowledge) associated with class identification. No clear differences were found between the rated class comprehension of blacks and whites or of men and women.

Another way of evaluating the degree of intrinsic meaning in people's responses to the class identification item is to ask them how strongly they feel about their responses. If class is meaningless or irrelevant, or if the class terms used in our item lack salience, people should express low intensity about their chosen class identification. To check on this, those who identified with a social class were asked immediately after the item, "How strongly do you feel you belong to the [class named]–very strongly,

---

[5]The percentage of each subjective class rated as having had problems is as follows: poor = 21.5; working = 15.3; middle = 12.1; upper-middle = 10.5; upper = 21.1. Upper-class identifiers were as likely as the poor to be rated as having had problems understanding the class terms, a datum that supports our earlier observation that the composition of that subjective class is sufficiently irregular to warrant treating the upper-class responses with extreme caution.

TABLE 2.3
INTENSITY OF SUBJECTIVE CLASS IDENTIFICATION

		Intensity			
	Very strongly	Somewhat strongly	Not too strongly	Don't know	Base N
Total sample	49.6%	28.8	19.8	1.8	1,864
Poor	58.0%	18.2	21.7	2.1	143
Working	61.3%	23.7	12.8	2.3	697
Middle	39.0%	34.3	24.9	1.8	826
Upper-middle	43.9%	32.9	23.2	0.0	155
Upper	52.6%	31.6	15.8	0.0	19
Whites					
Poor	50.6%	20.3	25.3	3.8	79
Working	60.1%	24.5	12.8	2.6	587
Middle	38.1%	34.5	25.5	2.0	762
Upper-middle	44.2%	33.3	22.4	0.0	147
Upper	56.3%	31.3	12.5	0.0	16
Blacks					
Poor	73.6%	11.3	15.1	0.0	53
Working	74.1%	16.0	9.9	0.0	81
Middle	51.2%	30.2	18.6	0.0	43

somewhat strongly, or not too strongly?" Table 2.3 presents the data from this item. Just under one half of the sample said they felt "very strongly," while only a little over one-fifth said "not too strongly" or "don't know" (we assume that in this context "don't knows" reflect a lack of salience of social class similar to the "not too strongly" response). Thus, almost 80 percent of the sample feel at least somewhat strongly about their class identification. There is some association between intensity of class identification and respondents' apparent understanding of the class terms: respondents who did not feel at least somewhat strongly about their class identification were about twice as likely to be rated as having had difficulty in understanding the class terms (22 percent versus 12 percent).

The distribution of intensity of class identification by subjective class suggests that class is more likely to be salient to people who identify with classes at the lower end of the categorization (if we disregard the upper-class respondents). Poor and working-class respondents are more likely than those identifying with the middle or upper-middle class to identify with their subjective class very strongly. Overall, social class appears to be most salient to working-class respondents and least salient to middle-class respondents, but class differences are not dramatic.[6] Even in the middle class, just under three-quarters of the respondents feel at least somewhat strongly about their class identification.

If one breaks down each subjective class by race, blacks within each class express stronger intensity about their class identification than do whites (there is an insufficient number of blacks identifying with the upper-middle or upper classes to analyze them separately). Class differences in intensity are also slightly greater among blacks than among whites: middle-class blacks differ more from their poor and working-class counterparts than do middle-class whites. No differences were found between male and female identifiers with each class.

In sum, we have found that the overwhelming majority of respondents had no apparent difficulty understanding the class terms used in the class-identification question. Further, class membership is at least somewhat salient to over three-quarters of the sample, and almost one-half express strong feelings about their class identification. Social class hardly seems remote from the consciousness of most Americans.

THE SUBJECTIVE MEANING OF SOCIAL CLASS IDENTIFICATION

To probe the meaning of class identification more fully, we turn now to an examination of the ways respondents assign occupations to classes, and of the range of criteria respondents use to define their own class. Our analysis proceeds as follows.

We begin with the basic step of evaluating the way Americans assign occupations to classes, because occupation has traditionally been regarded as a key element of socioeconomic status. If the terms used in class-identification questions are as meaningless to the mass public as some investigators have argued, we would expect respondents to waver a good deal in trying to assign occupations to classes, and to express widely varying ideas about the class location of occupations. On the other hand, a ready consensus about the social class placement of different occupations would suggest that class is relatively well defined in the public's awareness.

---

[6]These results are similar to those reported by Centers (1956) for a representative sample of Americans interviewed in 1950. If anything, feelings of class identity appear just slightly stronger in the present data. Centers reported that 34 percent expressed "very strong" feelings and 37 percent "fairly strong" feelings about their class identification.

Beyond the basic issue of whether social class terms have any common meaning lies the question of the form that such meaning takes. We probe that form in two ways. First, the data on the class assignment of occupations are reexamined to assess the rules that appear to underlie the way occupations are assigned to classes. Particularly important here is the degree of popular sensitivity to the qualitative blue-collar/white-collar distinction versus socioeconomic hierarchies based on income, status, job authority, skill, and level of education. Theorists of "postindustrial society" have argued that the relative increase in the size of the white-collar sector implies an expanding middle class and a decline in class divisions (e.g., Bell 1973). This argument would be weakened, however, if people were found to be more sensitive to socioeconomic hierarchies rather than to the blue-collar/white-collar dichotomy, since it is among lower-level white-collar jobs that the expansion has been greatest. In fact, Centers (1949) argued that such routine white-collar work was becoming "proletarianized."

The second way that we probe interpretations by Americans of their class identification is by examining the kinds of criteria they use in defining membership in their own social class. The central issue here is whether class membership is seen strictly in terms of shared objective characteristics, such as type of occupation or income, or whether it extends to encompass cultural and expressive characteristics, such as shared life-style or common beliefs and feelings. The former pattern would suggest that class is defined somewhat narrowly, conforming more to the Weberian notion of class as an economic category only (Weber 1946). The latter conception, however, would make class membership a more significant *social* affiliation, suggesting that class incorporates the Weberian description of a status group, as well as being more consistent with Marxist and interest-group arguments that class is both a social and an economic unit (Centers 1949; Marx 1964).

Centers's survey of American white males, conducted in 1945, provides important baseline data on the subjective meaning of social class identification. Comparison with data from the present study, gathered thirty years later, is complicated by differences in the samples (the present study does not exclude women or blacks) and in the wording of the items (the present items are an extension of those used by Centers). Nonetheless, some interesting comparisons between the two surveys are possible.

Perceived Class Location of Occupations: Agreement or Disagreement?

Occupation is of central significance to social class. The readiness with which people assign occupations to classes and the amount of agreement they express in the way they do it bear fundamentally on the degree to which class is meaningful and salient to the American public. A wide inability to associate occupations with classes or a broad divergence in views of the class location of various occupations would seriously question the importance of class as an element in the public's consciousness. This would, of course, be consistent with the prominent argument that class is of little significance or relevance to most Americans (see, e.g., Rosenberg 1953; Case 1955; Haer 1957; Wilensky 1966; Nisbet 1970; Bell 1973). Our analyses, however, do not support such an argument. Instead, they suggest that social class is a familiar concept to most Americans, and that significant agreement exists on the basic issue of how occupations are associated with classes.

Centers (1949) sought to isolate people's occupational definitions of their own subjective class by asking respondents to select from a list of eleven occupation groups those that they thought belonged to the class with which they identified. We extended this by giving respondents an "occupation-class sort board," with twelve occupation cards to be sorted among the five classes.[7] This provides data not only on respondents' perceptions of the occupations belonging to their own class but also on their images of the match between occupations and classes throughout the class structure.

The occupation-class sort board was introduced by the interviewer as follows:

> There is sometimes disagreement about what social classes peo-
> ple with different occupations belong to. Each of these cards has a
> group of occupations on it. Please look at this board with a slot for
> each of the social classes we have been talking about, and sort
> each card into the slot you think it belongs to.

In devising the twelve occupation cards, the main concern was to represent the major occupational categories of the civilian labor force with occupational titles that would be widely recognized by a cross-sectional sample of Americans. The occupations identified in the twelve cards are listed in table 2.4. They were not presented to the respondent in any fixed order, but they represent a broad range of prestige, income, skill, and job authority—from "migrant farm workers" to "corporation directors and presidents." In addition, different cards represent the blue-collar/white-collar distinction (e.g., "assembly-line factory workers" and "workers in

---

[7]The yellow sort board contained a row of pockets representing the five classes, and respondents inserted the red occupation cards into the pockets.

offices and stores"), as well as the professional/business distinction (e.g., "doctors and lawyers" and "corporation directors and presidents").

Most respondents completed the occupation-class sort board with little or no hesitation, and very few "don't know" responses were elicited by any of the occupations. In a structured question, interviewers were asked to report how much the respondent hesitated on the sort-board task. They were instructed to look for such signs of uncertainty as switching cards from one slot to another or taking more time to decide where to place each card. According to the interviewers' observations, fewer than 7 percent of the respondents hesitated "a lot" on the task, while 11 percent hesitated "quite a bit"; over 50 percent did not hesitate at all, and an additional 31 percent hesitated no more than "a little."[8] The small proportion of "don't know" responses (less than 2 percent for any occupation) is consistent with the interviewers' observations.[9]

Beyond the issue of the ease and familiarity with which Americans associate occupations with classes, the data in table 2.4 display a striking amount of popular agreement about how occupations are associated with classes. For all but two occupations, a single class location is selected by a clear majority of respondents. For six of the twelve occupation cards, one contiguous class absorbs almost all of the other responses, and for the other occupations, most of the remaining responses are absorbed by two contiguous classes. This amount of agreement is especially notable given the loose specification of some of the occupational categories. Because of the constraint that the occupational titles had to be sufficiently colloquial to be familiar to a cross section of the population, many of the titles inevitably encompass some internal variance in prestige, job authority, educational attainment, and income. Thus, the convergence of class assignments in table 2.4 is probably as strong as could reasonably be expected.

The level of agreement about the class location of different occupations seems to vary as a function of three factors that are not entirely separable in these data. Disagreement increases with occupations (a) that are in the middle, as opposed to the top or the bottom, of the hierarchy, (b) that

---

[8]Further breakdowns of hesitation by class and race indicate, first, that there were no race differences in hesitation within classes. Second, the poor hesitated on the sort-board task more often than the remaining four classes (among whom there are no systematic differences in hesitation). For the poor, interviewers reported hesitation as follows: a lot = 23 percent; quite a bit = 20 percent; a little = 32 percent; not at all = 25 percent.

[9]This is also consistent with pretest interviewers' reports that the sort board task provided an alternative response format that was enjoyed by respondents and that broke up the interview and enlivened respondents' motivation and interest in the interview. Note, further, that the missing data on the sort board derive predominantly from interviewers' errors in recording responses, rather than from respondent refusals.

encompass more internal variance in socioeconomic characteristics, and (c) that present conflicting cues for class categorization.

The three occupations that generate the most agreement in class assignments are migrant farm workers, corporation directors and presidents, and assembly-line factory workers. Each of these occupations is placed in a single class (the poor, the upper class, and the working class, respectively) by about three-quarters of the respondents. Migrant farm workers and corporation directors and presidents mark the two extreme ends of the class categorization, and perhaps this contributes to the high agreement about their class location. This interpretation is supported by the fact that all six occupations that generate the highest agreement are at the bottom or the top of the list in table 2.4. Since the occupation cards were not presented to respondents in any fixed order, this suggests that there is more spontaneous consensus about the class location of occupations with clear low or high status, and more disagreement about occupation-class images in the intermediate range.

TABLE 2.4

ASSIGNMENT OF OCCUPATIONS TO SOCIAL CLASSES (PREDOMINANT CHOICES ITALICIZED)

	Social class						
Occupations	Poor	Working	Middle	Upper-middle	Upper	Don't know	Base N
Migrant farm workers	73.3%	21.7	2.2	0.5	0.5	1.7	1,846
Janitors	25.2%	66.6	6.1	0.5	0.2	1.4	1,840
Assembly-line factory workers	5.0%	75.1	16.0	1.7	0.7	1.6	1,862
Workers in offices and stores	1.5%	59.9	33.4	3.4	0.8	1.0	1,843
Plumbers and carpenters	1.1%	43.9	40.0	11.7	1.9	1.3	1,853
Foremen in factories	0.6%	39.5	47.7	9.7	1.0	1.5	1,857
Schoolteachers and social workers	0.4%	18.7	59.7	17.4	2.5	1.2	1,858
Small businessmen	1.7%	17.6	60.5	17.7	1.2	1.3	1,859
Supervisors in offices and stores	0.1%	16.7	56.2	22.5	3.2	1.3	1,853
Business executives and managers	0.1%	3.0	13.8	55.8	25.7	1.6	1,861
Doctors and lawyers	0.0%	1.8	3.9	35.6	57.1	1.7	1,866
Corporation directors and presidents	0.4%	1.3	3.0	21.5	71.8	1.9	1,852

The two occupations at each end of the list, however, are also relatively homogeneous in terms of socioeconomic status, job authority, and type of work, and thus constitute less ambiguous stimuli. In this connection, note that doctors and lawyers, about whom there is less occupation-class agreement than about corporation directors and presidents, constitute a less homogeneous group than the latter. An equivalent elite subgroup of doctors and lawyers might be top surgeons in major hospitals and senior corporation lawyers in large law firms. Assembly-line factory workers—one of the three occupation groups about which there is the highest agreement—occupy a fairly constrained range of SEI scores, and present a straightforward stimulus in terms of type of work and level of job authority. There appears to be a common conception that relatively unskilled, low-authority, blue-collar work that is organized in group settings should be included in the working class. There is less consensus that workers in offices and stores belong in the working class. Apart from the blue-collar/white-collar distinction between this group and assembly-line factory workers, office and store workers constitute a slightly broader range of occupations in terms of type of work (e.g., secretaries, office clerks, typists, sales clerks) and individual task discretion.

Turning to the six occupation cards about which there is lower agreement (plumbers and carpenters through business executives and managers), we find that not only do these occupations fall in the middle of the list but also that each of these cards presents a more ambiguous stimulus by incorporating multiple occupations, authority levels, education and skill levels, incomes, and/or SEI scores. Each of these cards has considerable internal variance on at least three of those five dimensions. Plumbers and carpenters have similar NORC Prestige Scale scores (Siegel 1971), but the SEI score for carpenters is about half that for plumbers. In addition, "carpenters" may be interpreted as skilled tradesmen with wide individual task discretion, or as group-organized workers. School teachers and social workers have similar Prestige and SEI scores, but each occupation incorporates considerable variation in terms of job authority, educational level, and income. "Small businessmen" encompass a broad range from marginal economic ventures with the owner as the sole employee to fairly prosperous businesses with several employees, and the term covers a wide variation of occupations, incomes, education and skill levels, and spheres of authority. Foremen in factories and office and store supervisors also represent multiple occupations, authority levels, levels of skill and education, and incomes. Business executives and managers represent considerable variation in level and scope of authority, income, and education.

    The two occupation cards that generate the most disagreement, in that their prevailing assignments were split almost evenly between two classes, are plumbers and carpenters and foremen in factories. They are the only two occupation cards that represent skilled blue-collar work, and the assignments of both are split between the working class and the middle class. This doubtless reflects popular disagreement about the importance of the blue-collar criterion versus average job authority, skill level, and income in distinguishing working-class from middle-class occupations.

    The data in table 2.5 are helpful in trying to assess the sources of agreement and disagreement about the class location of occupations. This table reports the percentage of each subjective class assigning each of the

TABLE 2.5

Assignment of Each Occupation to Own Subjective Class
(by Subjective Class, with Predominant Choices Italicized)

	Social class				
Occupations	Poor[a]	Working[b]	Middle[c]	Upper-Middle[d]	Upper[e]
Migrant farm workers	*71.9%*	25.4	3.1	0.7	5.6
Janitors	48.2%	*69.6*	9.2	1.3	0.0
Assembly-line factory workers	16.5%	*80.6*	20.0	3.9	5.6
Workers in offices and stores	7.4%	*71.2*	42.0	5.3	0.0
Plumbers and carpenters	3.6%	*52.5*	47.2	12.0	0.0
Foremen in factories	2.2%	*48.4*	*53.5*	15.7	5.6
Schoolteachers and social workers	1.4%	33.4	*71.8*	25.3	0.0
Small businessmen	9.4%	28.9	*67.9*	31.8	0.0
Supervisors in offices and stores	0.0%	26.3	*63.9*	32.9	5.6
Business executives and managers	0.0%	4.8	12.1	*69.1*	29.4
Doctors and lawyers	0.0%	3.3	2.8	45.8	*82.4*
Corporation directors and presidents	2.2%	2.0	2.8	19.0	*76.5*

[a] Base *N* for poor ranges from 136 to 139.
[b] Base *N* for working class ranges from 682 to 690.
[c] Base *N* for middle class ranges from 802 to 817.
[d] Base *N* for upper-middle class ranges from 150 to 154.
[e] Base *N* for upper class ranges from 17 to 18.

occupation groups to their own class. Note, first, that the pattern of prevailing class placements remains the same in table 2.5 as in table 2.4. That is, the class to which an occupation card is predominantly assigned by respondents as a whole is also the class most likely to claim that occupation. Second, disagreements in table 2.4 tend to be reflected in table 2.5, with each of the classes involved in the disagreement being more likely to claim the disputed occupations than are respondents as a whole to assign the occupations to those classes. Thus, occupations with the widest spread in class assignments in table 2.4 tend to be "over-claimed" by the most classes in table 2.5. Three of the occupation cards whose assignments are spread over three classes in table 2.4 (school-teachers and social workers, office and store supervisors, and small businessmen) are overclaimed by all three classes in table 2.5. Small businessmen are also slightly overclaimed by a fourth class, the poor. This pattern of results supports the interpretation that disagreements about the class location of occupations derive substantially from within-occupa-tion variance in education, income, job authority, task direction, and skill: respondents identifying with different social classes are likely to use different levels of occupation titles as their reference in completing the occupation-class sort board.

There are no major differences between blacks and whites in the patterns we have just described, and we therefore do not present data equivalent to tables 2.4 and 2.5 by race. The most notable discrepancy is in the class assignment of schoolteachers and social workers: while 62 per-cent of the whites assign this occupation to the middle class (and another 16 percent assign it to the upper-middle class), blacks are less likely to see this as a middle-class occupation (42 percent) are more likely to assign it to the upper-middle class (28 percent). This pattern is also reflected in the proportions of each class assigning teachers and social workers to their own class, by race. Such race differences are not, however, found for the occupations adjacent to schoolteachers and social workers in table 2.4 (foremen and small businessmen). The other minor differences between blacks and whites occur for two low-status and two high-status occupa-tions. Blacks are more likely than whites to assign janitors and (to a lesser extent) factory workers to the poor over the working class, but the *overall* proportion assigned to both of these classes combined does not vary by race. Similarly, blacks are more likely to assign business executives and doctors and lawyers to the upper over the upper-middle class, but again the overall proportion of these occupations assigned to the upper-middle and upper classes combined does not vary by race. These patterns sug-gest a *slight* tendency for blacks to assign occupations to the lowest and highest classes more frequently than whites. We emphasize, however, that these differences are marginal. The most striking feature of the data is the similarity in the ways both blacks and whites assign occupations to classes.

To summarize these analyses, we employ a measure of people's agreement with the modal class assignments across all twelve occupations. This is calculated as follows. Those respondents who assigned occupations to the modal class choice are given a score of 0; an individual's disagreement is defined to increase directly with the unpopularity of her chosen class assignment. For example, disagreement over the class location of janitors is scored as follows: 0 = working class; 1 = poor; 2 = middle class; 3 = upper-middle class or upper class, or don't know. These scores are summed over the twelve occupations to give an overall occupation-class assignment score for each respondent that ranges from 0 (perfect conformity with modal assignments) to 37 (highly deviant class assignments).[10]

This scoring procedure imposes stringent criteria. In order to get a total score of 0, a respondent cannot make a single "error" across twelve tasks. In view of the accepted levels of unreliability in survey data, a perfect score seems unrealistic–indeed, only 2 percent obtained such a score. Despite this, most scores are low, which indicates that most respondents only sporadically make assignments that deviate from the mode. Very few *systematically* depart from the modal assignments of the twelve occupations. Fully 40 percent of the sample have scores no greater than 3, 65 percent score no higher than 5, and 81 percent have scores no higher than 7. At the other end of the distribution, only 6 percent have scores greater than 11, and barely 3 percent score higher than 14.

Table 2.6 reports the mean level of agreement on the class location of occupations by race and class (omitting the groups with very small Ns). It is evident from these figures that there is little variation in agreement by class and none by race. Among whites, there is a slight class effect, in the sense that the most "errors" in class assignments are made by the poor and the fewest are made by the middle and upper-middle classes. But regression analyses that allow for all possible class and race effects (not displayed here) show how weak this pattern is: the R^2 is only .037. In

---

[10]For the two occupation cards for which a single class location is not chosen by a majority (plumbers and carpenters and foremen in factories), we take either a working- or a middle-class assignment as a modal response. Respondents with missing data on any of the occupational assignments were excluded from the analysis. Valid data were available for a total of 1,719 respondents. We experimented with plausible variations on this measure, but alternative versions give the same results. For example, instead of ranking responses by their popularity, we tried ranking them by their proximity to the modal response. Note also that we obtain the same results if we exclude plumbers and carpenters and foremen in factories, and focus instead on the remaining ten occupations.

TABLE 2.6
MEAN LEVELS OF AGREEMENT ON CLASS LOCATION OF OCCUPATIONS (BY CLASS AND RACE)

	Poor	Working	Middle	Upper-middle
Whites	7.59	5.35	4.48	4.32
	(5.85)	(4.30)	(4.09)	(3.85)
	[74]	[545]	[693]	[134]
Blacks	7.48	6.14	5.44	
	(4.98)	(4.23)	(3.74)	
	[48]	[72]	[32]	

NOTE: Numbers in parentheses are standard deviations, numbers in brackets are cell *N*s.

general, the high degree of consensus on the class location of occupations is shared by all classes.

Occupational Characteristics and Social Class: Prevailing Perceptions

We turn now to an examination of the prevailing class assignments of the twelve occupation cards. While recognizing that each card encompasses some internal variance in socioeconomic characteristics, this analysis is useful in trying to assess the rules that seem to underlie the way occupations are associated with classes. A question that is of particular significance is the degree of popular sensitivity to the blue-collar/white-collar distinction versus socioeconomic hierarchies based on income, status, education, skill, or authority.

The blue-collar/white-collar dichotomy has frequently been treated by students of social class as synonymous with the working-class/middle-class distinction. The advent of the Duncan Socioeconomic Index (Duncan 1961) and the NORC Prestige Scale (Siegel 1971) led to some diminution of emphasis on the blue-collar/white-collar dichotomy, since it does not accurately reflect differences in SEI and Prestige scores. Of course, it had been argued much earlier that lower-level white-collar work was undergoing gradual routinization and proletarianization (Centers 1949:82-85; Mills 1956; see also Glenn and Feldberg 1977). Work by Laumann further discouraged emphasis on the blue-collar/white-collar distinction: he found no significant difference between people's feelings of social distance toward the lower-level white-collar occupation of sales clerk and the blue-collar occupations of machine operator in a factory or truck driver (1966:59). Use of SEI and Prestige scores brought more attention not only to the notion of occupational status, independent of whether the work was manual or non-manual, but also to the average educational attainment and income associated with occupations. Job authority is an additional occupational characteristic that has been stressed as an important aspect of class (Dahrendorf 1959; Robinson and Kelley 1979).

The blue-collar/white-collar distinction has recently been revived, however, as an indicator of working-class or middle-class membership (Giddens 1973; Dalia and Guest 1975; Vanneman and Pampel 1977; Gagliani 1981). In addition, the relative increase in the size of the white-collar sector makes the assessment of respondents' sensitivity to the blue-collar/white-collar dichotomy especially important. While most of this increase has taken place in lower-level white-collar jobs, it has been interpreted by theorists of "postindustrial society" as an expansion of the middle class with a subsequent increase in societal well-being and decrease in the probability of class conflict (e.g., Bell 1973).

Of particular relevance to the blue-collar/white-collar issue are the class assignments of five occupation cards: assembly-line factory workers, workers in offices and stores, plumbers and carpenters, foremen in factories, and supervisors in offices and stores. The first two occupation groups provide the blue- and white-collar counterparts of routine work with low responsibility, although assembly-line factory workers constitute a more homogeneous group and have somewhat lower mean SEI and Prestige scores than do workers in offices and stores. The predominant assignment of both occupations is to the working class, although this is done with more agreement for factory workers. Skilled blue-collar occupations with more responsibility (plumbers and carpenters and foremen in factories) are more likely than routine white-collar jobs to be associated with the middle class. Recall, however, that skilled blue-collar occupations are the only ones that generated pronounced disagreement about their class affiliation. Clearly, some people have difficulty associating even skilled blue-collar jobs with anything other than the working class. On the other hand, routine white-collar work (where most of the white-collar expansion has taken place) generally receives a somewhat lower class affiliation than skilled blue-collar work. Thus, in the majority view, the fact that an occupation is nonmanual is insufficient in itself to make it middle class. Supervisors in offices and stores might be seen as the white collar counterparts of foremen in factories, in terms of line of command on the job, although their equivalence on other socioeconomic characteristics is difficult to assess because they are not given separate titles in the census occupational classification. In fact, the class assignment of supervisors in offices and stores tends to be somewhat higher than that of factory foremen.

The blue-collar/white-collar distinction appears to play, at best, a limited role in the way occupations are associated with classes. Its clearest effect seems to be in lowering the class assignment some people give to skilled blue-collar occupations, rather than in raising the class affiliation of routine white-collar work. A comparison can be made with some of Centers's data as a way of evaluating his argument that routine white-collar work was gradually becoming increasingly proletarianized (1949:78-85). Centers's data are for white males only; he employed a different class categorization (lower, working, middle, and upper); most of his occupational titles are dissimilar to those in the present study; and he measured only the assignment of occupations to the respondent's own subjective class. Within these constraints, we can compare the proportion of the white male members of the working and middle class, respectively, placing "factory workers" and "office workers" in their own class in the 1945 survey, and the proportion of the white male identifiers with each of those classes in the 1975 survey claiming "assembly-line factory workers" and "workers in offices and stores" for their own class. The proportions claiming factory workers/ assembly-line factory workers are very similar in the two surveys (82 percent of the working class and 24 percent of the middle class in 1945 versus 84 percent and 21 percent for the two classes in 1975). The proportions claiming office workers/workers in offices and stores, however, are substantially different in the two surveys (48 percent of the working class and 53 percent of the middle class in 1945 versus 76 percent of the working class and 36 percent of the middle class in 1975). While these data should be interpreted with caution, they lend support to Centers's argument that lower-level white-collar occupations were acquiring an increasingly working-class affiliation.

A related issue is the extent to which people with blue-collar and white-collar occupations appear to follow the same rules in assigning occupations to classes. It has been argued that people in white-collar occupations are more sensitive to prestige criteria, while blue-collar workers are more likely to make a categorical distinction between the working and middle classes on the basis of the manual/nonmanual dichotomy (Dahrendorf 1959:280-289; Ossowski 1963; Goldthorpe et al. 1969:118-121; Vanneman and Pampel 1977). Is there any evidence of such a duality in the way blue- and white-collar workers assign occupations to classes? In brief, the answer is no. We compared the class assignments of occupations made by the blue- and white-collar members of the working and middle classes, respectively. It is the members of these two classes that are critical to the argument, and these are also the only two classes that contain a sufficient number of both blue- and white-collar workers to sustain reliable inferences. There are 439 blue-collar workers and 195 white-collar workers identifying with the working class; the middle class includes 299 blue-collar workers and 446 white-collar workers. Apart from the fact that so many blue-collar workers clearly abandon the manual/nonmanual distinction in identifying themselves with the middle class, there is no evidence that they are any more likely to use that criterion in sorting occupations generally into classes. The class assignments made by the blue- and white-collar members of each class are essentially similar, even for such critical occupations as workers in offices and stores, foremen in factories, and plumbers and carpenters. There is no evidence of different rules being applied by blue- and white-collar workers in assigning occupations to classes.

The prevailing class assignments of all twelve occupation cards appear to reflect primarily their overall socioeconomic characteristics rather than whether they are blue collar or white collar. In table 2.4 the occupation groups are listed in approximate ascending order according to their prevailing class assignments, and this ordering is eminently reasonable in terms of the prestige, educational attainment or skill, income, and sphere of authority associated with those occupations. That migrant farm workers is the only occupational group placed in the poor by a majority of respondents suggests that this social class is predominantly reserved for marginal occupations that provide irregular employment. Occupations that are predominantly assigned to the working class appear to be characterized by low job authority (whether blue or white collar), low skill, and low socioeconomic status. Skilled blue-collar jobs are split more or less evenly between the working class and the middle class. Occupations that are placed predominantly in the middle class are white-collar jobs with moderate job authority, lower-level professionals, and the petty bourgeoisie. The prevailing assignment of upper-level (but not top-level) positions in business is to the upper-middle class. Occupations that are placed predominantly in the upper class are elite positions at the topmost level of big business, and (with less agreement) high-level professionals.

Criteria for Class Membership

The way people define membership in their own class provides an important insight into their interpretation of social class. Especially significant is the extent to which people define their class narrowly in terms of objective factors or more broadly to include cultural and expressive factors as well. Weber reserved the term *status group* to denote a collectivity with a shared life-style and set of values, and he distinguished status groups from classes by defining the latter solely in terms of common economic fate (Weber 1946). Marxist and interest-group perspectives have maintained that this distinction is false and that classes are, indeed, *social* as much as economic collectivities (e.g., Marx 1964; Centers 1949; Portes 1971). All parties agree, of course, that without the social component, class is robbed of its political significance.

Centers (1949) pursued the question of how Americans conceive of their subjective class by excluding occupation and by asking respondents, "In deciding whether a person belongs to your class or not, which of these other things is most important to know: who his family is, how much money he has, what sort of education he has, or how he believes and feels about certain things?" Respondents could name more than one criterion. His results suggested that cultural and expressive aspects of class are subjectively more important than any of the others: 47 percent of his white male respondents named "how he believes and feels about certain things" as most important in deciding whether a person belongs to their class. Differences among the other three criteria were not nearly as great: education was mentioned by 29 percent of the respondents, family background by 20 percent, and money by 17 percent.

In the present study, separate data were gathered on the rated importance of each of six possible criteria for membership in one's own social class, including occupation. To avoid introducing a bias in favor of naming occupation, these questions were asked before the occupation-class sort board was administered.

> In deciding whether someone belongs to the [class with which R has identified], how important is each of these things to you?
> The person's occupation? . . .
> What sort of education the person has? . . .
> How much money the person has? . . .
> How the person believes and feels about things? . . .
> The person's style of life? . . .
> The kind of family the person comes from? . . .

For each criterion, the respondent was asked, "Is this very important, somewhat important, or not important to you in deciding whether someone belongs to the [class with which R has identified]?"[11] In drafting these questions it was intended that the first three criteria (occupation, education, money) reflect more objective characteristics, and that the next criteria (beliefs, style) reflect more expressive or cultural characteristics.

---

[11]Only 19 percent of the sample responded affirmatively to a follow-up question— "Is there anything else that you think is important . . . ?", and these respondents provided a total of more than twenty alternative additional criteria.

The last criterion (family) deals with inheritance and socialization, and it is more ambiguous whether this might be interpreted as an objective and/ or a cultural factor.[12]

TABLE 2.7

CORRELATIONS AMONG SIX CRITERIA FOR MEMBERSHIP IN OWN SUBJECTIVE SOCIAL CLASS

	Occupation	Education	Money	Beliefs	Life-style	Family
Occupation	—					
Education	.424	—				
Money	.298	.251	—			
Beliefs	.147	.286	−.019	—		
Life-style	.206	.278	.240	.354	—	
Family	.218	.321	.158	.287	.327	—

NOTE: Each correlation excludes the missing data from that pair of variables only. Ns range from 1,839 (r between family and beliefs) to 1,857 (r between education and occupation). All criteria are scored so that "don't know" is given the same score as "not important."

Before examining the rated importance of these six possible criteria for class membership, we can check their validity by investigating the degree to which respondents differentiated among them.[13] The correlations among the criteria (in table 2.7) provide data on their empirical grouping and aid in interpreting their meaning to respondents. The highest cor-

---

[12]Note the parallels between our procedure here and that employed by Klugel et al. (1977:601). They followed their "standard" measure of class identification with the four questions below:
1. Which social class is your *occupation* most like?
2. Which social class is your *income* most like?
3. Which social class is your *way of life* most like?
4. Which social class is your *influence* most like?
Like ours, these questions seek to pursue the validity of Weber's distinctions. They do not, however, identify the extent to which people think, for example, that occupation is a more important criterion than way of life in defining social class. In addition, the form of these questions implicitly suggests to respondents that their personal characteristics cannot conform to any single class.

[13]A count of responses over the six criteria suggests that the overwhelming majority of respondents found the criteria meaningful and differentiated among them. Only about 7 percent of the respondents said "don't know" to any of the six items, with 4 percent saying "don't know" to only one criterion and one half of the remainder saying "don't know" to two criteria. Fewer than 4 percent of the respondents said that all six criteria were "very important"; only another 6 percent rated five of the criteria as "very important" and 9 percent gave this response for four criteria. Less than one-sixth thought three criteria were "very important," and approximately one-fifth each rated two criteria or only one criterion as "very important." Another one-fifth rated none of the criteria as "very important." A count of the responses "somewhat important" and "not important" over the six criteria yielded parallel figures.

relation is between occupation and education (.424), followed by that between beliefs and life-style (.354). Occupation and money both correlate more highly with each other and with education than they do with the other three criteria. Education, however, has its highest correlation with occupation but its lowest correlation with money. These results suggest that, of the first three criteria, occupation and money may be interpreted as objective status criteria, while education is primarily an objective criterion that has a significant cultural and expressive component as well. This interpretation is supported by the fact that the last three criteria (beliefs, life-style, family) all correlate more highly with education than with the other two objective criteria. Of the last three criteria, beliefs has its highest correlation with life-style, followed by those with family and with education; life-style has its highest correlations with beliefs and family, and family has its highest correlations with life-style and education. Thus, beliefs and life-style group together, while family may be interpreted as predominantly an expressive and cultural criterion but with a small objective status component. In short, the six criteria do form two broadly interpretable groups. At the same time, of course, the correlations between the objective and cultural criteria suggest that they are far from mutually exclusive.

We turn now to the importance of these six criteria in Americans'

TABLE 2.8

RATED IMPORTANCE OF SIX CRITERIA FOR MEMBERSHIP IN OWN SUBJECTIVE SOCIAL CLASS
(PERCENTAGE DISTRIBUTIONS FOR ALL RESPONDENTS)

Criteria	Very important	Somewhat important	Not important	Don't know	Base N
Occupation	37.0%	30.8	29.8	2.4	1,864
Education	33.2%	35.6	29.7	1.6	1,859
Money	28.9%	30.9	38.1	2.0	1,856
Beliefs and feelings	40.0%	28.5	27.9	3.6	1,852
Style of life	38.6%	34.0	24.1	3.3	1,855
Kind of family	21.4%	27.6	49.2	1.8	1,849

definitions of their social class. Table 2.8 presents the percentages of respondents rating each criterion as "very important," "somewhat important," and "not important" (as well as those saying "don't know"). The three factors most likely to be considered "very important" are "how the person believes and feels about things," "style of life," and "occupation". Each is rated "very important" by approximately two fifths of the respondents. Education is only slightly behind in rated importance, and it is as likely to be considered at least "somewhat important" as the three criteria above. Money and family background are the least likely to be considered important, with almost four out of ten and five out of ten, respectively, saying these two factors are "not important" in the way they define their social class.[14]

These data indicate that cultural and expressive factors weigh at least as heavily as objective status characteristics in Americans' conceptions of their social class. These results are fairly consistent with those obtained by Centers thirty years earlier, although the emphasis on cultural and expressive factors is less exclusive in the present data.[15] Recall that the correlations among the six criteria indicate that few people mentioned exclusively cultural or objective factors. Indeed, a separate analysis indicates that only about 8 percent of the sample (excluding missing data) limited their choices to occupation, education, and/or money, and only about 10 percent limited their choices to beliefs, life-style, and/or family. As many as 80 percent chose at least one criterion from the first group *and* at least one from the second group. These patterns imply that class is indeed popularly interpreted as a social as well as an economic phenomenon. The set of criteria people use to define class membership exceeds the narrow Weberian definition of class and incorporates the criteria associated with Weberian status groups.

Examination of the criteria for class membership in each of the subjective classes indicates only a slight variant on this general theme. Table 2.9 presents the mean rated importance of each of the six criteria by subjective class and race. Weber argued that people in higher status groups would be more inclined to define group membership in terms of cultural characteristics, as a way of keeping their membership more exclusive (Weber 1946:192-193). Consistent with this argument, there is a slight tendency among whites for the relative mean importance assigned to expressive, rather than objective, criteria to increase with ascending subjective class. Blacks are more likely to rate all criteria except money as "very important," with no consistent class differences in the relative ranking of objective and cultural criteria. Reading across the rows for whites, the highest mean

---

[14]These patterns undermine the suggestion by Goldthorpe et al. (1969:147-150), Coleman and Rainwater (1978), and Bell and Robinson (1980:341-342) that money is the critical ingredient of social standing. Note also that Americans' conceptions of class pay little attention to a person's family background. Social mobility appears to be both expected and accepted. This is consistent with Centers's results, although the rated importance of family background seems to have fallen more sharply behind other factors in the present study.

[15]The results in the present study for white males only are essentially the same as those for the full sample.

TABLE 2.9
MEAN RATED IMPORTANCE OF SIX CRITERIA FOR MEMBERSHIP IN
OWN SUBJECTIVE SOCIAL CLASS (BY SUBJECTIVE CLASS AND RACE)

	Occupation	Education	Income	Beliefs	Life-style	Family
Whites[a]						
Poor	2.17	2.23	2.34	1.96	2.09	1.82
Working	2.12	1.95	1.76	2.06	1.98	1.66
Middle	1.93	1.96	1.94	2.07	2.19	1.69
Upper-middle	1.97	2.03	1.94	2.13	2.14	1.57
Upper	2.00	2.44	1.69	2.25	2.56	2.06
Blacks[b]						
Poor	2.28	2.42	2.13	2.37	2.21	1.94
Working	2.20	2.26	1.77	2.36	2.33	2.05
Middle	2.28	2.14	1.86	2.30	2.16	1.84

NOTE: Criteria scored as follows: "Not Important" and "Don't Know" = 1, "Somewhat important" =
2, "Very Important" = 3.
[a]Base Ns for each of the classes among whites range as follows: poor (76–78), working (580–588),
middle (758–761), upper-middle (147–149), upper (16). Note that the upper-class N is too small to be
reliable.
[b] Base Ns for each of the classes among blacks range as follows: poor (52–53), working (80–81), middle
(43). Since only 3 blacks identified with the upper-middle class and 3 with the upper class, means for
these groups are not presented.

ratings among those identifying with the poor are for two objective
criteria: money and education. For working-class identifiers, the two
criteria with the highest mean ratings are occupation and beliefs–one
objective and one expressive criterion. Among those identifying with
either the middle or the upper-middle class, the two criteria with the
highest mean ratings are both expressive: life-style and beliefs.[16] These
class differences should not, however, be overstated. There is only slight
variation by class around the more persistent pattern of both objective and
expressive criteria being prominent in the definition of class membership.

CONCLUSIONS

This chapter has explored cognitive interpretations of five common
social class terms: poor, working class, middle class, upper-middle class,

---

[16]These small class differences in the importance of objective and expressive criteria are not
affected by controlling for respondents' blue-collar/white-collar status.

and upper class. Although these terms are frequently used, there has been no thorough analysis of their meaning to Americans since Centers's classic study published over thirty years ago. Such an analysis is especially germane since some have argued that social class has become meaningless or irrelevant to most Americans.

Direct comparison with Centers's study is complicated by differing samples and items, but the general pattern of our results suggests that social class is no less significant to Americans in the 1970s than it was in the 1940s. About eight out of ten Americans feel at least somewhat strongly about their identification with a social class, and as many as five out of ten feel very strongly about it. More important, the critical exercise of associating occupations with classes elicits little or no confusion from most respondents, who also demonstrate considerable agreement about how occupations are affiliated with classes.

The way Americans (both white and black) associate occupations with classes suggests that they are more sensitive to socioeconomic hierarchies based on occupational prestige, education, skill, income, job authority and task discretion than they are to the blue-collar/white-collar dichotomy. The only occupations, however, that elicit sharp disagreement about their class location are the skilled blue-collar occupations. Thus, while white-collar status is most commonly considered insufficient for middle-class membership if the work is routine, it is also true that many Americans cannot think of manual work as middle class, even if it is skilled.

Beyond the basic issue of the perceived affiliation of occupations with classes, Americans' broader definitions of criteria for membership in their own social class indicate clearly that class is experienced as a social or cultural affinity as much as an objective, economic affinity. Such cultural and expressive criteria as "how the person believes and feels about things" and "the person's style of life" are as likely to be considered important in defining subjective social class as "the person's occupation." While the relative importance assigned to cultural and expressive factors increases somewhat with ascending social class, the emphasis on cultural or objective criteria is far from mutually exclusive in any class.

In short, the analyses of this chapter suggest that there is reasonable agreement about the basic issue of the association between occupations and classes, and that popular notions of this association are guided by standard socioeconomic criteria. They also suggest a widespread tendency to define class membership more broadly than by objective status characteristics alone. These patterns are at variance with the idea that there is considerable confusion about class; nor do they support the more general argument that social class is of dwindling significance in the

United States. On the contrary, they suggest that class has a subjective meaning that transcends the economic sphere and incorporates factors normally associated with status groups.

3

Affective and Interpretive Implications of Class Identification

We have established that social class has a ready interpretation for most people, an interpretation that includes both objective and cultural ingredients. In this chapter, we go beyond the issue of cognitive identification to examine the extent to which Americans attach emotional significance to class and interpret social life in class terms.

As we have already noted, cognitive identification is a necessary first step for class consciousness. If people have difficulty identifying with a social class or appear confused about what social classes are, then class as an issue of any subjective significance would be moot. Once cognitive identification has been established, however, it is important to know whether it ends with that fact as a dry datum in the person's mind, or whether this identification provides a basis for affective bonds and interpretations of social life. In other words, is class simply a cognitive label that the person perceives without difficulty, or is it a more central part of the person's identity?

In addressing this question, it is productive to compare class identity with racial identity. Race provides an important criterion because the basis for membership in racial groups is more clear-cut than it is for class. Indeed, the issue of how people choose a group label is moot for race, since the cues for racial group membership are sufficiently delineated so that few people can make "errors" in assigning themselves or others to groups. This, coupled with the long-standing visibility of race as a policy issue, doubtless accounts for the fact that race has been more widely recognized by scholars as an important source of group identity in American society. Racial identity thus provides a useful comparative reference

against which the pervasiveness of class identity can be more meaningfully evaluated. At the same time, a comparison of the relative power
of race and class affiliations in generating affective bonds and interpretations of social life bears critically on the long-standing issue of the relative
significance of culturally and structurally based cleavages.

We address the depth and significance of class identity in the following
ways. First, we examine affective class bonds through an analysis of
people's feelings of warmth toward and closeness to their social class. We
then explore the extent to which differences are seen between social
classes, and the ways that people interpret and explain such differences.
Finally, we investigate the extent to which people interpret economic
practices in terms of class interests. These factors are all important elements of class consciousness. The development of emotional bonds to
people of one's own class and the perception of class interests have always
been central to discussions of class identity. Similarly, the perception of
class distinctions and the interpretation of those distinctions in ways that
reflect one's own class interests bear directly on any assessment of the
depth of class identity.

AFFECTIVE CLASS BONDS

The issue of whether subjective social class encompasses a feeling of
emotional attachment is perhaps more critical than any other factor in
assessing whether class is more than a nominal identification. Certainly,
this issue is central to the debate about the significance of social class.

Consider the simplest argument that class is of limited or dwindling
significance in advanced industrial societies (e.g., Nisbet 1970; Bell 1973).
This view anticipates that even nominal identification is lacking for many
or most people. Consistent with this, many analysts have argued that
apparent nominal identification with a social class is an artifact induced by
forced-choice questions (e.g., Gross 1953; Rosenberg 1953; Haer 1957).
From this perspective, the class identification elicited from respondents
with such questions should completely lack any emotional overlay. If class
identification is peripheral, even at a cognitive level, then that identification cannot be emotionally invested.

A second argument, expressed most directly by Lane (1962:chap. 4), is
that in a society that boasts equality of opportunity, people in lower social
classes can gain little intrinsic satisfaction from their class position. Con-
fronted with their own low status and with an ideology that provides no
easy "excuse" for that fact, individuals from lower classes are faced with
the uncomfortable task of rationalizing their position. Lane suggests that

a variety of strategies are used to this end, most notably the denial of the significance of class. His discussion implies that for people in higher classes, the consonance of the ideology of opportunity and their own position should produce positive feelings associated with their class identification. For those in a less fortunate position, their class is at best a factor to be minimized, and at worst an active source of discomfort.

Although seldom explicitly discussed, the same configuration of class and affect is implied by the more general argument that there is at least a reasonable degree of consensus in American society about the ideology of opportunity. As many analysts have noted (e.g., Marx 1964:78-80; Dahrendorf 1959:280-289; Parkin 1971:79-82), it is in the interest of dominant groups to foster an ideology that stresses the equity of the status quo. While common acceptance of this ideology promotes stability, it must do so at the expense of the self-esteem of lower classes. If, as some would have us believe (e.g., Davis and Moore 1945), the social structure is indeed interpreted in functionalist terms by all elements of society, individuals from lower classes would be left with little cause for positive feelings of group identity.

In contrast to these views is the representation of social class as a source of positive affective bonds for all classes. If we approach class either from a Marxist perspective or as a prime example of a Weberian status group, we would expect subjective social class to be associated with a sense of emotional belongingness. It is clear from Marx's discussion that the transition from being a "class in itself" to a "class for itself" necessitates the development of emotional bonds within that class. Similarly, if classes are to conform to Weber's (1946) criteria for status groups, they must constitute emotionally bounded communities. Weber emphasized that this is true even for negatively privileged status groups: "Even pariah people who are most despised are usually apt to continue cultivating . . . the belief in their own specific 'honor'" (1946:189). He argued that while high status groups could derive their sense of "honor" from their present role and their great past, low status groups would base their honor on an anticipated future glorious role. There is an interesting parallel between this and the Marxist view that the positive connotations of working-class membership are associated with a future revolutionary role that will transform society. While Marx recognized that there would be many obstacles to this development among the proletariat, these obstacles would be gradually overcome. In the advanced stages of capitalism, when the proletariat's revolutionary role is imminent, the proletariat should display stronger affective bonds than the now-weakened bourgeoisie. These two views, along with their derivative, the interest-group perspective, anticipate that social class identification should minimally have a positive affective overlay for all classes.

Our measures of affective class and race bonds are from a self-administered booklet which the interviewer introduced as follows:

> The questions in this booklet ask about various feelings people might have toward different groups. On the first page, you are asked generally how warm or cold you feel toward different groups. The warmer you feel toward a group, the higher the number you should select from the scale at the top of the page. The colder you feel, the lower the number you should select.

Questions were of the form, "In general, how warm or cold do you feel toward poor people?" Respondents were asked about their warmth toward each of the five social classes, and toward blacks and whites, always starting with the subordinate group in each setting. The questions on warmth were followed by a parallel set of questions, "In general, how close do you feel to _____?" Respondents selected their responses from a nine-point scale extending from left to right that was printed at the beginning of each set of questions, and they recorded responses in the box next to each question. The left-hand pole of the scales was labeled 1 (*very cold/not at all close*), and the right-hand pole was labeled 9 (*very warm/very close*). The intervals between were marked 2 to 8, and the midpoint (5) was labeled *neither cold nor warm/neither one feeling nor the other*.

Warmth and closeness reflect two primary emotions in discussions of group consciousness. The warmth/coldness dimension is essentially a positive/negative one, which is clearly at the heart of affect. The closeness items are more a reflection of feelings of affinity. A related distinction between the two sets of items is that those for warmth do have a clear negative pole ("very cold"), whereas the opposite pole for "very close" expresses lack of feeling of affinity, rather than explicitly negative feelings. Yet we do not wish to overstate the differences between the warmth and closeness items. We would expect the two kinds of emotions to be strongly associated with each other, as indeed they are: the correlations between feelings of warmth toward and closeness to each of the five classes and the two racial groups range from .66 to .76, with a mean of .70.

Since we are concerned with affective boundaries between groups, our primary interest is not in *absolute* feelings of warmth toward or closeness to individual groups. Instead, the critical issue is the extent to which people *differentiate* their feelings toward their own and other groups. For example, it is difficult to interpret a response that a person feels "not at all

TABLE 3.1
MEAN SCORES FOR FEELINGS OF PREFERENCE FOR OWN CLASS AND RACE (BY CLASS AND RACE)

	Whites				Blacks		
	Poor	Working	Middle	Upper-middle	Poor	Working	Middle
Warmth toward own class minus warmth toward:							
upper	2.12	1.63	1.08	0.60	1.92	1.74	1.12
upper-middle	1.62	1.14	0.61	—	1.56	1.35	0.60
middle	1.04	0.54	—	−0.05	1.15	0.67	—
working	0.21	—	0.00	0.02	0.27	—	−0.49
poor	—	0.38	0.18	0.05	—	−0.06	−0.40
Warmth toward own race minus warmth toward other race	1.70	1.28	1.16	1.10	1.90	1.53	2.00
Closeness toward own class minus closeness toward:							
upper	2.21	1.86	1.38	0.85	1.98	1.92	1.19
upper-middle	1.83	1.34	0.78	—	1.67	1.68	0.88
middle	0.89	0.58	—	0.07	1.26	1.03	—
working	0.26	—	0.23	0.58	0.35	—	−0.74
poor	—	0.62	0.69	1.04	—	−0.04	−0.62
Closeness toward own race minus closeness toward other race	2.40	1.76	1.79	1.52	2.19	1.79	2.49

NOTE: Means are calculated from difference scores ranging in one-point intervals from +8 (warmer toward or closer to own class or race) to −8 (warmer toward or closer to other class or race).

close" to another class without also knowing how the person feels toward her own class, and so on.

Accordingly, our measure of affective class bonds reflects the difference between people's feelings toward their own class and their feelings toward each of the other classes. By subtracting the latter from the former, we obtain four scales for people from each class, with possible ranges from -8 (strong preference for other class) through 0 (no differentiation in class feelings) to +8 (strong preference for own class). The same procedure is used to measure the own-race preference of blacks and whites. The measures allow us to assess both the direction and strength of class (or race) preference.

Table 3.1 presents mean feelings of own-class and own-race preference in warmth and closeness, by subjective class and race. Given the large number of comparisons involved here, means rather than percentage distributions are reported, in order to simplify the presentation. Our discussion, however, incorporates both the means and the percentage distributions.

Three main patterns are clear in table 3.1. First, there is pronounced evidence of affective class bonds. Second, affect for other classes is determined by two concurrent tendencies: one is to prefer classes closer to one's own over those that are farther away, and the other is to prefer lower classes over higher ones. Finally, there are important differences between blacks and whites in the pattern of class bonds. Let us elaborate.

Contrary to the common argument that social class has become an archaic concept, the data in table 3.1 suggest that affective class bonds are substantial. There is considerable evidence of own-class preference in feelings of both warmth and closeness, but affective bonds are especially pronounced in the closeness items. Notice also that among both whites and blacks, these class bonds become stronger among lower classes. For example, if we calculate the average of the four mean preference scores in warmth and in closeness for each class, we find that for whites on warmth, this average increases monotonically from .16 for the upper-middle class to 1.25 for the poor. For feelings of closeness, the comparable averages range from .64 to 1.30.

The strength of these class bonds becomes clearer if we consider the percentage distributions on which these means are based. Almost all of the variance in each distribution is bounded by the range between no class preference (the neutral point) and some degree of own-class preference. Even for mean scores of 0, such as the one reported for feelings of relative warmth toward their own and the working class by white middle class respondents, very few respondents venture into other-class preference. Of these individuals, 72 percent are neutral, with the remainder divided equally between own-and other-class preference. Higher mean scores reflect distributions in which a trivial minority (between 5 and 8 percent) display other-class preference, and an increasing number display own-class preference. For example, among white poor respondents, the mean closeness preference score between their own and the upper class of 2.21 reflects a distribution where 34 percent are neutral, and fully 63 percent display own-class preference.

Thus, the means in table 3.1 summarize a pronounced inverse relationship between subjective class and affective class bonds. This, of course, provides little support for the second argument outlined earlier that individuals from lower classes try to minimize their status given their "failure" in a society that stresses equality of opportunity. Instead we find that such individuals are *more* likely to have positive feelings of group identity.[1]

Within each class, affective class bonds are more sharply expressed in differentiation from some classes than from others. There is a general tendency for affective differentiation to increase monotonically as classes become less proximate to one's own. There is also a general tendency for a stronger degree of own-class preference to be displayed when *high-er*classes are the referent than when lower classes are the referent. As a result of these two tendencies, the own-class preference of the poor has its weakest expression when they compare themselves to the working class; in comparisons with each higher class, own-class preference among the poor gradually increases until it reaches its strongest expression when the upper class is the referent. Similarly, members of the white middle class display greater affective differentiation from the poor than from the working class, and greater differentiation from the upper class than from the upper-middle class; at the same time, they differentiate themselves more from the upper and upper-middle classes than they do from either the poor or the working class.

There are interesting differences between blacks and whites in these patterns. Essentially, these patterns take an exaggerated form among blacks. Blacks who identify with the poor express class bonds comparable to those of their white class peers, and working- and middle-class blacks draw much the same affective boundaries between their own and *higher* classes as do their white class peers. In their expression of feelings for classes *lower* than their own, however, the black members of the working and middle classes draw *no* affective class boundaries. Working-class blacks tend to feel just as warm toward and close to the poor as they do to their own class, and middle-class blacks actually tend to express a preference for the poor and the working class *over their own class*.

Finally, a useful way of evaluating the strength of class bonds is to compare them with the strength of race bonds. Among poor and working-class whites, the figures in table 3.1 suggest that class bonds are at least as strong as race bonds, if not stronger. For feelings of warmth, both of these groups show slightly more own-class preference when comparing themselves with the upper class than they show own-race preference. The corresponding figures for closeness suggest that own-class and own-race preference are of roughly equal magnitude. The relative magnitude of own-class preference decreases as the referent classes become more proximate. Among upper-middle-, and to a lesser degree, middle-class

---

[1]Recall from chapter 2 that the same pattern was found, in weaker form, for intensity of class identification.

whites, own-race preference remains at a level similar to that for the working class, but this level exceeds their own-class feelings. This of course reflects the fact that the magnitude of class bonds varies inversely with class; but at the same time, feelings of distance from the upper class among the upper-middle class are as strong as the feelings of distance from any other contiguous class in the table. Among blacks, the figures for the poor and working class have a pattern similar to that for whites. The black middle-class identifiers, however, exhibit a radically different pattern, suggesting a level of race preference that is approximately twice as high as their own-class preference vis-a-vis the upper class. This would seem to be further support for the argument that, despite their cognitive identification with the middle class, these individuals do not have a middle-class identity.

To pursue these issues farther, we rearrange the data in order to make an explicit comparison at the individual level between people's affective bonds to their class and to their racial group. For each respondent, we calculate the difference between her feeling of warmth (or closeness) for her subjective class and for her racial group. This procedure yields two trichotomies, which are reported in table 3.2: those who feel warmer (or closer) toward their *class* than their race; those who feel *equally* warm (or close) toward their class and their race; and those who feel warmer (or closer) toward their *race* than their class. The distributions on these trichotomies, by race and by class, are most revealing.

Among whites, the prevailing tendency is for a higher proportion to express stronger class feelings (first row) than to express stronger race feelings (third row), and this tendency is especially pronounced among lower social classes. For both warmth and closeness, the poor are approximately four times more likely to express stronger bonds toward their own class than toward their own race, and over 40 percent of them express such class bonds. The working class is almost three times as likely to express stronger class bonds. In contrast, among both the middle and upper-middle classes, the tendency to prefer class over race is only barely larger than the opposite tendency. The poor are almost twice as likely as the middle and upper-middle classes to prefer their own class over their own race, with the working class falling in between. Finally, it should be emphasized that among whites, only a small minority of any class (but especially of the poor and the working class) express stronger race than class bonds. For the overwhelming majority of whites, class bonds are at least as strong as or stronger than race bonds.

The prevailing tendency among blacks is the opposite of that among whites: stronger race bonds (third row) exceed the expression of stronger class bonds (first row). Among the black poor, class bonds either balance

TABLE 3.2

COMPARISON OF FEELINGS TOWARD OWN CLASS WITH FEELINGS TOWARD OWN RACE
(BY CLASS AND RACE)

	Whites				Blacks		
	Poor	Working	Middle	Upper-middle	Poor	Working	Middle
Warmer toward class	40.6%	33.9%	24.8%	23.0%	17.3%	12.7%	4.7%
Equal (class and race)	49.3	52.8	55.6	56.1	65.4	57.0	46.5
Warmer toward race	10.1	13.3	19.6	20.9	17.2	30.4	48.8
Base *N*	(69)	(570)	(746)	(148)	(52)	(79)	(43)
Closer to class	45.5	35.1	26.3	27.4	19.2	11.7	4.8
Equal (class and race)	42.4	52.4	53.5	51.4	75.0	61.0	35.7
Closer to race	12.1	12.5	20.2	21.2	5.8	27.3	59.5
Base *N*	(66)	(569)	(746)	(146)	(52)	(77)	(42)

NOTE: Warmth toward and closeness to one's own class was subtracted from warmth toward and closeness to one's own race.

off or are greater than race bonds. The relationship between subjective class and the relative strength of class and race bonds, however, follows an exaggerated pattern among blacks. Thus members of the black working class express stronger race bonds by a ratio of more than two to one, and members of the black middle class display stronger race feelings by a ratio of at least ten to one. Thus, fully 60 percent of the black middle class feel closer to their racial group than to their class, while a mere 5 percent express the opposite feeling. This provides even stronger and more direct evidence than the data in table 3.1 that for the black middle class, racial bonds overwhelm their feelings of class identity.

What light do these results shed on the affective significance of social class in America? Most clearly, they provide evidence of considerable feelings of class identity, despite the common argument that class is peripheral to most people in advanced industrial societies like the United States. The pervasiveness of these feelings of class identity is underscored by the fact that whites overwhelmingly express feelings for their subjective class which are at least as strong as or stronger than their feelings for their racial group.

Beyond this, the patterns displayed in people's affective class bonds reveal important information about the nature of social class. First, there is no evidence of a "deference-achievement" syndrome in people's class feelings. There is no support for the view that, in a society that stresses an ideology of equality of opportunity, class bonds will be strongest among higher classes (the "successful") and weakest among lower classes (the "failures"). On the contrary, there is an *inverse* relationship between class and strength of class bonds, such that lower classes express the *most* own-class preference. In addition, far from expressing a preference for higher classes, it is in relation to higher classes that people draw sharper affective boundaries.

The inverse relation between class and strength of class bonds presents a superficial parallel to aspects of the Marxist perspective, but we should emphasize that we do not take this as evidence that the proletariat's revolutionary role is imminent. Among other things, too many differences between blacks and whites remain to sustain such an interpretation. Rather, we take this pattern, along with the corresponding one for affective race ties, to suggest that subordinate group members are more likely to feel strongly about the intergroup context as a whole than are dominant group members.

In any context, those in a subordinate status are likely to feel more keenly the significance of the status differentiation, because the negative accruements of low status are more sharply experienced than are the benefits of high status. Thus, racial status differentiation may seem more significant to blacks, who experience the resulting constraints to their opportunities and life-style, than it does to whites, who enjoy the concomitant privileges. Similarly, social class has more salience to those who experience its constraints than to those who enjoy its privileges. The sharper differentiation of own-class feelings from higher classes than from lower classes (even among the middle and upper-middle classes) reinforces our interpretation that people are more aware of the boundaries that separate them from those with higher status than from those who are less privileged. In this way, a sense of shared fate is likely to develop among subordinate groups before dominant groups develop a conscious feeling of group identity. In fact, as Mannheim (1936:229-232) noted, it is only when subordinate groups challenge the status quo that dominant groups are prompted to develop a conscious group identity.

A second revealing pattern in these data is that class is not treated as a single "us/them" dichotomy by any class.[2] If it was, people's feelings would not differentiate among classes other than their own. Instead, not only do people differentiate more from higher classes than from lower ones, but they also differentiate more from classes as they become more distant from their own. It seems that as classes become more proximate,

---

[2]This parallels the conclusion reached by Bell and Robinson (1980:337-341) in their exploratory study of the United States and England.

people assume they have more in common with the members of those classes, with the most positive feelings being reserved for their own class. This graded pattern in people's feelings indicates that the five classes are treated as distinct entities rather than being merged into a simple us/them dichotomy. This reinforces our argument that social class should not be defined in terms of any single dichotomous criterion (such as blue collar/white collar or workers/owners) but is instead an ordered series of status groups.

Finally, the differences in patterns of class identity between blacks and whites have interesting implications. The most dramatic of these involve black middle-class identifiers, who display more affect toward *lower* classes (the poor and working class) than toward their own class, and who claim closer bonds to other blacks than they do to their class. This suggests that for these people, affective class bonds are distinctly secondary to their racial identity. A less dramatic coupling of weak class bonds and strong race bonds is found among working-class blacks, and it is only among the poor that blacks treat their class identity comparably to whites.[3] This pattern bears on the argument advanced by Wilson (1980) that as blacks increasingly enter middle class positions, the significance of race is yielding to class within the black community. To the contrary, we find that even the fact of a cognitive middle class identification does not imply the development of stronger class feelings among blacks, but seems instead to be associated with weaker feelings of class identity.

Consistent with the inverse relationship between class identification and strength of affective class bonds, blacks express more emotional preoccupation with their racial-group membership than do whites. Blacks who identify with the poor make an especially instructive case, because they have two subordinate statuses, one "cultural" and one "structural." Their prevailing response is to express equally strong feelings for their racial group and their class, a response that distinguishes them both from the white poor (who are more likely to express stronger feelings for their class than for their race) and from blacks in the working and middle classes (who are increasingly likely to be emotionally preoccupied with race). To the extent that blacks in the working and middle classes do express sensitivity to their class membership, it is restricted solely to differentiation from *higher* classes. Contrary to the pluralist argument, not all group memberships have equal weight, and hence it is easy to overestimate the significance of crosscutting affiliations. Instead, these results

---

[3]Given the strength of race bonds among blacks, their feelings toward various social classes are doubtless influenced by the wide differences in the racial composition of those classes. Thus, middle class blacks may feel warmer toward classes lower than their own in part because lower classes include more blacks, and so on.

reaffirm our argument that subordinate statuses are more likely to be keenly experienced than dominant statuses. They also help explain the failure of earlier research to find linkages between socioeconomic status and class identification for blacks that parallel those found for whites (Jackman and Jackman 1973, and several studies since), a subject to which we return in the next chapter.

INTERPRETATIONS OF CLASS DISTINCTIONS

How do people perceive and interpret differences among the social classes? The perception and causal attribution of group differences are important factors in the ideology of group consciousness. To bolster their advantaged position, dominant groups should promote the belief that the system functions equitably; observable differences between groups should be explained as the natural outcome of biological and subcultural distinctions. If subordinate groups are persuaded that the system is fair, an atmosphere of consensus flourishes; but it would be more consistent with their interests for subordinate groups to challenge the equity of the system by interpreting group differences in terms of a biased opportunity structure.

The critical distinction is between those who think group differences are intrinsic to the groups themselves and those who believe they are the product of a social structure that provides different groups with unequal opportunities. The first type of argument legitimizes the status quo by implying that any change in the social structure would have no effect on important group differences. This legitimizing approach has two main variants. One asserts that group differences are not only intrinsic but immutable, that is, they have a biological or genetic basis. Such an argument is associated most readily with social Darwinism (e.g., Sumner 1883), but more recently the argument has been made by Jensen (1969) that there are genetic differences in intelligence between both classes and races. Certainly, there is no more extreme way to claim the justice of social inequality than to assert that it reflects a "natural sorting" on the basis of genetic differences in human potential.

A less extreme legitimizing belief is that there are critical differences in the values and habits that are fostered by group subcultures. While the values and habits of groups need not be seen as immutable, the onus for change is still within the groups themselves, not the social structure. This viewpoint was given much expression during the 1960s when the "culture of poverty" thesis promoted the idea that unproductive values and habits among the poor create a self-perpetuating cycle of poverty from one generation to the next (e.g., Lewis 1966). Such an explanation of inequality should be a convenient one for dominant groups in advanced industrial societies, since it leaves the social structure free of blame while avoiding the blatant extremism and simplicity of the genetic argument, which may be more vulnerable to challenge. Indeed, there is some scattered survey evidence to suggest that Americans generally attribute poverty more to such individual factors than to structural forces (e.g., Feagin 1975; Huber and Form 1973:chap. 6).

Against either of these legitimizing arguments is the challenging view that the social structure itself is the source of group distinctions, with the implication that most important group differences could be eliminated by a change in the social structure. While the functionalist approach to stratification assumes there is consensus around the belief that the current social system is fair (e.g., Davis and Moore 1945), the Marxist position of course argues that a characteristic feature of the development of pro-letarian class consciousness is the perception of the social structure as biased against their interests. The interest-group approach has similarly argued that among those who have enjoyed fewer of society's rewards, inequality is more likely to be interpreted as structurally caused and less likely to be seen as a function of individual attributes (e.g., Huber and Form 1973). From these perspectives, any lack of conflict about the basic causes of group differentiation reflects the success of the dominant group in maintaining ideological control rather than any spontaneous con-sensus about the equity of the social system (e.g., Parkin 1971). Before subordinate groups can offer a competing interpretation, they must learn to base their observations of social life directly on their own experiences rather than filtering those experiences through the framework provided by the dominant ideology.

In our study, we approached this issue by asking respondents how many important differences they believe there are between the social classes, and then asking for their interpretation of what causes those differences. To measure the extent to which they perceived important class differences, respondents were asked the following question:

> Remember I asked you about the poor, the working class, the middle class, the upper-middle class, and the upper class. Do you think there are many important differences between these classes, some important differences, a few important differences, or no important differences?

(Perceived race differences were measured in the same way, except that the item began, "Apart from differences in appearance between blacks and whites, do you think . . . ?') Those who saw at least "a few" important differences were then asked:

> People disagree about why there are differences between these classes (blacks and whites). Which of the statements on this card comes closest to what you think? Just tell me the letter of your answer.
>
> X. Most differences are there because they're born different.
>
> Y. Most differences come from the way they're brought up at home.
>
> Z. Most differences come from the different opportunities they have in America.

Respondents could choose one or more of the three response options. The first response option represents the biological type of explanation, the second the socialization explanation, and the third the structural explanation. The attribution of differences to multiple types of factors is more difficult to interpret, both because they reflect more complex reasoning and because the meaning of the component factors may be altered as they are joined with other factors. (For example, people who explain differences in terms of groups both being "born different" and having "different opportunities" may be referring to socioeconomic [rather than biological] inheritance along with subsequent opportunities.) Fortuitously, respondents were usually content to endorse a single argument.

We begin by reviewing people's responses to the first question. Most people, whatever their race or class, believe there are at least a few important differences between the social classes. Fewer than one in ten respondents believe there are no important class differences, about one in five say there are "a few" important differences, just under one-half say "some," and about one quarter think there are "many" important class differences. There is only trivial variation around these proportions by class or race. That so many people perceive class differences that they consider important reaffirms our earlier observations that far from being nebulous, class is readily construed by Americans. In this context, it is significant that among both blacks and whites, the belief that there are important class differences is a little more prevalent than the belief that there are important differences between blacks and whites.

The way people interpret these perceived differences gives us insight into the shape and meaning of their perceptions. Table 3.3 presents the

TABLE 3.3

EXPLANATION OF CLASS AND RACE DIFFERENCES (BY CLASS AND RACE)

	Whites					Blacks			
	Poor	Working	Middle	Upper-middle	Total	Poor	Working	Middle	Total
Explanations of class differences									
Opportunities	60.9%	48.2%	45.9%	34.1%	46.3%	55.3%	50.7%	56.4%	53.5%
Home	26.6	33.5	35.3	37.8	34.5	12.8	36.6	23.1	26.1
Born different	6.3	6.3	7.4	8.1	7.0	4.3	5.6	2.6	4.5
Combination of reasons	1.6	11.0	10.5	17.0	10.9	25.5	2.8	15.4	12.7
Don't know	4.7	1.0	0.9	3.0	1.3	2.1	4.2	2.6	3.2
Base N	(64)	(508)	(700)	(135)	(1,407)	(47)	(71)	(39)	(157)
Percentage of total seeing any class differences	91.0%	89.3%	93.4%	92.6%	91.7%	88.9%	90.0%	93.0%	90.4%
Explanations of Race differences									
Opportunities	29.3%	26.4%	32.3%	23.8%	29.2%	43.8%	42.4%	39.4%	41.9%
Home	32.8	38.7	36.0	34.9	36.7	21.9	35.6	27.3	29.8
Born different	29.3	21.6	14.5	17.5	18.0	6.3	10.2	12.1	9.7
Combination of reasons	5.1	11.8	16.7	23.8	15.1	28.1	11.9	21.2	18.5
Don't know	3.4	1.5	0.5	0.0	0.9	0.0	0.0	0.0	0.0
Base N	(58)	(473)	(650)	(126)	(1,307)	(32)	(59)	(33)	(124)
Percentage of total seeing any race differences	84.6%	82.9%	88.0%	85.9%	85.8%	59.3%	73.7%	76.7%	70.0%

percentage endorsing each of the possible explanations of class and race differences, by class and race. The first pattern to observe in these figures is that the three explanations of class differences vary considerably in their likelihood of being endorsed. Only a tiny minority from any class (8 percent or less) attribute class differences to genetic factors. The most popular explanation of class differences among all classes (except the upper-middle class) and among both races is in terms of varying opportunities.

The extent to which this structural interpretation of perceived class differences is favored among whites varies inversely with social class: among the poor, it is preferred over the subcultural explanation by a ratio of more than two to one (61 percent *vs.* 27 percent), but the gap between the popularity of the two explanations gradually shrinks until it disappears among the upper-middle class (34 percent *vs.* 38 percent). The argument that both subcultural and structural factors are at work accounts for most of the "combination" responses given. This explanation, which tempers criticism of the status quo with claims of intrinsic group differences, is somewhat more popular among whites identifying with the upper-middle class (12 percent *vs.* 1.6 percent of the poor), but its overall popularity is about on a par with the genetic argument. Thus, while the relationship of social class to the interpretation of perceived class differences is not dramatic, it does follow a steady pattern among whites that is consistent with the interest-group perspective. Indeed, the general popularity of the structural interpretation and the increasing edge that it enjoys with descending social class—despite a pervasive dominant ideology of equality of opportunity in America—may be taken as evidence of a significant failure of that ideology to persuade all citizens (especially the less privileged) of its veracity.

Among blacks, identifiers with the poor and working class offer the various explanations of perceived class differences with about the same frequency as their white class peers. (The only distinction is that about 14 percent fewer of the black poor than the white poor endorse the subcultural explanation, opting instead for the subcultural and structural factors jointly.) Middle-class blacks, however, resemble poor blacks more than middle-class whites in the way they explain perceived class differences—a behavior pattern consistent with the class feelings expressed by middle-class blacks.

A comparison of the class data with people's interpretations of perceived race differences suggests two interesting points. First, any black challenge to whites' beliefs is more likely to be in the form of a denial that there are any race differences than to be in terms of an alternative interpretation of what causes such differences. Blacks are less likely than whites to believe there are important race differences, but among blacks who do see differences, their explanations of these differences vary less from whites' explanations than poor people's explanations of class differences vary from those given by the upper-middle class. The genetic explanation is the least favored by both blacks and whites, although whites are somewhat more likely to use it. Of the other two explanations, whites show a slight preference for the subcultural one, and blacks slightly prefer the structural one. The second interesting point is that among both whites and blacks, race differences are somewhat less likely to be explained in structural terms than are class differences, and while the biological argument is still unpopular, it receives more frequent endorsement in the context of race differences than class differences. In short, class differences are more likely than race differences to be perceived, more likely to be interpreted as structurally caused, and more likely to induce a subordinate-group interpretation that challenges the interpretation asserted by the dominant group.

PERCEPTION OF CLASS INTERESTS

We now turn to a direct assessment of the way people perceive the interests of their own and other classes. Do they see the classes as having opposed interests? or do they interpret economic issues as affecting all classes in much the same way? The degree to which people explicitly perceive social classes as having distinct or shared economic interests has traditionally been seen as vital to the politics of class consciousness. The relationship of social class to the expression of class bonds and to the interpretation of class differences suggests that there is an increasing sense of shared fate with descending class. Yet these patterns need not reflect an explicitly articulated (and therefore more sophisticated) awareness of class interests.

There are two facets to the expression of class interests. First, to what extent is social life interpreted in class terms? Do people believe that classes have mutually opposed, special interests, or do they think all classes have the same interests? Second, how much disagreement is there in the perspectives of various social classes? Is the perception of class interests marked by consensus across classes, or are class interests perceived differently by dominant and subordinate groups?

Theoretical expectations about how these factors translate into evidence for or against group consciousness are not clear-cut, but several possibilities are apparent. At one extreme we have a picture of dominant and subordinate groups polarized by an awareness of mutually opposed interests. Conflict is based on zero-sum interpretations of class interests in which each group believes that its interests can be advanced only at the expense of the other. Polarization of this kind suggests a situation of explicit class hostility and conflict, such as that envisaged by Marx when revolution is imminent. There are, however, two less blatant forms of ideological conflict that have been taken as evidence of group consciousness. In one case, the dominant group generalizes its own interests to everyone, but the subordinate group believes that class interests are distinct. In the other case, each class denies the existence of special class interests and instead generalizes its own interests to all classes. Thus, dominant groups interpret the status quo as beneficial to all classes, but subordinate groups see it as hurting all classes. Finally, there is one case that presents unambiguous evidence against group consciousness, namely, where consensus embraces the status quo and all classes agree that current arrangements are beneficial to everyone. Let us examine the arguments that have been made about each of these possibilities.

Two arguments about the perception of group interests are associated with Marx. First is the zero-sum set of interpretations mentioned above, where prerevolutionary polarization leads each class to define its own interests sharply in opposition to the other. Another well-known argument by Marx is that the dominant group has a natural control over prevailing ideology. As a result, it will be more subtle in the way it propagates its position: the dominant group does not justify the major institutions of society in terms of its own selfish interests, but in terms of their generally beneficial properties for society as a whole.

> The ideas of the ruling class are, in every age, the ruling ideas . . . .
> The dominant ideas are nothing more than the ideal expression of
> the dominant material relationships . . . . During the time that the
> aristocracy was dominant the concepts honor, loyalty, etc., were
> dominant; during the dominance of the bourgeoisie the concepts
> freedom, equality, etc . . . . Each new class which puts itself in
> place of the one ruling before it is compelled, simply in order to
> achieve its aims, to represent its interest as the common interest
> of all members of society. [Marx, 1964:78-80]

The task of the subordinate group, then, is to reinterpret those same institutions as beneficial only to the dominant class at the expense of the remainder of society; in other words, to develop a sense of grievance about the status quo. Thus, from Marx it is not clear whether group consciousness implies zero-sum interpretations by both sides, or whether it is advantageous only to the subordinate group to emphasize special group interests.

This last pattern is one that has been stressed as evidence of ideological rift between dominant and subordinate groups by more recent writers (e.g., Dahrendorf 1959:280-289; Parkin 1971:chap. 3; Huber and Form 1973). Since ideology functions at least partly as a persuasive tool, it would seem rational for a well-entrenched dominant class to argue the merits of the status quo in terms of its generally beneficial effects; but for those in a subordinate position, it is more rational to draw attention to the ways in which the social order systematically works to their disadvantage. From this point of view, it makes sense for the dominant group to promote an ideology of individualism and opportunity, and carefully to avoid presenting the world in group terms. Exactly the opposite holds for the subordinate group. Dahrendorf writes:

> The dominant groups of society express their comparative gratification with existing conditions *inter alia* by visualizing and describing these conditions as ordered and reasonable; subjected groups, on the other hand, tend to emphasize the cleavages that in their opinion account for the deprivations they feel. [1959:284]

In contrast, in a highly polarized setting where the dominant group feels threatened by subordinate-group challenge and hostility undermines complacence, the definition of group interests may become more starkly cast on both sides.

The argument that no group cares to represent itself as pursuing purely its own selfish interests has been made by Gamson (1968:53-54). To be sure, dominant groups will deny their special interests with arguments such as "What is good for General Motors is good for the country." At the same time, however, Gamson implies that subordinate groups can turn this type of argument on its head: what is good for factory workers is good for the company, and hence the country. Apart from such materialist arguments, it is interesting to remember that socialist ideology emphasizes the benefits for all humanity which are to be derived from a socialist state. Perhaps a distinction is needed here between short-run material interests and broader conceptions of the quality of life. Thus, for example, Marxist ideology has long emphasized that the competitiveness inherent to capitalism is ultimately as destructive to the mental health of capitalists as it is to that of the proletariat. It seems unlikely, however, that such esoteric concerns will figure prominently in subordinate-group attitudes given the more immediate material issues that they confront.

Against all these views is the model that anticipates no group consciousness: all groups agree that the status quo serves everyone's interests. The best-known expression of this argument remains the functionalist one, with its denial that classes exist as meaningful groups. The emphasis on the functional interdependence between different positions in society, coupled with the underlying notion of societal equilibrium, clearly implies both that there can be no special class interests and that people will not perceive any such interests (Davis and Moore 1945). A consensus view is also implied by more general arguments either that class does not exist (e.g., Nisbet 1970) or that in postindustrial societies the perception of special class interests has eroded in favor of more individualistic orientations (e.g., Bell 1973). Of course, what these theorists characterize as a natural lack of perceived group interests is what other analysts would describe as an ideological victory for the dominant class.

Despite the widespread importance that has been attached to these issues, direct empirical evidence on the extensiveness of perceived class interests is sorely lacking. Instead, existing evidence bears on these issues only in an oblique way. For example, some studies look for class differences in partisan attitudes, in attitudes about various policy areas, or in beliefs about the opportunity structure (e.g., Centers 1949:107-140; Huber and Form 1973; Butler and Stokes 1974:86-94). Any observed class differences are then taken as a display of perceived class interests. But while such patterns are intrinsically interesting, they do not give us direct evidence on the degree to which people have an explicitly articulated view of distinctive or common class interests. For example, even if we find that the proportion favoring private ownership of industry increases with social class, we have no evidence on whether people believe private ownership affects each class in a distinctive way, or whether they see its effects as universally beneficial or harmful.

Accordingly, both of our measures of perceived class interests have two components. For a given economic arrangement, we asked, first, who (if anyone) *benefits* from this practice, and who (if anyone) is *hurt* by it? As we shall see below, such a format is necessary to an evaluation of the extent to which each of the social classes perceives distinctive group interests. The items themselves were introduced by the following statement:

People have different opinions about who benefits and who is hurt by certain policies and practices in America today. I am going to read you a short list of such policies and practices and ask you for your opinion about who benefits and who is hurt by each of these.

The specific items were, in turn:

1a. How about private ownership–rather than government ownership–of business corporations? Who benefits from private ownership of business corporations–upper-class people, upper-middle-class people, middle-class people, working-class people, poor people, everyone, or no one?

1b. Who is hurt by this?

2a. Who benefits from the tax policy that reduces taxes for some types of business investment–upper-class people, upper-middle-class people, middle-class people, working-class people, poor people, everyone, or no one?

2b. Who is hurt by this?

The response options listed in the items were also listed on a show card for respondents, who could name any one or combination of the five classes, or could give one of the alternative responses (interviewers were instructed to mark *all* mentions).

The first of these items is pivotal to most discussions of class interests. From a Marxist point of view, of course, private ownership of the means of production is the central issue in the definition of class interests in capitalist society. From a capitalist perspective, private ownership is seen as superior to government ownership on the grounds that it is driven by neutral market forces, which are seen as more efficient and productive. This, in turn, is regarded as beneficial to all sectors of society. The rationale behind the second item is similar. The tax policy referred to is justified on the grounds that it provides an incentive for investment, which by stimulating the economy leads to increased productivity and employment opportunities. A more critical view is that such tax policies merely provide "welfare for the rich." In short, these items are designed to reflect perspectives about classic issues in the debate over class interests. The first is broad in focus; the second addresses a specific economic policy.

Responses to the two item-pairs are presented in tables 3.4 and 3.5, by class and race. The first three rows report responses that reflect a stark zero-sum view in which these policies are seen as benefiting higher classes and hurting lower classes. We have classified the dominant groups as the upper and/or upper-middle classes; in the first row, the subordinate groups are the poor and/or the working class; in the second row, the subordinate groups are interpreted less restrictively as including the middle class as well. The third row displays another response pattern which we interpret as a zero-sum answer, where the upper class only is seen as benefiting, and everyone is seen as being hurt. While this could reflect a more complex perspective in which the upper class is seen as benefiting in some ways and being hurt in others (along with everyone else), we think it more likely that in the context of these interdependent items "everyone" is shorthand for "everyone else," especially since the upper class constitutes such a tiny minority of the population. A less extreme version of zero-sum views is displayed in row four: the perception that only the upper and/or upper-middle classes benefit, but no one is hurt. The next three rows represent alternative ways of denying special class interests: in turn, that the policy is detrimental to everyone's interests, that it is universally beneficial, or that it is universally neutral (almost all the "neutral" responses were that no one benefits and no one is hurt). The next row (responses of "don't know" to both items in the pair) also represents a failure to see special class interests, although that failure stems from uncertainty about either the question or the issue rather than from an active denial of class interests.

The last row in tables 3.4 and 3.5 includes an amalgam of other combinations of responses (eighty-six separate combinations on "private ownership" and seventy-five separate combinations on "tax policy"). Some of these responses suggest confusion, some are ambiguous, and some represent zero-sum interpretations that draw the boundary between who benefits and who is hurt differently from the way we have (for example, ten respondents thought that private ownership hurts the poor and benefits all other classes). These alternative combinations of responses do not merit separate attention because they are so dispersed: more than three-quarters of them attracted only between one and five respondents, and the bulk of the remainder attracted fewer than fifteen respondents. In other words, they offer no systematic pattern. Responses that fall into the "other" category should be seen as a function of the stringent criteria that we have used to interpret responses as clearly meaningful.

To what extent are these issues interpreted in class terms? and how much disagreement is there across classes? Table 3.4 reports the patterns of the pair of items on private ownership. Views about private ownership do vary somewhat with class. Among whites, about one-third of the poor, the working class, and the middle class view private ownership of business corporations in stark, unambiguous zero-sum terms, as compared to fewer than one-fifth of the upper-middle class (see the first two rows of

TABLE 3.4

THOSE WHO BENEFIT AND THOSE WHO ARE HURT BY PRIVATE OWNERSHIP OF BUSINESS CORPORATIONS (BY CLASS AND RACE)

	Whites				Blacks		
	Poor	Working	Middle	Upper-middle	Poor	Working	Middle
UUM#PW[a]	29.3%	29.8%	22.8%	13.4%	18.5%	39.5%	27.9%
UUM#MWP	2.7	5.2	7.5	5.4	16.7	5.3	14.0
U#EV	5.3	5.2	4.8	4.7	7.4	9.2	7.0
UUM#NO	4.0	4.5	5.9	8.7	3.7	1.3	2.3
NO#EV	1.3	0.2	0.1	0.0	1.8	0.0	0.0
EV#NO	10.7	20.6	28.6	36.9	5.6	7.9	7.0
Neutral[b]	2.7	1.7	1.3	2.0	3.7	1.3	2.3
DK#DK	24.0	9.9	6.7	2.7	14.8	17.1	16.3
Other	20.0	23.0	22.3	26.2	27.8	18.4	23.3
Total	100.0%	100.1%	100.0%	100.0%	100.0%	100.0%	100.1%
Base N	75	578	749	149	54	76	43

[a] Notation is in the form of "Benefiting Group#Hurt Group." Key: UUM = UM or UMU or U; PW = P or PW or W; MWP = MWP or MW or M; U = Upper Class; EV = Everyone; NO = No One.
[b] Neutral consists of the following responses: NO#NO; EV#EV; DK#NO.

the table). If one interprets the third row as a zero-sum view, this pattern is not significantly altered, since only about 5 percent of each class express this sentiment. The main alternative view that private ownership is universally beneficial becomes more prevalent with ascending social class: the proportion increases monotonically from about one-tenth of the poor to over one-third of the upper-middle class. In other words, these data support the argument that those in lower classes are more inclined to endorse the zero-sum view of class interests, and those in higher classes are more likely to see private ownership as universally beneficial. We do not, however, wish to overdraw the extent to which each class behaves in accordance with the expectations of this argument. In no case does an absolute majority of any class express a single view.

Table 3.5 reports the corresponding patterns for the pair of items on taxation policy. A higher proportion of people interpret this specific economic policy in zero-sum terms. Indeed, for whites between 40 and 55 percent of each class unambiguously hold this view (see the first two rows of the table). If one includes the "upper class benefits/everyone is hurt" response, over 60 percent of working- and middle-class identifiers take this position, along with 54 percent of the upper-middle class and 45 percent of the poor. The obverse side of these results is that no more than

TABLE 3.5

THOSE WHO BENEFIT AND THOSE WHO ARE HURT BY TAX DEDUCTIONS FOR BUSINESS INVEST-
MENT (BY CLASS AND RACE)

	Whites				Blacks		
	Poor	Working	Middle	Upper-middle	Poor	Working	Middle
UUM#PW[a]	34.2%	40.5%	32.7%	28.6%	29.6%	50.0%	34.9%
UUM#MWP	5.3	13.8	19.3	16.3	18.5	10.3	27.9
U#EV	5.3	6.7	8.5	8.8	11.1	9.0	2.3
UUM#NO	0.0	3.3	5.4	6.8	1.9	0.0	0.0
NO#EV	0.0	0.7	0.5	0.0	0.0	0.0	2.3
EV#NO	9.2	4.8	6.6	12.9	0.0	2.6	2.3
Neutral[b]	1.3	1.9	1.5	2.7	0.0	1.3	4.7
DK#DK	26.3	10.7	7.3	5.4	16.7	9.0	16.3
Other	18.4	17.5	18.2	18.4	22.2	17.9	9.3
Total	100.0%	99.9%	100.0%	99.9%	100.0%	100.1%	100.0%
Base N	76	578	741	147	54	78	43

[a] Notation is in the form of "Benefiting Group#Hurt Group." Key: UUM = UM or UMU or U; PW = P
or PW or W; MWP = MWP or MW or M; U = Upper Class; EV = Everyone; NO = No One.
[b] Neutral consists of the following responses: NO#NO; EV#EV; DK#NO.

13 percent of any class sees the taxation policy as universally beneficial.
Given the visibility of the standard justification that tax deductions for
business investment benefit everyone by stimulating the economy, it is
striking that so many people from every class, including the upper-
middle class, see this policy as benefiting solely higher classes at the
expense of lower classes.

In addition to these patterns, several other points are clear from tables
3.4 and 3.5. First, virtually no one in any class, not even the lower classes,
endorses the view that these policies are universally harmful (see the fifth
row). Second, very few people see these policies in neutral terms, and
only a slightly higher proportion see them as benefiting the upper and
upper-middle classes without hurting anyone else. Third, uncertainty
about these issues is expressed by about one- quarter of the poor, but by
only 3 to 11 percent of the other classes. This uncertainty might be seen as
another form of neutrality, although only a passive form: the higher
incidence of this response among the poor, combined with the low
incidence of the explicitly neutral response, suggests that the "don't
knows" stem primarily from the relative difficulty of these items. Finally,
between about one-fifth and one-quarter of the respondents in each class
give "other" responses. As noted earlier, these are dispersed over a

variety of responses that range from apparent confusion to alternative zero-sum interpretations.

Taken as a whole, the distributions in these tables provide no support for the argument that the perception of class interests is absent in the United States. To the extent that one finds evidence of the status-quo assertion that these policies are universally beneficial, this is more prevalent among higher classes. Even then, this view has only limited support, and on the specific tax-policy item this support largely evaporates. Nor is there evidence that each class generalizes its own interests to society as a whole. Lower classes refrain from this tendency almost entirely (see the tiny incidence of the "no one benefits/everyone is hurt" response), and as already noted, the obverse view that everyone benefits and no one is hurt receives only restricted support from the upper-middle class. The most common response is to see class interests as mutually opposed. On the issue of private ownership, there is a tendency for this interpretation to be more popular among lower classes, and the status-quo denial of special interests is more prevalent among higher classes. A majority of respondents from all classes, however, interpret the tax policy as benefiting higher classes at the expense of lower ones.

Among black respondents, the same patterns generally prevail, with two main exceptions. First, on both issues, blacks are somewhat more likely than their white class peers to see class issues in mutually opposed terms. Correspondingly, the status-quo denial of class interests is even less popular among blacks than among whites. Second, for blacks (as with whites) the special interests interpretation is more prevalent on the tax issue than it is on the private ownership issue, but for blacks, adherence to this view is unrelated to class in either case. This lack of even a moderate relationship to class on these issues among blacks is consistent with the pattern of results earlier in this chapter.[4]

To gain additional perspective on the extent of perceived class interests, we now briefly compare the patterns just described with comparable data on the perception of race interests. These data are from two item pairs of the form discussed above, and come from the same part of the questionnaire. They are worded as follows:

3a. If blacks generally live in black neighborhoods and whites live in white neighborhoods, who benefits from this– whites, blacks, everyone, or no one?

---

[4]It is also consistent with our earlier speculation that blacks care more about lower social classes (and hence take a political perspective in line with this), in part because they view lower classes as disproportionately black.

TABLE 3.6

THOSE WHO BENEFIT AND THOSE WHO ARE HURT BY RACIAL SEGREGATION IN
NEIGHBORHOODS AND IN SCHOOLS (BY RACE)

	Neighborhood Segregation		School Segregation	
	Whites	Blacks	Whites	Blacks
Whites#blacks[a]	6.8%	18.3%	8.7%	24.4%
Everyone#no one	38.4	14.1	34.3	8.3
No one#everyone	19.5	27.7	21.9	23.8
Whites#no one	1.5	0.5	1.2	0.5
Neutral[b]	14.2	16.2	15.3	15.5
DK#DK	5.7	5.8	6.3	6.2
Other	13.9	17.3	12.4	21.2
Total	100.0%	99.9%	100.1%	99.9%
Base N	1,623	191	1,614	193

[a] Notation is in the form of "Benefiting Group#Hurt Group."
[b] Neutral consists of the following responses: No one#No One; Everyone#Everyone; and DK#No One.

3b. Who is hurt by this—whites, blacks, everyone, or no one?

4a. If blacks generally go to some schools and whites go to other schools, who benefits from this—whites, blacks, everyone, or no one?

4b. Who is hurt by this—whites, blacks, everyone, or no one?

Table 3.6 reports the distributions for each pair of items on race interests, by race. The pattern of these responses is quite distinct from that found for class interests in three main ways. First, there is less perception of race interests in mutually opposed terms. This position is rarely taken by whites, and even among blacks, class interests are more likely to be seen as opposed than are race interests. Second, there is more evidence of both dominant and subordinate groups generalizing their own interests on race issues to society as a whole. Among whites, the most common view is that everyone benefits and no one is hurt by racial segregation in neighborhoods and schools. Whereas upper-middle-class identifiers express this type of view about as often as whites on one of the class issues, approximately 40 percent of whites take this position on both of the race issues. Among blacks, the two most common views are that blacks and whites have mutually opposed interests, or that they are both hurt by segregation, with about one-quarter giving each of these responses. Third, there is less conflict in the perception of race interests than in class interests. Both blacks and whites are more likely than dominant and subordinate classes to take positions that do not reflect group consciousness. Just under one-quarter of whites believe that racial segregation benefits no one and hurts everyone, and about one-third of blacks see segregation as either universally beneficial or as neutral in its impact. In this connection, note that passively neutral responses ("don't knows") are more evident in relation to class issues, but race issues are more likely to be actively interpreted as neutral in their impact, by both blacks and whites. In general, there is more evidence of conflict between classes than there is between blacks and whites. Even blacks appear more polarized from the upper-middle class in their perception of class interests than they are from whites in their perception of race interests.

The prevailing pattern in the perception of class interests is for those interests to be seen as mutually opposed. There is no evidence for the argument that each class will generalize its interests to everyone; only limited evidence exists for the expectation that dominant classes will see the status quo as universally beneficial and subordinate classes will see distinctive class interests. Instead, the prevailing theme is for both dominant and subordinate classes to believe that they have special interests that are mutually incompatible.

This pattern clearly implies an interpretation of inequality in relational terms: that the gains of some occur at the expense of others. At the same time, while the items require respondents to draw a categorical line between who benefits and who is hurt, people differ in where they draw that line. This reinforces our view that there is no single, commonly recognized dichotomy in popular conceptions of class. Some distinguish the upper class from all other classes; at the other extreme are those who separate the poor from all other classes; still others explicitly reject a dichotomy by excluding some classes from the benefits/hurts equation. For example, all responses in the top row of tables 3.4 and 3.5 minimally treat the middle class in this way: these responses imply that the said policies benefit higher classes and hurt lower classes, but that their impact on the middle class is relatively neutral. They suggest that people have a gradational notion of the *degree to which* each class participates in the benefits or costs of the status quo.

CONCLUSIONS

What do the analyses in this chapter tell us about the emotional and interpretive significance of social class in America? We can begin to answer this question by assessing our results for class against those for race. In feelings of group identity, in the interpretation of group differences, and in the perception of group interests, social class is at least as strong a factor as race, and is often stronger. We therefore conclude that social class is a major source of group identity in the United States.

Our results suggest that class is especially salient to those in lower classes; affective class bonds are stronger among lower classes than higher ones; class differences are more likely to be interpreted as resulting from biased opportunities by those in lower classes; and the perception of mutually opposed class interests is more prevalent in lower classes. These three patterns all support the argument that class is more keenly felt by those who experience its deprivations than by those who enjoy its privileges. For those in higher classes, it is both easier and more rational to minimize class membership as a factor in social life, and instead to promote the equity of the status quo. For those in a subordinate position, class presents itself as a less avoidable social fact. But even though those in higher classes (especially the upper-middle class) give several indications of minimizing the significance of class, they are hardly oblivious to its impact on social life. Many members of the upper-middle class believe that class differences are caused by differential opportunities rather than by factors intrinsic to the classes themselves, and many subscribe to the interpretation that classes have special interests that are mutually incompatible. Bearing these qualifications in mind, social class clearly retains more overt emotional and interpretive significance for those in subordinate positions.

Finally, the analyses reported in this chapter again suggest that social classes function much like a series of graded status groups. The expression of class bonds indicates, at a minimum, a feeling of affinity with those in the same class. The way class differences are interpreted and class interests are perceived suggests further that class membership (especially in lower classes) produces a sense of shared fate. These results do not fall into a pattern that supports any of the traditional class dichotomies. Instead, class feelings are graded according to the proximity and relative status of the referent class. Variation across classes in the explanation of class differences and the perception of class interests follows a monotonic rather than a dichotomous pattern. By the same token, people's definitions of the beneficiaries and losers from inequality appear more gradational than dichotomous. Because this graded series of status groups is generated by economic forces, it represents something with broader implications than that envisaged by Weber–a merging of his two dimensions of class and status.

4

Socioeconomic Standing and Class Identification

In the last two chapters we have examined cognitive identification with and emotional attachments to social class. We now turn our attention to the issue of how people convert their own experience into an identification with a social class. As a first step in the analysis, we explore in this and the next chapter the effects on class identification of the three main components of objective social standing: occupational status, education, and family income.

While most observers would agree that these are the three basic elements of objective social standing, there is less agreement about how they should be defined and the nature of their effects on class identification. In particular, occupation and income have proved to be complex phenomena from which observers have adopted a variety of emphases. Different notions about how the various aspects of occupation and income impinge on the definition of one's own social standing have, indeed, been central to debates about the very nature of class structure.

The most controversy has centered on the question of which elements of occupational standing are critical. Specifically, is occupational standing best seen as categorical or continuous? Is it more important to know the *type* of work people do or the *prestige* of the jobs they hold?[1] As we have already seen, those who emphasize the former typically place considera-

---

[1]For present purposes, the terms *occupational prestige* and *occupational status* are used synonymously.

ble stress on the qualitative distinction between blue-collar or manual and other types of occupations. Those who emphasize the latter argue that this distinction is nothing more than a crude indicator of occupational status. We begin this chapter by examining the merits of these two views of the role of occupational standing.

Following this, we turn to the effects of education and income, along with occupational standing. In this chapter, we confine our attention to earned income, as conventionally understood, reserving until the next chapter a discussion of income and assets, more broadly conceived. The third major issue we discuss here concerns the extent to which the effects of education, occupational standing, and earned income vary for blacks and whites, for women and men, and for people at different stages in their career cycle.

THE EFFECTS OF OCCUPATIONAL STANDING

In his seminal study, *The Psychology of Social Classes*, Richard Centers set the stage for most subsequent empirical work on the effects of occupational standing on class identification. From his analysis of a 1945 national quota survey of white males, Centers concluded that this effect was strong. For example, his tabulation of class identification against seven occupational categories for nonfarm respondents (Centers 1949:86, table 20) shows that fully four-fifths of all manual workers identified with either the working or the lower class, compared with only one-quarter of all business, professional, and white-collar workers. That this effect is pronounced is evident in the gamma correlation of .69 (and the tau-b of .49) which can be calculated for his table. More significant, perhaps, Centers's data pointed to the potential importance of the manual/nonmanual distinction in separating working-class from middle-class identifiers.

In the years since, of course, this distinction has become widely accepted. Indeed, some have argued that it is more important than occupational prestige. For example, Dalia and Guest have suggested that white-collar workers "are becoming more homogeneously middle class in orientation, while blue-collar workers show very minor shifts from their working-class orientation" (1975:303). So central is this distinction, according to Dalia and Guest, that the effects of continuous measures of occupational prestige on class identification observed by others are probably spurious and result from the manual/nonmanual dichotomy.

Taking a slightly different tack, it has been suggested that the two groups have different views of the class structure (Dahrendorf 1959:280-289; Ossowski 1963; Goldthorpe et al. 1969:118-121; Vanneman and Pampel 1977). For manual workers, that view is a dichotomous one ("us versus them"), but nonmanual workers are more sensitive to gradations in prestige. Consistent with this view, Centers's original table (1949:86) showed that the percentage identifying with either the working or the lower class among blue-collar workers varied over the rather limited range of 72 to 82 percent. In contrast, the corresponding figures for white-collar workers vary much more substantially, from 7 percent among those in "large business" up to 35 percent among those in simple "white-collar" occupations.

Against these arguments, we found no evidence in chapter 2 that manual and nonmanual workers define classes differently. Both groups appear to be more sensitive to gradational socioeconomic criteria than to the manual/nonmanual split, and both groups see the same range of criteria as important in defining class membership. Remember, too, that there was no evidence in chapter 3 that *any* group reacts to classes in a dichotomous "us versus them" form. Instead, affect toward classes other than one's own is expressed more in terms of gradations. While these results do not bear directly on the way people convert their own occupational standing into a social class, they do imply that the significance of the manual/nonmanual distinction may be overstated in the sense that these two groups do not have different views of social classes. A similar conclusion can also be drawn from Centers's original analysis, which showed that the relation between social standing and class identification was the same whether the former was defined in terms of "occupational, economic, or power stratification" (1949:109-114). That Centers obtained the same results with each of three different measures of social standing implies that the manual/ nonmanual distinction may not be as critical as often supposed.

How Significant is the Manual/Nonmanual Dichotomy?

To address this question, we cross-classified class identification by occupational category. To measure the latter, we used the Occupational Classification System developed by the U.S. Bureau of the Census, restricting our attention to civilian, nonfarm occupations. This restriction follows the common practice in discussions of the manual/nonmanual dichotomy (e.g. Hamilton, 1972:chap. 4), and is consistent with most analyses of the relation between occupational standing and class identification (e.g., Centers 1949; Vanneman and Pampel 1977). Specifically, we employed the following eight-category classification of occupational types: professional, technical, and kindred workers; managers and administrators (except farm); sales workers; clerical and kindred workers;

TABLE 4.1

CLASS IDENTIFICATION BY HEAD OF HOUSEHOLD'S CENSUS OCCUPATIONAL
CATEGORIES, FOR NONFARM, CIVILIAN OCCUPATIONS

	Class Identification							
Occupation	Poor	Working	Middle	Upper-middle	Upper	Total	N	Working and poor
1. Professionals	0.7%	17.3	61.6	19.7	0.7	100.0%	289	18.0%
2. Managers	0.9%	20.2	58.8	18.0	2.1	100.0%	233	21.1%
3. Sales	3.3%	22.0	61.5	12.1	1.1	100.0%	91	25.3%
4. Clerical	6.6%	42.9	41.2	9.3	0.0	100.0%	182	49.5%
5. Craftsmen	4.5%	53.0	39.3	2.9	0.3	100.0%	313	57.5%
6. Operatives	9.9%	53.0	35.0	0.7	1.4	100.0%	283	62.9%
7. Service	21.9%	45.9	29.5	2.2	0.5	100.0%	183	67.8%
8. Laborers	17.1%	51.3	30.3	1.3	0.0	100.0%	76	68.4%
Total	6.9%	38.4	45.2	8.7	0.8	100.0%	1,650	45.3%

NOTE: This table excludes respondents with missing data on either of these variables, as well as those with farm or military occupations.

craftsmen and kindred workers; operatives; service workers; and nonfarm laborers.

Since ours is a sample of the whole adult population (as opposed, say, to a sample of white male adults), we focus on the occupational standing of the head of household. To identify this individual, we asked all respondents (apart from those living alone, who we assume *are* heads) to identify the head of the household. Approximately 85 percent of these respondents named themselves or another individual, and most of the rest claimed joint headship. For these latter respondents, we took the head of household's occupational code to be either the occupational title of the husband's job (where both heads were currently in the labor force), or the occupational code of the individual currently in the labor force (where one head was not currently in the labor force).

Table 4.1 reports class identification cross-classified by head of household's census occupational category. The first point to note in this table is that the effect of occupational standing is pronounced and largely monotonic. For example, laborers are over three times as likely to think of themselves as working class or poor as are professionals and managers. Similarly, managers and professionals are approximately ten times more likely than service workers or laborers to identify with the upper-middle class. A comparison with Centers's results indicates that the relationship was somewhat stronger in 1945 than in 1975.[2] Nonetheless, it remains a pronounced one.

The more striking and interesting difference between the figures in table 4.1 and those reported by Centers is that our data provide no evidence for a manual/nonmanual split in class identification. Instead, we find half of the *clerical* workers identifying as either working class or poor, which is close to the proportion of craftsmen who classify themselves similarly (58 percent), and quite different from the proportion of sales personnel who classify themselves in this way (25 percent). To the extent that there is a split in this table, then, that split occurs *within* nonmanual occupations between sales and clerical workers, not between white- and blue-collar workers. This pattern contrasts starkly with Centers's figures showing that "skilled manual" workers (his highest manual labor category) were twice as likely to identify with the working or lower classes as were "white-collar" workers (Centers's lowest nonmanual category). Our results imply instead that the class boundary between the working and middle classes is not coterminous with the usual manual/nonmanual distinction. This, of course, is also consistent with our results in chapter 2.

Finally, the change in the importance of the manual/nonmanual distinction suggested by the general comparison of Centers's figures with our own has interesting implications for the "postindustrial society" argument. In the past several decades, the occupational distribution has shifted substantially away from manual to nonmanual occupations (see, e.g., Blau and Duncan 1967:90–113; Hauser and Featherman 1973). This fact has led some to argue that as the size of the manual sector diminishes, so too does the force of class perceptions, especially working-class perceptions (notice the way that manual occupations are assumed to define working-class membership). In the place of the old occupational structure is a new one dominated by white-collar jobs (with special growth in the white-collar service sector) in which the "traditional" problems of job security, income, worker alienation and the like are presumed to be solved. Hence, the irrelevance within postindustrial societies of the working-class issues, demands, and conflict endemic to "industrial" societies (see, e.g., Bell 1973; Hancock 1971; and for a critical review of this literature, Straussman 1975). The figures in Table 4.1 belie the postindustrial

---

[2]We again emphasize, as we did in chapter 2, that comparisons between our results and Centers's must remain approximate, given the fact that each is based on different samples and differing items. Note, however, that our discussion of table 4.1 is not dependent on the inclusion of women and blacks in that table: removing these respondents to make our sample more comparable with Centers's has no effect on the distributions reported in table 4.1.

argument that the shrinking proportion of the labor force in manual occupations has reduced the salience of social class.

In short, table 4.1 suggests that while there is a strong relationship between census occupational classification and class identification, the manual/nonmanual distinction is not crucial. Insofar as there is a break in this table, it occurs between sales and clerical workers (both of which are white-collar categories). This could be taken to indicate that instead of an embourgeoisement process among manual workers, what may be occurring is a proletarianization process among the lower echelons of the nonmanual labor force (see Centers 1949; Goldthorpe et al. 1969:158; Giddens 1973:221; Glenn and Feldberg 1977).

Socioeconomic Status and Class Identification

While they may be useful for locating potential occupational boundaries, the categories in the census occupational classification of table 4.1 are broad and internally heterogeneous. The occupations included within each category (especially the white-collar categories) are diverse in terms of their socioeconomic status or prestige. For example, specific occupational titles within the sales workers' category range from real estate agents and brokers to newsboys to hucksters and peddlers. Within the clerical and kindred workers' group, these titles range from stenographers to messengers and office boys. Heterogeneity of this kind suggests that the ratio of within-census category variance in status to between-category variance in status is unnecessarily high.

We therefore turn to an alternative and more discriminating measure of occupational status, namely, the Duncan Socioeconomic Index (SEI). Duncan created this measure by regressing prestige ratings for forty-five occupations on the education and income levels of those occupations. The regression coefficients thus estimated were then used to assign scores to all census occupational titles on the basis of their aggregate education and income characteristics, which results in a two-digit status index ranging from 4 to 96.[3]

The superiority of this index as a measure of socioeconomic status over the census occupational classification becomes apparent when we con-

---

[3]For full details on the construction and properties of the Duncan SEI, see Duncan (1961) and Blau and Duncan (1967:117-128). We employ the updated SEI scores for the total labor force reported in Hauser and Featherman (1977). As we were going to press, Stevens and Featherman (1981) published two new versions (for males and for the total labor force) of the Duncan SEI based on 1970 Bureau of the Census figures. The new scores are very highly correlated with those we employ. We have reestimated our results in this and subsequent chapters with the new scores, and unless specifically noted, the differences are trivial or nonexistent.

sider specific occupational titles such as those mentioned above. Within the sales workers' group, the SEI score for real estate agents and brokers is over 60, that for newsboys is less than 30, and the SEI score for hucksters and peddlers is in the bottom decile. Similarly, within the census clerical group, the score for stenographers is over 60, and that for messengers is less than 30. These differences make intuitive sense. It is clear from these examples that the SEI captures much of the within-group heterogeneity in socioeconomic status of the census occupational categories.

Of course, we are not trying to claim that the SEI tells us *all* we would like to know about socioeconomic status. Within specific occupational titles, the SEI may not be sensitive to variations in such factors as income, job authority, and the like, factors whose impact we will examine more closely later in this and the next chapter, and factors whose weight cannot be determined from knowledge of occupational title alone. Instead, we are simply suggesting that the SEI is a more informative measure of socioeconomic status than is census occupational classification, in the sense both that it makes more use of the occupational title data and that occupations with similar SEI scores are less heterogeneous in terms of their prestige than are occupations within a given census classification.

Table 4.2 reports class identification cross-classified by head of household's SEI decile score.[4] Perhaps the most obvious difference between this and the previous table is that SEI is more closely related to class identification than is census occupational classification.[5] This is evident from the fact that respondents in the bottom decile of head of household's SEI are almost *eight* times as likely to consider themselves either working class or poor as are those in the top decile (the corresponding ratio in table 4.1 was only four to one). Similarly, the SEI is more effective in isolating upper-middle class identifiers and, to a lesser extent, the poor. Whereas only 20 percent of "professionals," taken as a group, identify with the upper-middle class (table 4.1), fully 43 percent of the highest SEI decile have this identification, and the corresponding figure for the second-highest SEI

---

[4]Note that head of household's SEI is defined the same way as is head of household's census occupational code, with one exception. For married respondents who claim joint headship and who are both currently in the labor force, head of household's SEI is defined as the mean of the respondent's and spouse's individual scores.

[5]Unlike those in table 4.1, the figures in table 4.2 include respondents from farm occupations for the simple reason that the results of a similar classification restricted to heads of household with nonfarm occupations are almost identical to those reported in table 4.2 (farm laborers and foremen fall into the lowest decile of the Duncan SEI, and farmers and farm managers are classified in the second lowest decile). Of course, there is no a priori reason to exclude the farm population if the emphasis is on occupational status rather than on the manual/nonmanual distinction. In this sense, occupational status conceptually extends beyond industrial relations to incorporate the full labor force.

TABLE 4.2
CLASS IDENTIFICATION BY HEAD OF HOUSEHOLD'S
DUNCAN SEI SCORE FOR CIVILIAN OCCUPATIONS

Duncan SEI score		Poor	Working	Middle	Upper-middle	Upper	Total	N	Working and poor
				Class Identification					
(high)	90–96.0	0.0%	9.5	47.6	42.9	0.0	100.0%	21	9.5%
	80–89.9	0.0%	5.8	66.7	27.5	0.0	100.0%	69	5.8%
	70–79.9	0.9%	8.0	72.6	16.8	1.8	100.1%	113	8.9%
	60–69.9	1.5%	24.6	55.6	16.7	1.5	99.9%	329	26.1%
	50–59.9	2.2%	36.7	47.8	12.2	1.1	100.0%	90	38.9%
	40–49.9	4.8%	48.5	39.6	7.0	0.0	99.9%	227	53.3%
	30–39.9	5.8%	39.7	51.9	2.6	0.0	100.0%	156	45.5%
	20–29.9	6.3%	51.4	38.2	2.8	1.4	100.1%	144	57.7%
	10–19.9	12.9%	51.4	32.6	2.3	0.8	100.0%	481	64.3%
(low)	0– 9.9	27.5%	45.9	26.6	0.0	0.0	100.0%	109	73.4%
	Total	7.4%	38.6	44.6	8.5	0.8	99.9%	1,739	46.0%

NOTE: This table excludes respondents with missing data on either of these variables, as well as those with military occupations.

decile is 28 percent (table 4.2). Similarly, 28 percent of the lowest SEI decile identify with the poor, as opposed to 17 percent of "laborers." In addition, the effect of SEI on class identification is largely monotonic and approximately linear.

In all, these figures suggest that class identification may be more a function of occupational prestige than it is of type of work. At least such an interpretation is consistent with the fact that SEI has a stronger effect than does census occupational grade, and with our failure to find any evidence of a manual/nonmanual split in class identification. Yet this is a provisional conclusion. While the analyses in this section are helpful in identifying the broad shape of the effects of occupational standing and in suggesting that the manual/ nonmanual distinction has no real bearing on class identification, further analyses are required to evaluate fully whether prestige or type of work is critical. Such analyses presuppose a more complete treatment of the effects of social standing, to which we now turn.

EDUCATION, OCCUPATIONAL STATUS, AND EARNED INCOME

As we have already made clear, occupational status is but one component, albeit a major one, of social standing. Following earlier research (e.g., Hodge and Treiman 1968; Jackman and Jackman 1973), we begin a more complete discussion of the way people convert their social standing into a sense of class identification by considering, along with occupational status, the effects of education and earned income.

These two factors are important because they help alleviate the limitation of occupational status noted in the last section. Specifically, while the Duncan SEI does convert detailed occupational titles into a useful measure of occupational standing, it is limited by its reliance on the occupational title data. For example, the possibility that some stenographers or real estate brokers are likely to have more social standing than others cannot be ascertained from knowledge of their occupational title alone. Of necessity, SEI scores are based on the modal status of each title. A more complete description of people's socioeconomic status requires information about them beyond their occupational title or that associated with the heads of their households. Education and earned income are obvious candidates in this regard.

The way in which the head of household's SEI is measured has already been discussed, but an explanation of the other two explanatory variables is in order. To measure a respondent's education, we first asked a question that identified the highest grade of school or year of college completed. To this we have added information from further questions that identify whether the respondent has high school equivalency, specific details on any college or advanced degrees held, and information on any other schooling (e.g., business training or nursing school experience). The result is a measure of years of formal education that ranges from one to twenty years.

Our measure of earned family income is based on data from a comprehensive "income sheet" that sought information on all sources of family income and assets. The income sheet was designed to maximize both respondents' comprehension of the questions and respondents' sense of privacy (and hence to maximize the response rate). To achieve this, the income questions were administered verbally by the interviewers, but instead of answering verbally, respondents recorded their answers directly on to the income sheet. On completion, the sheet was immediately placed in an envelope by the interviewer. Answers were recorded as letter values on the sheet, and these values ranged from 0 (no income) to A ($1 to $499) through W ($60,000 or more), yielding eighteen income categories. In the following analysis, these letter values are translated into their midpoint dollar values, except for the "$60,000 or more" category, which we code as $70,000.

We define "earned income" as income from earnings and transfer payments to the individual or family, as opposed, say, to income from assets or stocks. Specifically, earned family income comes from any or all of the following seven sources: respondent's main job; spouse's main job; respondent's and/or spouse's other jobs; retirement benefits, annuities, and Social Security; unemployment or workmen's compensation; welfare and public assistance; and other sources such as alimony, child support, veteran's benefits, and insurance benefits. The 165 respondents for whom values were not ascertained on any or all of these income sources (8.6 percent of the total sample) are excluded from the analysis. A small number of respondents who reported income from a source but who did not know the value of that income were assigned the median value for that income source, but this involves few cases. The largest number of "don't knows" occurred on the item for income from spouse's main job (N = 37), and the mean number of "don't knows" across the seven items is 18, which is less than 1 percent of the total sample. The resulting measure of earned family income is coded in thousand-dollar units.

Finally, it is important to note that we focus on the effects of *respondent's* education, *head of household's* SEI, and *family* income. For respondents who live alone, these figures all refer of course to their own social characteristics. For those living with families, we assume that since education is usually acquired in a finite period in the preadult or early adult years, people remain more sensitive to their own educational attainment than to that of other nuclear family members. We assume, however, that *currently* conspicuous status characteristics, such as occupational standing and income, are drawn from the family. Thus, for occupational status their referent is the status of the head of the household (this follows conventional procedure, the validity of which we pursue in chapter 7). Similarly, we focus on family earnings because the family is the unit of consumption.

The first column of table 4.3 reports the least squares estimates of the effects of respondent's education, head of household's SEI, and earned family income on class identification.[6] All three parameter estimates are of the expected sign, statistically significant, and moderately strong. Overall, the three explanatory variables account for 27 percent of the

---

[6]In passing, note that the summary statistics for the independent variables in table 4.3 (N = 1,607) are as follows. Education ranges from 1 to 20 years, with a mean of 11.8 (standard deviation = 3.11); head of household's SEI ranges from 4.1 to 96.0, with a mean of 39.9 (standard deviation = 23.37); and earned family income ranges from 0 to 97.5, with a mean of 13.5 (standard deviation = 11.3). The zero-order correlations among these variables are:

1. ClassID	1.00			
2. REduc	.41	1.00		
3. HHSEI	.42	.52	1.00	
4. FamInc	.38	.35	.37	1.00
	1.	2.	3.	4.

TABLE 4.3

REGRESSIONS OF CLASS IDENTIFICATION ON RESPONDENT'S EDUCATION,
HEAD OF HOUSEHOLD'S SEI, AND EARNED FAMILY INCOME

	Full sample	Farmers excluded
REduc	.052	.051
	(8.1)	(7.8)
HHSEI	.008	.008
	(8.8)	(8.8)
FamInc	.015	.015
	(9.6)	(9.2)
Constant	1.452	1.440
	(22.4)	(21.3)
R^2	.268	.267
N	1,607	1,525

NOTE: Main table entries are the metric regression coefficients; entries in parentheses are their t-ratios.

variance in class identification. It is interesting to note that these estimates are similar in magnitude to those we obtained earlier with a 1964 NORC national survey (Jackman and Jackman 1973), except that the amount of explained variance is higher with our more recent data (.268 versus .176). Notice also that the three explanatory variables account for more variance in class identification than does head of household's SEI alone: squaring the simple correlation of the latter with class identification gives a figure of .176, over which the R^2 of .268 reported in the first column of table 4.3 is a clear improvement. This is consistent with our argument that in evaluating people's social standing, it is important to focus on information besides that available from their occupational title alone. While education and earned income do not exhaust these additional possibilities, the estimates in table 4.3 do underscore the importance of their inclusion in descriptions of people's social standing.

The estimates in the second column of table 4.3 are restricted to respondents from the nonfarm population only. Comparing these with the estimates for the sample as a whole shows that the effects of education, occupational status, and income on class identification are the same whether or not persons from farms are excluded from the analysis. In fact, the parameter estimates for two of these three explanatory variables are identical in the two columns, and the estimates for the third parameter are only trivially different. In light of this, and in order to maximize sample size, we include respondents from farm backgrounds in the analyses that follow, unless otherwise noted.

Some might argue that a coefficient of determination of .268 leaves considerable variance unexplained and thus attests to the looseness of the socioeconomic status-class identification nexus (e.g., Hodge and Treiman 1968). Without advocating the extreme opposite of that position, it is important to point out the difficulties that such an argument entails. First, the estimates in table 4.3 are for a simple model only, which we will be elaborating in much of the book. Second, and apart from the general technical problems associated with overemphasizing the exact size of a given coefficient of determination, we emphasize that the reported R^2 of .268 assumes that all variables have been measured with perfect reliability, and is therefore a *lower-bound* estimate of the strength of the relationship. It certainly does not automatically imply that three-quarters of the variance remains "unexplained." To illustrate this, if we correct the correlations in note 6 for unreliability using reliability estimates reported by others, and then reestimate the model for the full sample, the R^2 increases from .268 to .450.[7] While different reliability estimates would lead to slight variants on this figure, the adjusted R^2 is at least firm qualitative support for our conclusion that socioeconomic status has marked effects on class identification.

Black/White Differences in Class Identification

In the preceding chapter we found that even though blacks and whites have similar cognitive interpretations of class labels, blacks differ from whites in their expressions of emotional commitment to their class. Specifically, while poor blacks express equally strong commitment to their race and class, working- and middle-class blacks express successively stronger race bonds and weaker class bonds. Along with this, and unlike their white counterparts, working- and middle-class blacks interpret class issues no differently than do poor blacks. These patterns support our argument that subordinate status is experienced more sharply than is

---

[7]The reliability estimates for socioeconomic status are from Duncan (1969:83) and are as follows: education = .93; SEI = .86; income = .85. The corresponding figure for class identification of .64 is the estimate reported by Klugel et al. (1977:609) for whites, and is as far as we know the only such estimate available. The correlations in footnote 6 were corrected using these estimates in the formula reported by Bohrnstedt (1970:84) prior to reestimating the regression model. We emphasize that we use these reliability estimates solely to gain a qualitative sense of the possible effects of unreliability, since these estimates come from measures that are similar, but not identical, to our own.

dominant status. In turn, this argument implies that there is a distinctive subculture or set of attitudes toward social classes among blacks.

Any such distinctive subculture should affect the way people convert their own social standing into a sense of class identification. In our earlier research we did find a pattern of this sort: among whites socioeconomic status had a pronounced effect on class identification, but among blacks the effects of socioeconomic status were weak or nonexistent. From these results, we concluded that as members of a group that is assigned low prestige on ascriptive, noneconomic grounds, American blacks are not sensitive to any prestige that may accrue from more "achieved" status. Instead, "the prestige of the [low] ascriptive status appears to assume such overwhelming significance that prestige resulting from achieved statuses takes on relatively minor significance in the individual's self-location in the socioeconomic structure" (Jackman and Jackman 1973:580; for similar results, see Evers 1975).

Notice how this argument contrasts with the pluralist (or cross-cutting cleavages) view, which sees all group memberships as entering into a person's identity in an equally weighted, additive way (e.g., Rosenberg 1953; Hodge and Treiman 1968). According to this view, the class identification of blacks should be lower (by a constant amount) than it is for whites at *any* level of socioeconomic status. For example, black professionals will identify with a lower class than their white counterparts, but with a higher class than black laborers. These differences in class identification by race will be the same whether the comparison is between professionals, laborers, or any other socioeconomic group. In other words, blacks' class identification scores should be lower than whites, but blacks are still sensitive to the overlapping effects of socioeconomic status, which means that they do not behave as members of a distinctive subculture.

To test for the presence of race differences in the effects of socioeconomic status on class identification, table 4.4 reports estimates of the effects of education, head of household's SEI, and earned family income separately for whites and blacks. These figures are fully consistent with those we reported in our earlier research and indicate that the class identification of blacks is insensitive to any potentially compensatory effects of socioeconomic status. While the parameter estimates for whites are similar to those reported in table 4.3 for the sample as a whole, socioeconomic status is completely unsuccessful in accounting for the class identification of blacks. None of the parameter estimates in the second column of table 4.4 is more than twice the size of its standard error. In fact, the largest t-ratio is only .99 (for head of household's SEI). Besides, the estimated equation for blacks is statistically insignificant at any meaningful test level (the F-ratio is 1.72).

TABLE 4.4

REGRESSIONS OF CLASS IDENTIFICATION ON RESPONDENT'S EDUCATION,
HEAD OF HOUSEHOLD'S SEI, AND EARNED FAMILY INCOME (BY RACE)

	Whites	Blacks
REduc	.056	.027
	(8.8)	(1.0)
HHSEI	.006	.005
	(7.5)	(1.0)
FamInc	.015	.003
	(9.6)	(0.3)
Constant	1.498	1.587
	(22.7)	(6.1)
R^2	.276	.032
N	1,393	159

NOTE: Main table entries are the metric regression coefficients; entries in parentheses are their t-ratios.

Some might conclude that these results simply reflect a more homogeneous class composition of the black population. The data, however, do not support such an interpretation. While it is true that the mean class identification of blacks (2.05) is slightly lower than that for whites (2.64), the standard deviation for blacks (.86) is slightly higher than it is for whites (.73). Indeed, as is clear from the figures we reported in chapter 2 (table 2.1), the results in table 4.4 cannot derive from a restricted variance in the class identification of blacks. Instead, we believe they support the idea that there is a distinctive set of attitudes toward social classes among blacks, with the result that many blacks do not convert their own social standing into a class identification in a way similar to whites.

Let us pursue this further. As we showed in the last chapter (table 3.2), middle-class blacks and, to a lesser extent, working-class blacks are much less likely to express strong class bonds than are comparable whites, and are much more likely to express strong race bonds. For these people, their class identity is decidedly secondary to their racial identity. In contrast, among those blacks identifying with the poor (i.e., those with two clearly defined subordinate statuses), race identity does not outweigh class identity.

Since feelings of class identity are strongest among the poor and weakest among the middle-class identifiers, we would expect the former to be the most likely to convert their social status into a class identification in a pattern similar to that for whites, while the latter should be the least likely to make such a conversion. Thus, if we restrict our attention to poor and working-class identifiers only, socioeconomic status should be related to the class identification even of blacks. But in restricting our attention to black working- and middle-class identifiers only, we should find no corresponding association.

The data are consistent with these expectations. For poor and working-class identifiers, each of the three components of socioeconomic status is positively correlated with class identification among both black and white respondents. When we confine our attention to working- and middle-class identifiers, however, among blacks none of the components of socioeconomic status is correlated with class identification, in contrast to the pattern obtained for whites.[8] To illustrate this pattern more fully, table 4.5 displays class identification by head of household's SEI (collapsed into four categories) and race. Comparing blacks and whites, two major points are clear. First, there is a stronger relationship between socioeconomic status and identification with the poor among blacks than among whites. For blacks, the percentage difference between the highest and lowest SEI categories is 39 percent (51.6 - 12.5), which is more than twice the comparable difference for whites of 16 percent. Second, while there is a clear monotonic relationship between socioeconomic status and a middle-class (or higher) identification for whites, there is no clear corresponding pattern for blacks.

Putting these two points together, it seems that the class distinction blacks make is between the poor and the nonpoor. In comparison, whites tend to avoid an identification with the poor and to orient themselves

---

[8]For poor and working-class respondents, the tau-b's between the three components of socioeconomic status and class identification, by race, are:

	Whites	Blacks
REduc	.23	.19
HHSEI	.13	.25
FamInc	.29	.32

Each of these associations is at least four times the size of its standard error of estimate. Among working- and middle-class respondents, the corresponding figures are:

	Whites	Blacks
REduc	.28	.03
HHSEI	.27	.05
FamInc	.17	−.13

The figures for whites are all statistically significant. For blacks, only the income-class identification association is statistically significant, but it is also of the wrong sign: inspection of the table on which this figure is based indicates that it does not represent a meaningful association.

TABLE 4.5
Class Identification by Head of Household's Duncan SEI Score (Collapsed) and Race ($N = 1,676$)

Duncan SEI score (collapsed)	Whites					Blacks				
	Poor	Working	Middle	Upper-middle & upper	N	Poor	Working	Middle	Upper-middle & upper	N
(high) 40–96.0	1.7%	26.6	55.0	16.7	783	12.5%	55.0	30.0	2.5	40
20–39.9	3.8%	44.5	48.3	3.5	263	25.9%	55.6	14.8	3.7	27
10–19.9	8.1%	53.4	35.7	2.9	384	29.3%	41.3	24.0	5.3	75
(low) 0–9.9	17.8%	49.3	32.9	0.0	73	51.6%	35.5	12.9	0.0	31
Total	4.5%	37.7	47.8	10.0	1,503	28.9%	45.7	22.0	3.4	173

primarily around three classes: the working, middle, and upper-middle classes. This is evident from the figures for blacks and whites identifying with the working class. For whites, the percentage making such an identification decreases with SEI, but among blacks this percentage increases with SEI. The net effect is that on the basis of their socioeconomic status, blacks make the poor/nonpoor distinction more "accurately" than do whites, but further distinctions among the nonpoor classes are made much more accurately by whites.

These patterns, taken together with those in chapter 3, suggest that while poor blacks may have a relatively well-defined class identity, among other blacks, feelings of racial identity overwhelm the subjective significance of any socioeconomic achievements. Since past studies of class identification have either restricted class to the working-class/middle-class dichotomy or have used the lower class as the bottom category (a label with which very few people identify), those studies have omitted the only class with which blacks have a feeling of identity. In general, these results support our argument in chapter 3 that subordinate statuses are more personally compelling–people are not equally influenced by all their group memberships, as pluralists assume, but instead are most sensitive to those that give them a subordinate status.

Gender Differences in Class Identification

Having determined that there are pronounced race differences in the effect of socioeconomic status on class identification, we turn briefly to see whether there are corresponding differences between men and women. A number of analysts have suggested such differences (e.g., Ritter and Hargens 1975), with some (e.g., Vanneman and Pampel 1977) arguing that attention is therefore most profitably confined to white males only. The exclusion of women from studies of class has indeed been a common procedure, and presumably reflects an implicit assumption that the socioeconomic sphere of life is outside the female's domain.

We postpone a full analysis of gender effects on class identification until chapter 7, where we examine such factors as the role of the family, of female labor force participation, and of marital status in some detail. Here we are concerned with the much simpler issue of whether the inclusion of women in the analysis influences the estimated effects of socioeconomic status. That is, would separate analyses by gender lead to different conclusions than those reached when gender is ignored?

To address this question, table 4.6 reports the estimated effects of socioeconomic status for white men and women separately (we confine our attention to gender differences among whites in light of the results of

TABLE 4.6
REGRESSIONS OF CLASS IDENTIFICATION ON RESPONDENT'S EDUCATION, HEAD OF
HOUSEHOLD'S SEI, AND EARNED FAMILY INCOME (BY GENDER FOR WHITES)

	Men	Women
REduc	.057	.055
	(6.6)	(5.8)
HHSEI	.0066	.0062
	(5.1)	(5.5)
FamInc	.018	.013
	(7.4)	(6.6)
Constant	1.382	1.586
	(15.6)	(16.0)
R^2	.329	.240
N	618	775

NOTE: Main table entries are the metric regression coefficients; entries in parentheses are their t-ratios.

the last section).[9] A comparison of the two columns in table 4.6 shows that there are no pronounced gender differences in the coefficients. Among both women and men, each of the three components of socioeconomic status has effects of the expected sign that in statistical terms are highly significant: all of the coefficients are at least six times as large as their standard errors. Indeed, the estimates for respondent's education and head of household's SEI are almost identical for women and men, and the family income coefficient for women is just a little smaller than that for men. The major difference between the two sets of estimates is that the model accounts for more variance in the class identification of men than of women. Thus, the main effect of ignoring gender is to reduce the R^2 over that which would be obtained were we to focus solely on white males. Compared with the race differences in the effects of socioeconomic status discussed in the last section, however, this difference is minor. Gender differences are explored further in chapter 7, but for present purposes it is clear that pooling men and women in the same analysis does not introduce serious biases into our basic model. At the same time, it is advantageous to make the sample as inclusive as possible. There are no grounds

[9]Separate analyses indicate there are no race-gender interactions in these coefficients.

for excluding such a large proportion of the population unless there is clear evidence that the group involved behaves distinctively.

Life-cycle Differences in Class Identification

The standard approach to estimating class identification from objective status is to assume that people draw on their current status characteristics. This approach, however, takes no account of career development over the life cycle. In this section we therefore explore the possibility that people's estimate of their social class is sensitive to their overall career rather than simply to their current attainments at a single point in time.

Studies of earnings across the life cycle show that earnings peak in mid-career, that is, in the age range from about thirty-five to fifty-four (Mincer 1974). Thus younger people have not yet attained the seniority or job experience that they may reasonably anticipate. At the same time, older people have a standard of living that has been established on the basis of their mid-career achievements. Major expenses such as housing and children are typically faced during the mid-career earnings peak. Successful capital accumulation (especially housing and savings) during mid-career allows older people to maintain their standard of living from lower current earnings (including retirement income), but failure to accumulate assets is more difficult to remedy after the earnings peak. For these reasons, differences in current annual earnings less accurately reflect differences in standard of living among those who are beyond the mid-career peak.

In view of these considerations, we would expect the impact of current status on class identification to vary across the life cycle. Of course, the aspect of objective status most subject to change of this sort is family earnings. Adults are more likely to establish their "permanent" standard of living during their mid-careers. Thus, at this stage in the life cycle, our measure of current earnings best reflects the income that is going to set the standard of living. If people are sensitive to their total career in this way, the fit of our basic model for class identification should peak at the same time as do people's careers—in the age range from thirty-five to fifty-four. The relation between current family earnings and class identification should also be the strongest for this group of people. Among those who are either younger or older, neither the coefficient for current family income nor the overall fit of the model should be as strong, because for these two groups, current family earnings are less salient since they do not reflect as accurately the standard of living that is either anticipated or previously established at the career peak.

TABLE 4.7

REGRESSIONS OF CLASS IDENTIFICATION ON RESPONDENT'S EDUCATION, HEAD OF
HOUSEHOLD'S SEI, AND EARNED FAMILY INCOME (BY AGE FOR WHITES)

	Less than 35 years	35 to 54 years	55 years or older
REduc	.056	.076	.064
	(4.2)	(6.6)	(5.6)
HHSEI	.006	.005	.007
	(4.6)	(3.2)	(3.9)
FamInc	.016	.018	.013
	(5.3)	(7.5)	(4.1)
Constant	1.424	1.203	1.570
	(9.4)	(10.2)	(15.2)
R^2	.221	.373	.293
N	489	432	413

NOTE: Main table entries are the metric regression coefficients; entries in parentheses are their t-ratios.

Table 4.7 displays the estimates for our basic model of class identification, for three age groups: less than thirty-five, thirty-five to fifty-four, and fifty-five or older. Blacks are excluded from these analyses, as are respondents who report that a parent, grandparent, or aunt/uncle is their head of household (since we are interested here in how people process their own adult-life achievements). The estimates follow the expected pattern. The fit of the model is indeed highest for those in the mid-career phase, and the coefficient for income is also highest for this group. The R^2 is lowest for the youngest group, which is consistent with the idea that for a larger proportion of this group, careers and standard of living are not yet settled. Thus, their current objective social standing is not so reliably converted into a class identification. The fit of the model almost doubles when we consider people in their mid-careers, and then drops to a value between the youngest and mid-career groups for those in the oldest age group. In this last group, the overall fit is better than for the young because their standard of living is more settled and predictable. The coefficient for income is lowest, however, among those fifty-five or older because it is in this age group that current income reflects current standard of living least accurately.[10]

We repeated the analyses of table 4.7 for blacks and for white men and women separately. The results (not displayed here) are congruent with the patterns reported in the last two sections. Objective status is unrelated to class identification for any age group among blacks. If one compares white women and men, the only systematic difference in the coefficients within each age group occurs with the income coefficients, which are consistently a little higher for men (as was true in table 4.6). The model is also consistently more successful in accounting for the class identification of men than of women. At the same time, the life-cycle effects that we observed for whites as a whole are also evident for each sex considered separately. Thus, the coefficients of determination for both men and women peak in the mid-career group, at .407 and .355, respectively, and the income coefficients are also highest in this age group for both sexes (.021 and .017, respectively).

These results suggest that in estimating their social class, people consider their current objective status characteristics within the broader context of their total career. Of course, life-cycle considerations do not introduce dramatic variation into the coefficients. In light of this, it is unnecessary to pursue the cumbersome procedure of breaking down our subsequent analyses by age. At the same time, it is important to bear in mind that the salience of current status characteristics does vary across the career cycle, so that our basic three-variable model does not fully reflect the effects of objective social standing on class.

A FINAL NOTE ON THE MANUAL-NONMANUAL DISTINCTION

Now that we have identified a basic model of class identification that draws on a person's educational attainment, the head of household's

---

[10]Our interpretation of these age differences as life-cycle effects is not, of course, the only logical possibility, since it is impossible to distinguish statistically life-cycle from cohort effects with the available data. On a priori grounds, however, the age effects we observe are much more plausibly attributed to life-cycle than to cohort effects. For example, the most common class-cohort argument is that class has become progressively less important to successive generations as the United States has become wealthier. If this were the case, the fit of our basic model should be highest among those aged fifty-five or more. After all, the members of this group were born no later than 1920 and therefore experienced most directly the years of the Great Depression and the New Deal, years in which political issues were most likely to be cast in class terms (see, e.g., Abramson 1975). But no such pattern is evident in table 4.7.

socioeconomic status, and the family's income, we must return to the blue-collar/white-collar issue. We argued earlier in this chapter that socioeconomic status is a more sensitive predictor of class identification than is census occupational category, and further, that the bivariate effect of census occupational category does not suggest a dichotomous split between blue- and white-collar occupations. The task that remains is to assess directly two arguments that a model of class identification such as ours is seriously misleading because it ignores the manual/nonmanual distinction.

One less extreme argument is that the effects of socioeconomic status on class identification vary with type of occupation, such that white-collar workers are sensitive to gradations in prestige, but blue-collar workers see the class structure in simple dichotomous terms (Dahrendorf 1959:280-289; Ossowski 1963; Goldthorpe et al. 1969:118-121). A second, more extreme, argument is simply that the observed association between occupational status and class is spurious, and really due to the manual/ nonmanual distinction (Dalia and Guest 1975).

Empirical assessment of these two arguments appears simple enough. A test of the first argument requires the addition of two terms to the basic model of class identification: a dummy variable that equals 1 if the household head has a blue collar occupation (and 0 otherwise), and a term that allows for a statistical interaction between this dummy variable and head of household's occupational status. Expectations for the additive effects of manual work are not clear-cut, but the interaction term should be negatively signed with an absolute value equal to that for the estimated coefficient for head of household's occupational status (so that the two coefficients sum to 0 for blue collar workers). An empirical test of the second argument requires the addition to the basic model of just the dummy variable for blue-collar occupation: if the argument is correct, this variable should have a significant negative effect on class identification, while the coefficient for occupational status should become statistically insignificant.

While the estimation of such models seems straightforward, there are two hidden problems. Most seriously, the blue-collar/white-collar distinction is highly collinear with occupational status: the correlation between the two variables exceeds .8. This makes it difficult to separate statistically the effects of the manual/nonmanual distinction from those of occupational status. It also suggests that the blue-collar/white-collar split is unlikely to represent a qualitative distinction that is clearly separable from a graded status hierarchy.

This problem is compounded by another issue that undermines the validity of the argument that only white-collar workers are sensitive to

status differences. Such a view assumes that the *range* of status differences
is similar for blue- and white-collar workers, and simply specifies greater
sensitivity to that range on the part of white-collar workers. However, this
assumption is incorrect: the variance in head of household's SEI scores for
nonmanual workers is 206, which is almost 40 percent higher than the
comparable figure for manual workers of 151. The difference is even more
dramatic when the revised SEI scores (Stevens and Featherman 1981) are
substituted for those we employ here (see footnote 3 above): the variance
in SEI scores for nonmanual workers becomes about 6 times greater than
that for manual workers. Given this, whether the two groups vary in their
sensitivity to status distinctions becomes a less interesting question.
Instead, it seems clear that the range of status distinctions to which blue-
collar workers could *potentially* be sensitive is restricted.

In spite of these difficulties, we made an attempt to test the two
arguments about the effects of blue-collar status on class identification.
We began with the argument that only white-collar workers are sensitive
to prestige gradations. Vanneman and Pampel (1977) had estimated this
model for white men, and they concluded that there is a statistical
interaction between occupational status and the manual/nonmanual distinction, such that status influences class identification only among nonmanual workers. In contrast, "for blue-collar workers ... the higher
prestige of skilled work makes little difference for their subjective identification" (1977: 432). In view of the problems we have raised above, such a
conclusion seems hasty, and, indeed, our attempt to replicate their results
revealed an instability in the estimates. For whites as a whole, our results
were generally consistent with their's: there is no additive adjustment for
blue-collar status, but the interaction term is significant and negative,
suggesting that the class identification of blue-collar workers is insensitive
to status gradations. However, when whites were broken into two groups
according to sex, the blue-collar "effect" disappeared in both groups.[11]
When we estimated the simpler model that tests the argument that the
manual/nonmanual distinction nullifies entirely the effect of socioeconomic status, the additive adjustment for blue-collar status became
significant, while the coefficient for head of household's SEI remained
significant but was reduced in size. Neither of these two models ac-

---

[11]Similar problems were encountered when we altered the simple manual vs. nonmanual
distinction to include clerical workers in the former category. This lack of consistency is
underlined when the model is reestimated substituting the revised Stevens-Featherman SEI
scores for the Duncan SEI. When the new male SEI scores are used, the same inconsistent
pattern emerges, and there is complete failure of the blue-collar terms to attain statistical
significance when the new total SEI scores are used.

counted for any additional variance in class identification over the basic three-variable model.

These results reflect empirically the problems that we raised earlier. Because blue-collar and white-collar workers occupy different segments of the socioeconomic index that only partially overlap, one can estimate a separate slope for each group (as in the second model of manual/nonmanual "effects") or one can estimate a single (steeper) slope for socioeconomic status that connects the two parts of the distribution (as in our basic model). Alternatively, because blue-collar jobs span a relatively restricted range of SEI scores, one may depict the adjustment for blue-collar status as either a "constant" one (as in the second model) or as an "interaction" (as in the first model).

The important point is that consideration of the manual/nonmanual distinction adds no new information to the model. Its introduction serves merely to split up the socioeconomic index into one group that spans a relatively narrow range of status scores at the lower end of the scale, and a second group encompassing a broader range of scores at the higher end of the status scale. There is no evidence of a categorical distinction between blue- and white-collar workers that nullifies or even modifies the effect of socioeconomic status on class identification. Proponents of the blue-collar/white-collar distinction urge us to believe that there is a dichotomous, qualitative break in the occupational structure according to the color of one's workshirt. We argued in chapter 1 that the conceptual basis for such a distinction is weak. The evidence in this chapter points to the same conclusion: the manual/nonmanual distinction is but a crude indicator of socioeconomic status.

CONCLUSIONS

This chapter has focused on the effects of occupation, education, and earned income on class identification. We began by examining the form and nature of the impact of occupational position. The analysis shows that there is a moderately strong relationship between census occupational grade and class identification for the sample as a whole, and that this relation is of a form similar to (although weaker than) that reported by Centers for his 1945 sample of white males. Our analysis, however, provides no support for the view that the class identification of manual workers is fundamentally different from that of nonmanual workers. While a majority of manual workers identifies with either the working class or the poor, so does a majority of those in clerical occupations (the lowest nonmanual census category). Insofar as there is an occupational split in the proportions identifying with the working and middle classes respectively, that split is between manual and clerical workers on the one hand, and other nonmanual workers on the other. This implies that the subjective class boundary defined by the working class versus middle class distinction does not arise out of the simple manual/nonmanual distinction.

Further analysis indicates that the relation between occupational grade and class identification is reflected better when the former is defined in terms of socioeconomic status rather than in terms of census occupational category. This suggests that occupation is more profitably treated as a continuous measure of status than as a dichotomy based on type of work, since the occupations in such categories are unnecessarily heterogeneous in their social status. This provides additional evidence that the manual/nonmanual split has no important bearing on class identification.

Occupational status, however, is only one aspect of socioeconomic status, and it is based on limited information–the occupational title. We therefore specified a simple model of class identification as a function of the respondent's education, and earned family income, as well as the head of household's occupational status, in order to incorporate additional information about the respondent's socioeconomic status. The estimates for this simple model indicate that each of the three variables has a pronounced effect on class identification, and the parameter estimates are similar to those obtained with data from earlier surveys. In addition, the model accounts for over one-quarter of the variance in class identification. Noting that this is a lower-bound estimate of the explained variance (since it is based on the assumption that the reliability of each of the variables in the model is perfect), we conclude that socioeconomic status has a marked effect on class identification.

We then turned to the question of whether this model applies equally well to whites and blacks, women and men, and people at different stages of the life cycle. The analysis points to major differences by race, in that objective status characteristics fail to account for the identification of blacks with any class other than the poor. Thus, while blacks choose between the poor and the nonpoor more "accurately" than do whites, their identification with classes within the nonpoor category is not related to their socioeconomic status. Consistent with the race differences we found in the last chapter, this is further evidence that class is interpreted quite distinctively by a group that has already been ascribed low status on the basis of other criteria. As we argued in the preceding chapter, low status is more keenly experienced than high status: for blacks with low socioeconomic status, there is less difficulty translating that socioeconomic status into an appropriate class identification, but for other blacks, their low racial status renders their socioeconomic status relatively insignificant.

In contrast to this pattern among blacks, the estimates for the model are similar for white men and women, although the model accounts for more variance among the former. As we have already noted, however, this does not exhaust possible gender differences in class identification. A more complete analysis of this issue is reserved for chapter 7. Life-cycle differences were found in the accuracy with which people translate their current objective status, and especially their income, into an identification with a class. These life-cycle effects suggest that people evaluate their current status characteristics within the context of their total career. It is among those in the critical mid-career years that current status characteristics most accurately match permanent social standing. Neither sex nor life-cycle differences are strong enough to warrant the separate treatment of these groups for the remainder of the analyses, but they do underscore our argument that the coefficient of determination for our basic model remains a lower-bound estimate of the predictive power of objective status for class identification.

With our basic model of class identification in place, we reconsidered the role of the blue-collar/white-collar distinction. The results indicate that incorporating this distinction into our model adds no new information. On the basis of this and earlier evidence, we concluded that the manual/nonmanual distinction is but a rough proxy for socioeconomic status.

5

Elaborating the Effects of Income and Occupational Status

Now that we have in hand a basic model of the effects of socioeconomic status on class identification, we introduce two sets of elaborations. In the first of these we go beyond a consideration of the effects of *earned* family income to examine the impact of capital ownership, that is, nonearned income and wealth. Second, we introduce a number of factors that isolate variations in work environments and experiences and that therefore elaborate the nature of occupational standing. These are important issues because they allow us to address some of the limitations inherent in the measures of earned income and occupational status that were mentioned in the last chapter. In the process, they help us to understand more fully *how* people convert their socioeconomic standing into an identification with a social class.

EFFECTS OF CAPITAL OWNERSHIP

Capital ownership is integral to discussions of social class. This originates with the well-known Marxist distinction betweeen owners and workers. According to this perspective, the fundamental cleavage in capitalist society is between those who own the means of production and those whose lack of capital forces them to become wage laborers. This cleavage is sharpened as those with small capital holdings are driven out of competition with more successful capitalists and forced into the ranks of the proletariat.

Capital ownership is rarely credited with such overriding significance in more recent approaches to class. Instead, capital holdings are seen primarily as a reflection of wealth that is more encompassing than earned income alone. Attention has turned to the ways in which capital ownership serves either to confound or to embellish socioeconomic distinctions among "wage earners."

The pluralist approach to social class has attempted to turn the Marxist argument about the importance of capital assets on its head. With their emphasis on the openness of the class structure, pluralists have maintained that access to capital is not restricted to the wealthy. Instead, most people have the opportunity to acquire at least some capital, so that capital ownership is widely distributed throughout the population. Many workers may own a small amount of capital in the form of rental property, stocks and bonds, savings bonds, or a small business, and this confuses their subjective class identification. Many who should "objectively" (given their low socioeconomic status) consider themselves in the working class instead develop a middle-class identification. No matter how limited in size, their holdings give them a sense of social participation as "owners."[1]

This, of course, is a well known argument that has been popular for some time. Indeed, one of the best discussions of it remains Hartmann and Newcomb's (1939) description of a hypothetical antiunion school teacher:

Examining his total annual income, we find it derived from the following sources:

Yearly amounts	Category	Origin
$1,800	Wages (salary)	School budget, i.e., taxes
100	Rent	Payment by tenants on father's farm
100	Interest or Profit	Dividends, etc., on investments or savings

Economically, this teacher is properly classified as a laborer, for 90 percent of his revenue comes from some definite service rendered under supervision. Nevertheless, he thinks as a member of the middle class hostile to the "encroachments" of other workers. Although no more than 10 percent of his purchasing power

---

[1]There is a loose but ironic parallel between this pluralist argument about the wide dispersion of capital and recent neo-Marxist class categorizations which assign as many (if not more) people to a "manager" class as they do to a "worker" class (e.g., Kalleberg and Griffin 1980:738). Either way, the class structure is characterized as having an unusually high officers/enlisted ratio.

originates from the return upon his small inherited or accumu-
lated capital, this amount is literally the tail that wags the dog.
This phenomenon occurs with such frequency that we are com-
pelled to acknowledge that the attitude here manifested must be
traced to certain "levels of aspiration," i.e., ideals, standards and
norms, which make the values of the employer more impressive
than those of the employee. [1939:196][2]

The alternative view, which we find more plausible on a priori grounds,
is that capital ownership is simply an additional reinforcing aspect of
socioeconomic status. Disregarding that very small segment of the population that controls a disproportionate share of the national wealth
through inheritance (a segment seldom included in sample surveys representative of the general population), we would expect capital ownership
to increase with earnings. Those with lower earnings have little surplus
income to save or invest, in contrast to those with higher earnings. Thus,
annual earnings may give a reasonable estimate of the net worth of those
with lower incomes (recall that our measure of annual earnings introduced in the last chapter includes transfer payments), but they are likely
to underestimate the net worth of those with higher incomes. If this is so,
including capital ownership should give us a more complete representation of a family's net worth than does family income alone, especially for
those families with higher social standing.

It then follows that far from weakening the socioeconomic status-class
identification linkage, the introduction of capital holdings should help to
strengthen that linkage. In this connection, of course, it is important to
know the size of people's capital holdings. Hartmann and Newcomb may
have been correct in their observation that many people hold small
amounts of capital, but if we are to learn whether this is really "the tail that
wags the dog," we have to go beyond the fact of mere possession. The
pluralist argument may well have overemphasized the implications of the
possession of small amounts of capital, and at the same time downplayed
the possibility that some shareholders are more equal than others.

---

[2]It is important to remember that this view anticipates a weak relationship between socioeconomic status and class identification because the class structure is characterized as
overwhelmingly middle class in orientation. Thus, those who "should" on the basis of their
objective status characteristics identify themselves as workers are instead pushed into a
middle-class identification, in this case because of the small amount of capital they possess.
At the same time, those who, given their socioeconomic status, should identify with the
middle class *do* have such an identification. The other way that a weak relationship between
socioeconomic status and class identification could occur is if many of those with higher
socioeconomic status identified with the working class. According to the pluralist approach,
however, any such pattern would be rare (see, e.g., Lipset 1960:253).

Despite their importance, these issues have received surprisingly little empirical attention. The only major empirical study was carried out by Hodge and Treiman (1968). In this analysis, responses to three items were examined from a 1964 national survey that identified respondents who owned stocks and bonds in private companies, savings bonds, and rental property. Their analysis indicated that ownership of such capital was largely independent of the main earner's occupation, the respondent's education, and family income. They also found that of the three forms of capital ownership, only possession of stocks and bonds in private companies had a statistically significant but modest effect on class identification. From these results, Hodge and Treiman concluded that

> various types of capital holdings do not appear to have any substantial, direct effect upon class identification. However, their dispersion throughout the objective class structure may serve to further confound the clarity of such objective features of the stratification system as education, occupation, and income as bases for class identification. [1968:541]

The parallels between this and the Hartmann and Newcomb position are self-evident.

Yet there are problems with the interpretation. First, if it is true that capital ownership is only weakly related to class identification, then it is difficult to see how the dispersion of capital holdings can confound the relationship between socioeconomic status and class identification. Instead, the dispersion of capital should have no bearing at all on the latter relationship. Second, while Hodge and Treiman's data identified those respondents possessing assets, they did not identify the value of those assets. This may account for the low correlations between family income, capital holdings, and class identification, and it may mask much stronger relations between family income, *size* of holdings, and class identification. As we have already emphasized, the value of capital holdings is critical to the issues at hand. Finally, even with this data limitation, Hodge and Treiman's analysis points to an interesting exception to their conclusion, since they found that ownership of private shares, stocks and bonds was significantly associated with family income, to the extent that almost 60 percent of the highest-income respondents reported owning such stocks, a rate that is almost eight times as large as the rate found for the lowest income group. Possession of stocks and bonds, in turn, was the only one of their three measures of capital holdings to have a direct effect on class identification.

In a reanalysis of the same 1964 data, we employed the three items already discussed, along with three others that identified respondents who owned local, state, or federal bonds, patents or copyrights, and partnerships in private companies (Jackman and Jackman 1973:575-576). We attempted to compensate for the lack of information on the value of capital holdings by summing the items to form a six-point index of capital ownership, on the assumption (possibly heroic) that those investing in more areas had probably invested more resources. Although this remains a crude measure that probably *understates* the sample variance in size of holdings, we found that education, occupation, and income had a moderately strong effect on this index of capital holdings, as reflected in a multiple correlation of .51. We also found that this variable had a modest association with class identification. It is important to emphasize, however, the tentativeness of these conclusions, given the weakness of the measure of capital holdings.

Measuring Capital Ownership

Data on capital holdings were collected along with the information on earnings introduced in the last chapter. Given the considerations just enumerated, we attempted to identify the existence, source, and value of any capital holdings. From these data, we have constructed three variables that we label value of assets, income from assets, and value of home. Let us briefly introduce these.

The first measure, value of assets, is generated from answers to the following four items in the questionnaire:

How much money do you (and your husband/wife) have invested in stocks and bonds?

How much money do you (and your husband/wife) have in savings, not counting stocks and bonds?

. . . do you own any other property–I mean real estate [apart from "your own home here"]? (If yes) . . . please write down the letter that comes closest to the estimated value of this property.

How much money did you (and your husband/wife) receive last year from gifts or inheritance?

Data on income from assets come from two questions. Respondents were first asked, "How much money did you (and your husband/wife) receive last year from dividends, interest, or rent paid to you?" In addition, a general item asked ". . . did you (and your husband/wife) receive money last year from any source we haven't already mentioned, like alimony, veteran's benefits, royalties, or anything else? (If yes) . . . how much money came from those sources?" Three such other sources were counted as income from assets: royalties, income from property sales, and income from "investments."

The final measure deals with the value of the respondent's home. While in principle, home ownership simply represents another type of asset (like the four listed above), we have separated it here for the *practical* reason that home ownership is generally regarded as the principal method of capital accumulation available to most families, especially for low-to-middle-income families (see, e.g., Kain and Quigley 1975). We therefore began with a filter question: "Do you own your own home here, or rent, or what?" Home owners were then asked, "Would you please write down the letter that comes closest to the estimated value of your home?" (For further discussion of this measure, see Jackman and Jackman 1980:1227-1228.)

Since the collection of such detailed data on income and assets is a sensitive issue for many respondents, and in order to maximize the chances of gaining accurate information, these questions were administered as part of the "income sheet" introduced in the last chapter. Recall that on this sheet, letter values were assigned to each of eighteen income categories. Responses to each income question were then recorded *by the respondents*, who assigned the appropriate letter value to a box on the income sheet that corresponded to the particular income question. (We translate these letter values into their midpoint dollar values.) At the end of the income questions, this sheet was immediately placed in an envelope containing other information from the interview. As we pointed out in the last chapter, this procedure was designed to compensate for the sensitivity of the information by maximizing respondents' sense of privacy.

The response rates to these questions were high. Less than 8 percent of the total sample are coded as "not ascertained" on any or all of the four items measuring value of assets. The corresponding figure for the measure of income from assets is just over 6 percent, and that for the home-value variable is just under 6 percent. All such cases are excluded from further analysis.

To measure value of assets, we first assigned median dollar values for those respondents who reported that they had a given asset, but who did not know its value. Again, few cases are involved: the largest number of "don't knows" occurred on the question concerning value of savings (N = 54), and the mean number of "don't knows" across the four items is 34,

TABLE 5.1
DISTRIBUTIONS AND SUMMARY STATISTICS FOR EARNED FAMILY INCOME, VALUE OF ASSETS,
INCOME FROM ASSETS, AND VALUE OF HOME (N = 1,530)

	FamInc	ValAssets	IncAssets	ValHome
none	1.0%	28.5%	56.4%	36.5%
1–499	1.1	9.5	24.6	.0
500–999	1.3	9.6	5.6	.1
1,000–2,999	8.6	12.8	6.9	1.2
3,000–4,999	11.0	6.8	2.6	1.4
5,000–8,999	15.8	6.2	2.1	3.9
9,000–12,999	17.8	5.3	.9	4.5
13,000–16,999	15.2	3.2	.3	5.8
17,000–24,999	18.4	5.5	.2	11.7
25,000–39,999	6.6	3.9	.2	20.5
40,000–59,999	2.2	2.4	.2	10.4
60,000 or more	.8	6.2	.0	4.1
	99.8%	99.9%	100.0%	100.1%
Observed maximum value		210	55	70
Observed minimum value		0	0	0
Mean		11.16	.83	18.51
Standard deviation		23.30	3.26	19.51
Restricted mean[a]		15.60	1.92	29.14

NOTE: The table excludes respondents with missing data on these variables and education, occupation, and class identification. Summary statistics are in $1,000 units.

[a] Restricted means are the mean values for respondents with nonzero values on these variables. They are based on the following Ns: ValAssets = 1,094; IncAssets = 667; ValHome = 972.

which is less than 2 percent of the total sample. Value of assets scores were then calculated by summing the dollar values of these four items for each respondent. The other two variables were constructed in the same manner. For the two income-from-assets items, this involved replacing "don't knows" with median values for 45 respondents on the first item, and for 14 on the second. For the home-value variable (which is based on a single item), median values were assigned to 27 respondents, or just over 1 percent of the total sample.

Given their intrinsic interest and their relative neglect in the sociological literature (see Henretta and Campbell 1978, for a recent exception), table 5.1 reports the distributions and summary statistics for each of these variables, along with the distribution of earned family income for comparative purposes. It is not surprising that each measure has a skewed distribution. This, of course, was also true for family earnings. The three new variables, however, are more heavily skewed than earnings, in the sense that their standard deviations are larger than the corresponding means.

Of the 1,530 people in the analysis, over 70 percent reported that they owned *some* assets, which at first glance appears consistent with the pluralist argument. In evaluating the meaning of this figure, however, it is important to recall that one of the four components of this index is the dollar value of *savings*. Fully 63 percent of this sample reported some savings, compared with 15 percent who said they had received gifts or inheritance money, 20 percent who said they owned additional real estate, and 26 percent who claimed to own some stocks and bonds. That the overall value-of-assets measure is skewed is evident from the fact that over two-thirds of the sample either have no capital holdings or the value of their holdings is less than $5,000, even though the maximum observed value is $210,000. Less than 13 percent report assets worth more than $25,000. The skewness is also evident from the fact that the standard deviation is more than *twice* as large as the mean (it is even one and a half times the size of the "restricted" mean, i.e., the mean for those *with* holdings).

One simple point follows from these patterns. Items that identify only whether respondents have any capital holdings probably conceal more information than they convey. That almost three-quarters of the sample report some capital holdings does not mean that three-quarters of the sample are substantial capitalists. The life-style of factory workers may well be insensitive to whether they have $1,500 deposited in an account at the local savings and loan association.

If value of assets is a skewed variable, income from assets is even more heavily skewed. More than half the sample report no such income, and another one-quarter report income from assets of less than $500. This pattern is hardly cause for surprise, since the income that *can* potentially be derived from small capital holdings (say, a savings account of under $1,000) is so small that it may even go unreported. We would therefore expect the skewness in the prior variable (value of holdings) to be compounded and magnified in the distribution of income from those holdings.

The behavior of the third variable, value of home, is quite different. Over 63 percent of the sample report that they are home owners, and for this group the distribution of value of the home is more nearly normal, with a mean of $29,140 (see the restricted mean in the last column of table 5.1) and a maximum value of $70,000.[3] This, of course, means that there is

---

[3]This is the dollar value we assign to the category "$60,000 or more." The one case in the last column of table 5.1 falling in the "less than $1,000" category is not a coding error but is the figure entered on the income sheet by a single, white, 59-year-old farm laborer residing in a southern state.

TABLE 5.2

RANK-ORDER CORRELATIONS BETWEEN THREE MEASURES OF CAPITAL HOLDINGS AND OTHER
COMPONENTS OF SOCIOECONOMIC STATUS (FOR BLACKS AND WHITES)

	REduc	HHSEI	FamInc	ValAssets	IncAssets	ValHome
REduc	1.0	.491	.354	.253	.166	−.138
HHSEI	.517	1.0	.370	.364	.256	.114
FamInc	.348	.374	1.0	.349	.251	.264
ValAssets	.250	.309	.349	1.0	.380	.175
IncAssets	.216	.261	.223	.579	1.0	.043
ValHome	.133	.261	.475	.382	.333	1.0
	REduc	HHSEI	FamInc	ValAssets	IncAssets	ValHome

NOTE: Correlations above the diagonal are for 148 blacks; those below the diagonal are for 1,331 whites. Respondents with missing data on class identification are excluded. With 148 cases, correlations greater than .162 are statistically significant at or beyond the .05 level.

some skewness in this variable, of an order of magnitude similar to that for family earnings. Whether or not nonowners are excluded, however, the skewness in the variable is much less severe than it is for either value of assets or income from assets.

Capital Ownership and Class Identification

We now turn to the two issues raised at the beginning of this chapter. First, how valid is the general pluralist claim that capital ownership is scattered throughout the population, and is therefore essentially independent of socioeconomic status? Second, what effects, if any, does capital ownership have on class identification?

We begin by examining the correlations among the three measures of capital holdings, and between them and respondent's education, head of household's SEI, and earned family income. Given the race differences observed in the last chapter, table 5.2 reports the intercorrelations separately by race: the figures above the main diagonal are calculated for blacks (N = 148); those below the diagonal refer to whites (N = 1,331). As we noted in the last section, two of the measures of capital holdings (value of assets and income from assets) are substantially skewed. It is therefore highly unlikely that these two variables are linearly associated with the other variables in table 5.2. Consequently, the entries in this table are Spearman's rank-order correlations rather than product-moment correlations (which assume linearity). Although we do not display them, the estimated product-moment correlations are very similiar to the figures reported in table 5.2, except that the product-moment correlations involving the skewed variables are much lower than the corresponding rank-order estimates (for example, the rank-order correlation between income from assets and head of household's SEI reported in table 5.2 for whites is .261, but the product-moment coefficient gives a figure of .129).

Looking first at the correlations for whites in the lower diagonal of the table, it is clear that all the coefficients are positive and moderately strong. The highest correlation is between value of assets and income from assets, this being consistent with the fact that the former is a logical prerequisite of the latter. Note also that the figures for whites suggest that the capital-holdings variables are more highly associated with earned family income than they are with either respondent's education or head of household's SEI. This, of course, reflects the fact that the holdings variables are intended primarily to supplement the income data. In general, the six intercorrelations among the capital-holdings variables and earned family income (the mean correlation is .39) are of the same size as the three intercorrelations among education, head of household's SEI, and earned income (the mean correlation is .41). To illustrate the relationships underlying these correlations, among those with earnings below $5,000, 38.2 percent report no assets, 35.5 percent report assets worth less than $3,000, and only 7.7 percent report assets worth more than $25,000. In contrast, among those with earnings greater than $25,000, only 9.5 percent report no assets, and 37.8 percent claim assets worth more than $25,000 (in fact, of this income group, over half claim assets worth more than $17,000). Similarly, among those with earnings below $5,000, over half do not own a home and only 11.3 percent report homes worth more than $25,000. Among those with earnings greater than $25,000, only 11.1 percent are *not* home owners, and fully 78.4 percent claim homes worth more than $25,000. These are relatively strong associations, and they indicate that the pluralist emphasis on the dispersion of capital holdings across all socioeconomic strata is substantially overstated. Instead, these correlations suggest that capital holdings constitute an element of socioeconomic status that *reinforces* other aspects of status in much the same way that occupational status reinforces educational attainment. This pattern is consistent with the emphasis of the interest-group approach.

Among the correlations for blacks in the upper diagonal, those involving income from assets should be treated with considerable caution, since the spread on this variable is very restricted for the black members of the sample. Only eighteen blacks (12 percent) report income from assets (the corresponding figure for whites is 48 percent), and only four (3 percent) of the blacks report income from assets greater than $1,000 (as opposed to 15 percent of the whites). Bearing this important caveat in mind, the entries in the upper diagonal of table 5.2 show that in general the intercorrelations among these six variables for blacks are quite similar to those for whites. This reinforces our earlier argument that the failure of so-cioeconomic variables to account for the class identification of blacks does not stem from a particularly unusual pattern of intercorrelations among the components of socioeconomic status for blacks.

The only systematic exception to this pattern occurs with the five correlations for blacks between value of home and the other variables: these are no more than half the size of the corresponding estimates for whites, and three of them are statistically insignificant at the .05 level. Some might take this exception among blacks as at least partial evidence for the pluralist view that capital ownership is readily accessible and therefore widely distributed. But more complete analyses of these data, along with external evidence, suggest that race differences in home ownership are most plausibly attributed to discrimination. Blacks are less likely to own homes than are whites of comparable socioeconomic status, and those who are home owners have homes of lower value than com-parable whites (Jackman and Jackman 1980; see also Henretta 1979). Thus, the figures for both blacks and whites are consistent with the emphasis of the interest-group approach. The apparent exception (that is, the figures involving value of home for blacks) is best seen as a function of discrimina-tion, not as evidence of the crosscutting cleavages envisaged by the pluralists.

Taken as a whole, then, the figures in table 5.2 provide little support for the pluralist contention that capital ownership is essentially independent of socioeconomic status. This brings us to the second question: how does capital ownership affect class identification? To address this issue, we expand the basic model of the last chapter by incorporating the three capital-ownership variables into that model.

At first glance, such an expansion would appear straightforward enough. We could simply add these three variables to the model, im-plicitly specifying linear effects. But the skewed distributions of the measures of capital holdings make such an approach quite misleading. We therefore experimented with a variety of plausible alternative specifi-cations, starting with a full dummy variable classification of each of the assets variables. This procedure indicated the breakpoints in the effects of these variables: for example, the net effects of having assets valued at between $1,000 and $2,999 and between $5,000 and $6,999 were the same, whereas the (larger) effect on class identification of assets valued from $7,000 to $8,999 did not increase with further increments in the value of assets. Value of assets is therefore most efficiently represented as two dummy variables, the first of which is equal to 1 when the value of assets is reported between $1,000 and $6,999 (and 0 otherwise), and the second of which equals 1 when assets are reported to be worth $7,000 or more (and 0 otherwise). Since income from assets that was less than $7,000 had no net effect on class identification once the value of the assets themselves was taken into account, income from assets is specified as a dummy variable that equals 1 if such income is reported to be $7,000 or more (and 0 otherwise). Finally, owning a home worth less than $50,000 had no net effects, so value of the home is set equal to 1 if respondents reported owning a home worth at least $50,000 (and 0 otherwise).

Table 5.3 reports three sets of estimates, for whites only. The first column contains estimates for a model with the parameters for the assets variables constrained to 0: it is similar to the first column in table 4.4 of the preceding chapter, except that respondents with missing data on any of the assets variables are excluded from the calculations. Estimates in the second column are for an unrestricted version of the model, and those in the third column are for a version with the effects of education and head of household's SEI restricted to 0. We do not report the corresponding estimates for black respondents, since the expanded model is as unsuccessful in accounting for the class identification of blacks as was the simpler model considered in the preceding chapter.[4]

The estimates in table 5.3 suggest that the three capital-ownership variables serve primarily to elaborate the effect of earned family income on class identification, and to a lesser extent the effect of occupational status. They also help increase the fit of the model. Let us elaborate.

A good way to start to gauge the impact of the capital-ownership variables in the model is to compare the first two columns of table 5.3. Note first that the estimated effects of respondent's education are unchanged by the addition of the three forms of assets to the model, which indicates that *none* of the effects of education are mediated by the assets variables. In fact, decomposing the effects of education according to the procedure discussed by Alwin and Hauser (1975) suggests that one-half of the total effect of education on class identification is direct, just under 40 percent is mediated by occupational status, and the remainder is channeled from education through earned family income. Education is therefore an important variable primarily because of its direct effects and its impact via occupational status. It does not have any indirect effects through the capital-holdings variables.

Comparing the estimates for occupational status in the first two columns of table 5.3 shows that including the assets variables reduces the effect of occupational status by almost 20 percent. That is, one-fifth of the effect of this variable is mediated by the assets variables. At the same time,

---

[4]Along with the factors discussed in previous chapters, this reflects the small number of blacks with assets noted earlier in this section.

TABLE 5.3
REGRESSIONS OF CLASS IDENTIFICATION ON RESPONDENT'S EDUCATION, HEAD OF HOUSE-
HOLD'S SEI, EARNED FAMILY INCOME, AND CAPITAL HOLDINGS (WHITES ONLY; $N = 1,331$)

REduc	.057	.055	
	(8.6)	(8.6)	
HHSEI	.0064	.0053	
	(7.4)	(6.1)	
FamInc	.015	.010	.017
	(8.9)	(5.6)	(9.5)
Assets $1,000–6,999		.164	.250
		(3.8)	(5.5)
Assets $7,000+		.246	.341
		(5.8)	(7.7)
IncAssets $7,000+		.393	.401
		(3.6)	(3.5)
ValHome $50,000+		.267	.313
		(4.0)	(4.4)
Constant	1.492	1.481	2.203
	(21.9)	(22.1)	(69.2)
R^2	.271	.312	.210

NOTE: Main table entries are the metric regression coefficients; entries below them in parentheses are
their t-ratios. All coefficients are statistically significant well beyond the .0001 level. Respondents with
missing data on any of these variables are excluded.

a comparison of the second and third columns shows that the estimates
for the two value-of-assets dummies are reduced substantially (by 35 and
30 percent, respectively) when education and occupational status are
added to the model. This means that one-third of the simpler association
between value of assets and class identification (in the third column) is
spurious and reflects instead the effects of occupational status. Note, in
contrast, that the addition of education and occupational status has only a
minimal impact on the estimates for income from assets and value of
home (these estimates drop by only 2 and 15 percent, respectively, from
the third to the second columns of table 5.3).

Finally, table 5.3 shows that including the capital ownership variables reduces the effect of earned family income on class identification by one-third (the coefficient drops from .015 to .010). In other words, one-third of the effect of earned income is indirect and mediated by the various measures of assets. This means that besides its direct impact, earned family income is important because it affects the size of capital assets and any income derived from them. At the same time, capital holdings have an independent effect on class identification, as is clear from the increment to the explained variance from the first to the second columns.

In short, the results in table 5.3 suggest that the capital-holdings variables do provide more information on the way in which income and wealth affect class identification than is available from standard measures of earnings. These results are more consistent with an interest-group view than the pluralist argument for two reasons. First, the pattern of intercorrelations among the indicators of capital holdings and the other components of socioeconomic status is not as loose as the pluralist argument anticipates. Second, over much of their range the assets variables have no marked effect on class identification. For example, the measure of home value has no effect until we consider those who own homes they value at *more* than $50,000, which means that this variable is important because it helps isolate those relatively wealthy individuals not adequately identified by measured family earnings alone. For the remaining 91 percent of the sample, home value has no effects independent of occupational status and earned income. A similar pattern obtains with the other two assets variables.

Contrary to the pluralist argument, then, the possession of small amounts of capital holdings does not seem to result in substantial defections to the middle and upper-middle classes by individuals who on the basis of their education, occupational status, and earnings would otherwise be considered working class. Contrary to Hartmann and Newcomb, few dogs appear in danger of being wagged by their tails. Instead, our measures of capital holdings serve primarily to elaborate the effect of earned family income by helping identify those relatively affluent persons not isolated by the cruder measure of earnings alone.

EFFECTS OF WORK EXPERIENCES

In the last chapter, we concluded that occupation is better represented by socioeconomic status than it is by the alternative census bureau classification of occupations. Contrary to many recent studies, our results also indicate that distinctions such as that between manual and nonmanual occupations have inconsequential implications for class identification, once socioeconomic status is taken into account. Yet these distinctions hardly exhaust the types of work experiences that may bear on class identification. Even if socioeconomic status is taken to reflect the single most important aspect of occupation, other characteristics of a person's work experience may also influence class identification.

To pursue this issue, we consider the ways that the effect of socioeconomic status may be conditioned by three overlapping sets of factors that identify variations in job experiences and environments. First, we seek to place a person's occupation in context, by considering any supplementary participation in the labor force. Next, we elaborate the nature of the main occupation itself with information on characteristics that are not encompassed by its socioeconomic status score but that have been regarded by some theorists as highly salient to the formation of class identification. The first of these is the organizational nature of the work setting, as identified by union membership and self-employment. The second is the amount of authority the person enjoys in the work place as an accruement to his job.

We continue to focus on the socioeconomic status of the head of household, since this is the best way to represent family social standing for those households consisting of more than one adult (for other households, of course, the respondent *is* the head). In other words, we assume that respondents who identify, say, a spouse as head of household estimate their own socioeconomic status as being that of the spouse. The factors we are now about to consider, however, reflect the experiences associated with a job rather than overall family social standing. It is unreasonable to assume that these factors are experienced by all the members of the household. Instead, they should only affect the way socioeconomic status is converted into an identification with a social class *by those who experience them directly.* In the remainder of this chapter, we therefore confine our attention to those respondents who are heads of households, as defined earlier.

Supplementary Labor Force Participation

Here we examine whether the head of household has a second job. There are two ways that a second job might affect class identification. First, from a pluralist perspective, it could be seen as a "noise" factor that weakens the relationship between occupational status from the main job and class identification. Because the main occupation does not constitute the entire current work experience of people who have a second job, it will play a less significant role in their estimate of their own prestige. Thus, they may see their own prestige as higher *or* lower than that of their primary occupation, since their second job has introduced some diversity into their work experience.

An alternative interpretation takes a less benign view of the second job. We assume that people take a second job to supplement the income received from their primary occupation, and that they perceive their second job in this light. Consequently, the second job is unlikely to be salient in itself as a source of socioeconomic status. Instead, it introduces a "strain" factor in people's work lives, because they must work at more than one job to maintain their desired standard of living. Thus, it tends to undercut any positive status benefits that may accrue from the main occupation. This effect should be felt more by those with main occupations of higher socioeconomic status. While having a second job is unlikely to drive people's identification from the working class to the poor (their overall status and income preclude this), it may lower the class identification of those who would otherwise consider themselves middle class. Indeed, having a second job appears more generally consistent with a working-class life-style and relatively incompatible with a middle-class life-style.

Of the 710 white respondents who are heads of households and for whom we have information on this variable (the question was asked only of those currently employed), 95 (13 percent) report having a second job. It is interesting to note that the probability of having a second job does not vary meaningfully with the socioeconomic status of the primary occupation. For example, of those whose main job has a Duncan SEI score lower than 50, 12 percent report a second job, as opposed to 15 percent of those with an SEI score of at least 50. At the same time, people whose main occupations have either very low or very high status rarely report a second job. Holding a second job is rare among women heads of households. Only 18 women (of those who are heads of households) report a second job, and further, such women are more likely to be supplementing part-time employment in their main job than to be using the second job to augment their income *beyond* that provided by regular full-time employment in the main job.[5]

We began by elaborating our basic model of class identification with two new terms: a dummy variable identifying those with a second job, and an interaction term allowing an adjustment to the slope of HHSEI for those with a second job. Estimates from that model indicated that of the two additional terms, only the interaction term approached statistical

---

[5]Of these 18 women, only one-third report working a total of more than 45 hours weekly; the corresponding percentage for men with a second job is just under 90 percent.

TABLE 5.4

REGRESSIONS OF CLASS IDENTIFICATION ON RESPONDENT'S EDUCATION, HEAD OF
HOUSEHOLD'S SEI, EARNED FAMILY INCOME, AND SUPPLEMENTARY EMPLOYMENT

	All whites	White men
REduc	.063	.065
	(6.7)	(6.4)
HHSEI	.006	.006
	(4.5)	(4.3)
FamInc	.018	.020
	(8.3)	(7.8)
2ndJob*SEI	−.004	−.005
	(2.7)	(3.2)
Constant	1.343	1.276
	(13.3)	(11.5)
R^2	.318	.360
N	648	476

NOTE: Main table entries are the metric regression coefficients; entries in parentheses are their t-ratios.

significance. Given this pattern, along with substantial collinearity between the two new terms, we reestimated the model omitting the additive
dummy variable, but retaining the interaction term. Estimates for this
model are displayed in table 5.4. The first column contains the figures for
all whites, while the second column is for white men (because of the small
number of women who have a second job and the different meaning that
this has for them, we do not report corresponding estimates for women).
These estimates show a substantial negative adjustment to the slope of
HHSEI for those with a second job (for all whites, .006 - .004; for white
men, .006 - .005).

Our results provide little support for the pluralist argument, since they
involve more than a simple weakening of the socioeconomic status-class
identification relationship. Instead, since there is no positive adjustment
to the intercept for those having a second job, the figures are more
consistent with our alternative view. That is, having a second job lowers
people's class identification, and this pattern becomes more pronounced

as the socioeconomic status of the main job increases (but remember that people with very high-status occupations are unlikely to hold a second job). The net result is that among those with low status, having a second job lowers their class identification only minimally; among those with higher-status main occupations, having a second job results in a marked devaluation of their social status. Apparently, having a second job is viewed as more consistent with a working-class than with a middle-class identification.

Organizational Nature of the Work Setting

Two aspects of the organizational nature of the work setting have received particular attention from students of class: union membership and self-employment. These two factors might be seen as polar opposites, representing on the one hand a politically organized group work force and on the other an individualistic petty bourgeoisie. In examining the effects of these two factors, however, we should bear in mind that such extreme representations are undoubtedly overdrawn. The large unions that account for most of the unionized work force in the United States are sufficiently impersonal and bureaucratized to limit the full grass-roots politicization of their rank and file. In parallel fashion, the economic position of many small businessmen who comprise the bulk of the self-employed is sufficiently insecure to prevent the emergence of a "capitalist" political outlook. Nonetheless, the two extreme portrayals of union membership and self-employment are commonly seen as containing a substantial element of truth.

What kinds of effects should these variables have? If unions mobilize their members into an awareness of their collective economic interests, we would expect those members to be more likely to identify with the working class than their nonunionized peers. This effect should be most noticeable among those whose socioeconomic status might otherwise lead them to identify with the middle class. For the self-employed, both pluralist and Marxist approaches imply that the small amount of capital that these individuals control should raise their class identification. In the simplest case, this would mean that regardless of their socioeconomic status, the self-employed will have a higher class identification than otherwise comparable individuals. The other possibility is that the self-employment effect will diminish with increasing socioeconomic status, because self-employment carries greater weight among those whose occupational status is relatively low.

Among whites who are heads of households (and for whom we have data), 217 (23 percent) are union members and 146 (15 percent) are self-employed. Union membership and self-employment are almost mutually exclusive, with less than 1 percent reporting both (these few individuals are truckers, painters, carpenters, and the like). It is not surprising that both union membership and self-employment are related to socioeconomic status. For example, union members constitute 29 percent of those with SEI scores less than 50 and 14 percent of those with higher SEI scores; the opposite pattern obtains with the self-employed, who constitute 11 percent of those with SEI scores less than 50 and 22 percent of those with higher SEI scores. In addition, women heads of households are only about half as likely as their male counterparts to be either unionized or self-employed. Gender differences in self-employment do not vary as a function of socioeconomic status, but for union membership, gender differences become larger for those whose SEI scores are below 50.

Table 5.5 reports the effects of union membership and self-employment on class identification. Since these two factors overlap so little, and in order to save space, we include them in the same equation. The first column contains the estimates for all white heads of households; the second is confined to men. We do not report separate estimates for women for two reasons: their lower rates of unionization and self-employment (regardless of their socioeconomic status), and the small absolute numbers of respondents involved.

In general, the estimates in table 5.5 are consistent with expectations, but the muted nature of the effects suggests that neither union membership nor self-employment are powerful factors. For union membership, there is no adjustment to the intercept, but a substantial negative adjustment to the slope (for men, the effect of HHSEI is reduced by two-thirds: .009-.006 = .003). This adjustment, however, is of only marginal statistical significance (p = .053). Thus, as expected, union membership lowers the class identification of those with higher socioeconomic status more than it does for others, but this effect is not very robust. For self-employment, the estimates for men show a clearly significant positive adjustment to the intercept (of .389). The estimates also suggest a negative adjustment to the effects of HHSEI, which is as large as in the case of union membership, but with a significance level that is slightly more marginal (p = .064). This means that self-employed men generally tend to identify with a higher social class than do otherwise comparable individuals, and there is weak evidence that this effect is more pronounced among those of lower socioeconomic status.

The results for union membership contrast slightly with previous research that found no effects at all (Hodge and Treiman 1968; Jackman and Jackman 1973). But given the modest nature of the effects just reported, this difference is minor. Instead, our results imply that unions

TABLE 5.5

REGRESSIONS OF CLASS IDENTIFICATION ON RESPONDENT'S EDUCATION, HEAD OF HOUSE-
HOLD'S SEI, EARNED FAMILY INCOME, AND ORGANIZATIONAL FEATURES OF THE WORK SETTING

	All whites	White men
REduc	.051	.052
	(6.3)	(5.7)
HHSEI	.007	.009
	(4.9)	(5.5)
FamInc	.015	.017
	(7.0)	(6.9)
Union member	.042	.188
	(0.4)	(1.6)
Union*SEI	−.004	−.006
	(1.6)	(1.9)
Self-employed	.195	.389
	(1.5)	(2.8)
Self-empl*SEI	−.002	−.005
	(0.6)	(1.9)
Constant	1.511	1.319
	(17.0)	(12.8)
R^2	.276	.346
N	848	570

NOTE: Main table entries are the metric regression coefficients; entries in parentheses are their t-ratios.

have not been especially successful in mobilizing their members into a working-class identification. They support the more tempered portrayal of contemporary unions as a moderate political force.[6] In a similar fashion, the effects of self-employment suggest that being one's "own boss" has only a moderate effect on class identification. Being petty bourgeois

[6]Macro-level research on income inequality indicates that unions have had, at best, a minimal impact. This provides alternative evidence that unions in the advanced industrial societies generally are moderate rather than radical forces for change (Jackman 1980).

does raise one's class identification, but the pattern is not dramatic. For many of the small businessmen who are self-employed, their independent economic position may feel sufficiently insecure to inhibit their identification with a higher class.

Authority in the Work Place

The amount of authority that a person commands in the work place constitutes a significant aspect of his objective status. The relevance of this for class has been emphasized by Dahrendorf (1959), who in fact defines class in terms of authority relations. Although it is reasonable to expect that job authority is related to the Duncan Socioeconomic Index, it is not directly addressed by that index. The prime emphasis of the Duncan SEI (as we have already noted) is on the status that accrues to the individual on the basis of his abstract occupational title, rather than the status he enjoys among his associates on the basis of his personal achievement within that title. Recent research has reemphasized the potential importance of individual job authority as a component of overall social standing.

Dahrendorf makes a simple distinction between those who command authority in the workplace and those who do not, the "command" and "obey" classes in Lopreato's (1968) terminology. The possession of authority over others places the command class in a dominant social position. In contrast, the obey class is socially subordinate because it lacks autonomy in the workplace. According to Dahrendorf, there are no distinctions within the command class by breadth of authority. More recently, however, Robinson and Kelley (1979) have argued that a distinction needs to be made between those in intermediate positions in authority hierarchies and those at the top, that is, between the "lower" and "upper" command classes.

In our conception, job authority does not define class. Rather, we view it as a component of objective status–a component to which the individual may be sensitive, along with her education, the prestige of her occupational title, and her income and assets. Job authority bestows two advantages: (1) the right to control the work activity of others, and (2) the right to greater discretion over one's own work activities.[7] Like Robinson and Kelley, we think that all those who have job authority are not equal. As one progresses up the chain of command, both the sphere of authority

---

[7]It is, of course, possible to have discretion over one's own work without exercising control over others. In general, however, authority and autonomy are logically interrelated: those who are subject to the authority of others *ipso facto* have curtailed task discretion.

and the degree of task autonomy increase. The resulting degree of job authority should be related positively to class identification.

Our measure of authority in the work place is drawn from responses to the following three items (asked only of those currently employed):

1. Are there any people with *more* responsible positions than you at the place where you work?

2. Are there any people with *less* responsible positions than you at the place where you work?

3. Are there any people at work with *about the same* amount of responsibility as you?

We use responses to these items to define three broad levels of job authority: those with high, intermediate, and no job authority. In the first category are those who said that they had subordinates but no superiors (i.e., those who answered "yes" to item 2 and "no" to item 1). Respondents were classified as having intermediate job authority if they reported (*a*) having both superiors *and* subordinates, (*b*) having solely coworkers with the same level of responsibility, or (*c*) working alone (i.e., those who answered [a] "yes" to items 1 and 2, [b] "no" to items 1 and 2 but "yes" to item 3, or [c] "no" to all three items). Third are those with no job authority: those who reported having superiors and no subordinates (i.e., those who said "yes" to item 1 and "no" to item 2).

While these categories do not capture fine gradations in job authority, they do identify the basic distinctions. The clearest distinction is between those at the top and those at the bottom of the authority hierarchy. The intermediate job category is more heterogeneous, for two reasons. First, it incorporates multiple levels in the chain of command. Second, people have intermediate job authority because either (*a*) they both exercise and are subject to authority, or (*b*) they lack authority over others but retain discretion over their own work.

Of the 696 respondents who are heads of households and for whom we have data, degree of job authority breaks down as follows: high, 11 percent; intermediate, 74 percent; and none, 15 percent. In addition, exercise of job authority bears a clear relationship to socioeconomic status, as anticipated. Among men, 27 percent of those with an SEI score of at least 50 are classified as having high job authority, as compared to 6 percent of men with a lower SEI score. At the same time, only 4 percent of those with an SEI score greater than 50 have no job authority, in contrast to 17 percent of men with a lower SEI score. The pattern is similar for women, but as in the last section, there are too few respondents to yield

TABLE 5.6
REGRESSIONS OF CLASS IDENTIFICATION ON RESPONDENT'S EDUCATION, HEAD OF HOUSE-
HOLD'S SEI, EARNED FAMILY INCOME, AND AUTHORITY IN THE WORK PLACE

	All whites	White men
REduc	.059	.064
	(6.0)	(6.2)
HHSEI	.005	.005
	(3.7)	(3.2)
FamInc	.017	.019
	(7.4)	(7.4)
HighJobAuth	.298	.374
	(2.9)	(3.3)
MedJobAuth	.098	.129
	(1.4)	(1.5)
Constant	1.336	1.188
	(12.1)	(9.4)
R^2	.304	.362
N	637	467

NOTE: Main table entries are the metric regression coefficients; entries in parentheses are their t-ratios.

reliable results: only 7 women heads of household have high job authority, and 45 have none.

Given this relationship with socioeconomic status, it makes little sense to examine whether the effect of socioeconomic status on class identification varies with degree of job authority, since any such variation would occur over a limited range of SEI scores. This is reflected in the fact that the interaction terms needed to test for such variation are so collinear with the additive terms for job authority that it is difficult to distinguish their effects statistically. We therefore restrict our attention to the additive effects of job authority. We add two dummy variables, for high and intermediate levels of job authority, to our basic model that estimates the effects of education, socioeconomic status, and family income on class identification.

Table 5.6 reports the estimates for all white heads of households in column one, along with those for white men in column two.[8] In this table, the constant term stands for those with no job authority, and the two dummy variables show the extent to which those with intermediate and high levels of job authority differ from those with none. If job authority influences people's class identification in the expected way, these coefficients should be positive, and the coefficient for high job authority should be larger than that for intermediate job authority. The coefficients in both columns of table 5.6 are consistent with this expectation, although the pattern is more pronounced where women are excluded. For those with intermediate job authority, there is a small positive adjustment (.129 for men) that is of borderline significance. For those with high job authority, the positive adjustment is more than twice as large (.374 for men) and is highly significant (p < .01 for the whole sample and for men only).[9]

These results show that while the effects of having an intermediate level of job authority are weak, high job authority has a clear impact on class identification. It is important to emphasize that this effect is net of the effects of the status of one's occupation, educational attainment, and family earnings. In other words, the exercise of high authority in the work place influences class identification over and above the effects of socioeconomic status, more conventionally defined.[10] At the same time,

---

[8]As in the last section, we do not report corresponding figures for women, since so few of them fall into either the high or the low job-authority levels that any such estimates are rather meaningless.

[9]Along with this test (which concerns the contrast between those with no job authority and those with high job authority), note that the difference between the high and intermediate levels of job authority is also statistically significant (beyond the .05 level for the figures in the first column and beyond the .01 level for men only).
Note also that our failure to find a significant difference between the intermediate- and no-job-authority levels is not the result of the relative heterogeneity (discussed above) of the former category. The 74 percent of the sample in the intermediate level of authority breaks down into 10 percent who work alone or with peers only, and 64 percent with both superiors and subordinates. But when these two categories are treated as separate dummy variables, the results are similar to those in table 5.6, and the coefficients for each category are almost identical in magnitude.

[10]By itself, job authority accounts for much less variance in class identification than do the other three components of socioeconomic status. For the 637 white respondents represented in table 5.6, the job-authority variables alone account for only .066 of the variance, and the corresponding figure for white men is .075 (N = 467). Additionally, these raw effects are in good part spurious: for white men, the gross estimates for HighJobAuth and MedJobAuth are .791 and .407, respectively, compared to the net estimates of .374 and .129 reported in table 5.6. This means that over half of the gross effects are spurious and are the result of the three components of socioeconomic status. Note also that adding the job-authority variables to the basic model has only a marginal effect on the R^2: for example, for the 467 white men the R^2 increases from .346 to .362. This small effect is similar to Robinson and Kelley's (1979:52) report that when added to the "basic Blau-Duncan model," authority increases the R^2 by less than .01.

these results underscore the importance of distinguishing different levels of job authority. Dahrendorf (1959) to the contrary, the exercise of limited job authority is not as compelling as being at the top (or the bottom) of the chain of command. The position of those at the top or the bottom in the authority structure at work is clear-cut. For those in the middle, however, there is more ambiguity: these people (who comprise the vast majority) may exercise some authority over others but may be constrained in their own task discretion, or they may enjoy task discretion but no authority. This ambiguity prevents these people from reacting clearly to their position of authority in deciding their class identification. Consequently, they are only marginally distinct from those who exercise no authority. Our results imply, then, that the essential distinction is between those who unambiguously exercise authority in the work place and those who exercise none.

CONCLUSIONS

The analyses of this chapter have helped us elaborate our basic model of class identification in several ways. First, we introduced the notion of capital ownership in order to elaborate the effects of earned family income. The results from these analyses provide little support for the pluralist view that access to capital is widely distributed throughout the population, and that the possession of even small amounts of capital leads those who would otherwise identify with a lower class to locate themselves in a higher one. Instead, our analyses lend more support to the interest-group perspective. Far from being widely dispersed throughout the population, capital ownership is systematically related to education, occupational status, and (especially) earned income. It thus helps to identify those relatively wealthy individuals who are not adequately isolated by the measure of earnings alone. Consistent with this, class identification seems insensitive to the possession of small amounts of capital: it is affected only by relatively substantial capital holdings.

In the second part of the chapter, we elaborated the role of occupational standing by examining characteristics of people's labor force experience that are not encompassed by a standard measure of occupational status. We examined the effects of the holding of a second job, self-employment, union membership, and job authority. As with capital ownership, our results in this section generally support the interest-group perspective. Whereas pluralists have emphasized factors that promote a middle-class identification among people who would otherwise be working class, we have analyzed two factors that point in the opposite direction: maintaining a second job and belonging to a labor union. While these effects are modest, they do identify characteristics that encourage a working-class identification in the face of apparent status gains. Our analysis of self-employment, however, did give mild evidence of an "ownership" effect: at *all* occupational status levels, people who work as their own boss have a tendency to identify with a higher class than they might otherwise. The effect of job authority is primarily to consolidate the already high status of those who constitute the bulk of the people exercising authority in the work place.

None of the factors we have considered in this chapter radically alters the basic model, and none should be seen as substitutes for that model. Indeed, many of the effects are modest and do not lead to marked changes in the coefficients for the basic model. In addition, many of these factors have only a minor effect on the amount of explained variance. This reflects the fact that in most cases, few respondents are involved: for example, a very small minority report income from assets worth more than $7,000 or homes worth more than $50,000, and few hold positions with high job authority.

Thus, the factors addressed in this chapter are best seen as illustrations of the ways in which basic components of objective status affect people's financial and employment experience. In this way, they help to interpret how people convert their social standing into a social class identification.

6

Cognitive and Affective Issues
in Class Identification

We now examine the relation between social standing and class identification from another perspective. In chapters 2 and 3 we addressed the ways people define classes, and the nature of their emotional bonds to those classes. The question that now arises is how do these factors bear on the relation between social standing and class identification?

A common argument has been that this relationship is weakened because of widespread confusion about and lack of emotional investment in class. Our basic goal in this chapter, however, is to show that people generally do convert their social standing into a class identification in a predictable and rational manner. We have already shown in chapters 2 and 3 that most people are far from confused about the definition of social class, and that many also attach emotional significance to their class affiliation. The issue that remains is how different conceptions of class influence the conversion of objective status characteristics into subjective class. Those conceptions vary in several ways. Some people use different criteria to define class than others; some are more confused about class than others; and some are more emotionally attached to class than others. We deal with these in turn.

PERSONAL DEFINITIONS OF CLASS

The analyses of chapter 2 showed that most people define class in terms of both objective and cultural criteria. But people vary in the relative weights they attach to these two types of criteria: for some, objective criteria are more likely to be seen as very important; for others, cultural criteria are more likely to be regarded as very important. Along with this, people vary in the relative weights they apply to each one of the objective and cultural criteria.

Our basic model of class identification does not take account of these distinctions. Instead, it assumes that all respondents define their class identification strictly in terms of objective factors, and that all respondents weight the relative importance of each of these objective factors similarly. We cannot incorporate cultural status characteristics directly into our model, but we can explore the extent to which varying weights attached to each of the objective criteria affect the conversion of personal social standing into a class identification. In addition, we can assess the role of cultural factors indirectly by comparing the estimates of the basic model for those who put more weight on cultural factors with the estimates for those who attach more significance to objective factors.

Such an analysis is important for several reasons. First, it allows us to assess the degree of rationality in the way people formulate their class identification. The criteria people consider very important in defining their social class should bear on the way they convert their own social standing into a class identification. For example, do those who consider education a major criterion weight their own educational attainment more heavily in their class identification? If a person's general definition of social class is separate from the manner in which he derives his own class identification, this would suggest a lack of rationality, or at least an inconsistency, in that person's approach to social class.

Second, this analysis bears on the question of how people resolve discrepant personal objective status characteristics when they settle on an identification with a social class. Some analysts have maintained that because educational attainment, occupational status, and family income are imperfectly associated with one another, people are unable to identify clearly with a single social class (e.g., Hodge and Treiman 1968). It is argued that because people's objective status characteristics do not always fall together in an identical way, there is widespread confusion over something as definitive as a social class identification. This view implicitly assumes that people attempt to draw evenly on all their objective status characteristics in formulating their class identification, and further that the relative importance attached to various objective characteristics does not vary from one person to another. The results we reported in chapter 2 undermine both of these assumptions. The issue that remains is whether people's general weighting of criteria for class membership is applied logically to their own case. If it is, then holding discrepant objective statuses should not confuse people. Instead, they should simply draw on those aspects of their status that are most personally salient.

Finally, this analysis allows us to assess the extent to which standard models of class identification exclude an important set of explanatory variables: cultural status characteristics. Since most people name some combination of objective and cultural criteria for class membership, it is important to examine the implications of omitting cultural status characteristics from the model. Of course, these are not readily measured at the individual level, and so it would not be feasible to incorporate these factors explicitly. Nonetheless, it is important to obtain a qualitative sense of their potential impact.

Recall from chapter 2 that the item we use here asks, "In deciding whether someone belongs to the [class with which R has identified], how important is each of these things to you?" This was followed by a list of six criteria: occupation, education, "how much money the person has," "how the person believes and feels about things," life-style, and "the kind of family the person comes from." Recall too that these six criteria formed two broadly interpretable groups: we labeled the first three "objective" and the last three "cultural and expressive" criteria. As we pointed out, however, these groups are not mutually exclusive, and two of the criteria (education and family) do not fit as neatly into the classification as do the remaining four.

Table 6.1 displays three sets of estimates of the basic model for whites. For each of the three objective criteria, separate regressions are reported according to the importance the respondent attached to that criterion. Thus, the top panel contains figures for those who think education is a very important criterion, for those who think it is somewhat important, and for those who regard it as unimportant. The second and third panels have the corresponding breakdowns for occupation and money, respectively.

For the education criterion, the pattern is straightforward. Those who regard this as a very important component of class also weigh their own educational attainment more heavily than do those who think it is only somewhat important. The latter, in turn, weigh their own educational attainment more heavily than those who regard education as unimportant. Thus, the education coefficient drops from .077 through .065 to .016 as we look down the first panel of the table. Along with this pattern in the regression coefficients for education, the amount of explained variance drops substantially from .352 through .294 to .190 as we move from the first to the third rows of the top panel of table 6.1. Thus, the degree to which the basic model can account for class identification is itself a function of the importance people attach to one of the objective factors as a criterion defining class. The key distinction is between those who con-

TABLE 6.1

EFFECTS OF EDUCATION, OCCUPATIONAL STATUS, AND FAMILY INCOME ON CLASS IDENTIFICA-
TION (BY IMPORTANCE ASSIGNED TO THREE CRITERIA FOR CLASS MEMBERSHIP; WHITES ONLY)

Criterion	REduc	HHSEI	FamInc	Constant	R^2	N	Percentage of total N
Education							
Very important	.077	.004	.018	1.266	.352	416	30.1
	(6.9)	(2.3)	(7.1)	(11.3)			
Somewhat	.065	.006	.014	1.525	.294	513	37.1
important	(6.1)	(4.4)	(5.4)	(13.4)			
Not important,	.016	.009	.012	1.830	.190	455	32.9
D.K.	(1.4)	(6.2)	(4.3)	(15.1)			
Occupation							
Very important	.065	.007	.013	1.345	.300	495	35.7
	(6.3)	(4.7)	(5.2)	(13.0)			
Somewhat	.053	.005	.021	1.563	.333	431	31.1
Important	(4.7)	(3.3)	(7.5)	(12.8)			
Not important,	.042	.006	.012	1.725	.175	460	33.2
D.K.	(3.5)	(4.5)	(4.2)	(13.4)			
Money							
Very important	.070	.005	.021	1.246	.383	400	29.0
	(5.6)	(3.2)	(7.5)	(10.0)			
Somewhat	.063	.007	.013	1.491	.323	443	32.1
important	(6.0)	(4.6)	(5.2)	(13.5)			
Not important,	.035	.007	.011	1.786	.142	538	38.9
D.K.	(3.2)	(4.7)	(3.9)	(15.1)			

NOTE: Main table entries are the metric regression coefficients; entries in parentheses are their t-ratios.

sider the criterion unimportant and those who assign it at least some importance.

A similar pattern in the coefficients of determination is evident in the second and third panels as well: where occupation is the criterion (second panel) the R^2 goes from .300 to .333 and then down to .175, and where money is the criterion (third panel) it drops from .383 through .323 and then to .142. In addition, the pattern in the income coefficients (third panel) is very similar to that for education: among those who regard money as very important, the income coefficient is .021, but the effect is only half the size (.011) for those who see money as unimportant in defining class. Only where occupation is the criterion (second panel) is there no clear pattern in the appropriate regression coefficients. The occupational status coefficients in this panel range from .007 (very important) through .005 to .006 (not important). While any interpretation of this (non)pattern is necessarily speculative, we think it may reflect a condition in which occupation is such a standard component of social class that people are unable to ignore their own occupational status, even when they downplay its importance. But the basic model explains less variance in class identification for the latter group, indicating that as the importance of occupation is downplayed, the conversion of social standing into class identification becomes less accurate.

Taken as a whole, then, the figures in table 6.1 suggest that people do respond in a consistent and rational way to class. The criteria they use to define classes are also important in the way they convert their own social standing into a class identification. Consequently, for example, among those who downplay the importance of money as a criterion for class, their own income is less important in determining their own class identification.

Two features of the estimates in table 6.1 are interesting because they suggest an alternative approach to the problem. First, as already noted, within each panel the coefficient of determination drops substantially when the criterion involved is regarded as not important. Second, there is a tendency for the regression coefficients for respondent's education and family income to follow the same pattern, even where these are not the criteria under consideration. Together, these features suggest that when *any* of these objective criteria are seen as less important, peoples' objective standing (as defined in our basic model) becomes less central to the way they themselves identify with a class. This is important because (as will be recalled from chapter 2) we did not restrict respondents to naming a single criterion as important or to providing a simple rank ordering of the criteria by their significance. Instead, respondents were free to say that each or several of the six criteria are very important, or that each or several of them are unimportant. Indeed, most people included both objective and cultural criteria in their definitions of class, although they did not necessarily assign them equal weight.

We now address these considerations directly. Instead of treating each of the objective criteria separately, as in table 6.1, we isolate two groups of respondents. The first of these, which we call the objective camp, consists of those who name any or all of the three objective but none of the cultural criteria as "very important." The other group, which we call the cultural camp, comprises those who fall into the opposite pattern, that is, those who regard any or all of the cultural but none of the objective criteria as very important.[1] Of the 1,365 whites for whom we have data, 529 (just under 40 percent) fall into one or the other of the two camps. Of these, 261 (19.1 percent) clearly assign more weight to objective criteria, and 268 (19.6 percent) clearly weight cultural and expressive criteria more heavily.

If our argument to this point is correct, we would expect the following pattern. Those in the objective camp should weigh their own social standing more heavily in forming a class identification. At the other end of the picture, those in the cultural camp should place much less emphasis on their personal socioeconomic characteristics in forming their class identification. In other words, the basic model should perform best for the former group and least well for those in the latter group.

As the estimates in table 6.2 show, the figures do generally conform to this pattern. Here we report the estimates of the basic model for the two pure cases: in the top row are the figures for the objective camp; those for the cultural camp are displayed in the bottom row. First, it is clear that in terms of explained variance the model performs much better in the top row than it does in the bottom row. The R^2 for those in the objective camp is .355, which is over two and a half times the size of the R^2 for those in the cultural camp (.140). Along with this, there are pronounced differences in two of the three regression coefficients. The coefficient for education drops by 40 percent from .075 to .045 between the two rows, and the income coefficient drops by almost 60 percent from .016 to .007. Only the coefficient for head of household's occupational status is the same in the two rows, which we believe reflects the factor we outlined earlier in connection with table 6.1: occupational status appears to be a robust element in the formation of subjective class.

The results of these analyses have important implications. First, it is evident that most people process the concept of class in a consistent and rational manner. When people see a given objective criterion as an important component of class, the factor involved generally becomes more influential in the conversion of their own social standing into a class identification. In addition, the social-standing/class-identification linkage is much stronger among those who emphasize objective criteria in defining class than it is among those who emphasize cultural criteria.

---

[1]Only about half of the people in each of these camps completely deny the importance of the other set of factors. The balance simply relegate the other factors to a secondary role.

TABLE 6.2

EFFECTS OF EDUCATION, OCCUPATIONAL STATUS, AND FAMILY INCOME ON CLASS
IDENTIFICATION (FOR THOSE WHO NAME AS EXCLUSIVELY IMPORTANT EITHER OBJECTIVE
CLASS CRITERIA OR CULTURAL CLASS CRITERIA; WHITES ONLY)

	REduc	HHSEI	FamInc	Constant	R^2	N
Only objective criteria very important[a]	.075 (5.2)	.0051 (2.6)	.016 (5.0)	1.212 (7.8)	.355	261
Only cultural criteria very important[a]	.045 (3.0)	.0058 (3.1)	.007 (1.7)	1.902 (11.6)	.140	268

NOTE: Main table entries are the metric regression coefficients; entries in parentheses are their t-ratios.

[a] Estimates in the first row are for respondents who rated any or all of the objective criteria (but none of the cultural criteria) "very important"; those in the second row are for respondents who rated any or all of the cultural criteria (but none of the objective criteria) "very important."

Second, these patterns suggest that holding inconsistent objective status characteristics does not confuse a person's class orientation: people weight various objective criteria differently and use each criterion accordingly in their own identification with a class. This undermines the pluralist contention that social class is weakened and obscured in the United States by the fact that there are imperfect relationships among different components of objective status.

Finally, these analyses suggest that an important set of variables—indicators of cultural status characteristics—is missing from standard models of class identification. One might conjecture that if measures of these factors could be added as explanatory variables to the basic model, then "social standing" in an expanded sense might account for more of the variance in class identification. Unfortunately, these factors are not susceptible to ready measurement.[2] We should, however, bear in mind that most people do consider cultural status characteristics a part of their subjective class, and that the relative importance they attach to these factors (as opposed to objective status characteristics) does influence dramatically the explanatory power of a standard model of class identification.

---

[2] But see Laumann and House (1970) for a novel attempt to measure one aspect of cultural status characteristics.

COMPREHENSION AND UNDERSTANDING OF CLASS

One element that emerges as intrinsic to people's personal identification with a class is occupation. Whether or not they explicitly name it as an important criterion for class, people seem implicitly to draw on their own occupational status in forming a class identification. The question we now explore is this: does confusion about the class location of occupations undercut the conversion of personal social standing into a class identification?

As we argued in chapter 2, most people have a clear conception of social class and display considerable agreement in the way they assign occupations to classes. This, of course, is not to say that perfect consensus reigns. Recall that we developed a measure of overall agreement in occupation-class assignments in chapter 2. The degree to which people deviated from the modal class assignment for each occupation card was summed over the twelve cards. The resulting measure ranges from 0 (for perfect conformity with the mode) to 37 (for highly deviant responses). Here we collapse this measure into three categories: 0 to 3 (representing the most accurate respondents), 4 to 7, and 8 to 37 (the least accurate).

To assess the impact of occupational accuracy, we estimate our basic model of class identification for whites who fall into each of the three categories of occupation-class accuracy. These estimates are displayed in table 6.3, and the results are straightforward. Comparing the first two rows shows that the estimates are the same for the first two groups, which account for about 84 percent of these white respondents. Indeed, the coefficients for each of the three components of socioeconomic status are virtually identical in the first two rows, as are the constant terms. Further, in each row the basic model accounts for approximately 30 percent of the variance in class identification.

Comparing each of these rows with the third, however, indicates that the performance of the basic model is quite different for those 209 white respondents we have classified as inaccurate. For this 16 percent of the white sample, the size of the education coefficient is halved, and the SEI coefficient is less than a one-sixth the size of those in the top two rows and is statistically insignificant. Along with this, the constant term in the third row is higher, and the R^2 is reduced by two-thirds to just .099. Only the family income coefficients are the same across the three rows of table 6.3. Thus, those respondents who do deviate significantly from the modal assignment of occupations to classes are much less likely to translate their social standing into a class identification in a straightforward manner. As

TABLE 6.3

EFFECTS OF EDUCATION, OCCUPATIONAL STATUS, AND FAMILY INCOME ON CLASS
IDENTIFICATION (BY DEGREE OF OCCUPATION-CLASS ASSIGNMENT ACCURACY; WHITES ONLY)

Occupation-class assignment accuracy score	REduc	HHSEI	FamInc	Constant	R^2	N	Percentage of total N
0–3	.063	.0072	.015	1.333	.311	554	43.1
	(6.0)	(5.6)	(6.9)	(11.0)			
4–7	.060	.0075	.015	1.413	.293	521	40.6
	(5.4)	(5.4)	(6.2)	(12.4)			
8–37	.034	.0012	.015	1.859	.099	209	16.3
	(2.2)	(0.5)	(2.6)	(12.6)			

NOTE: Main table entries are the metric regression coefficients; entries in parentheses are their t-ratios.

we noted in chapter 2, however, these respondents comprise only a small minority of the total.[3]

In earlier chapters we argued that the failure of the basic model among blacks does not reflect a lack of understanding of the class terms by black respondents. The present data reinforce that interpretation. Recall from chapter 2 that while blacks as a group deviate from the modal occupation-class assignments more than whites, the difference is not a major one, and it disappears when accuracy scores are broken down by race and class, since there is a modest association between class identification and accuracy. In addition, estimates of the basic model for blacks (paralleling those for whites in table 6.3) indicate that this model fails for blacks at all levels of occupation-class assignment accuracy. None of the coefficients is significantly different from zero in any of these regressions. This means that the nonconversion of their social standing into a class identification cannot be attributed to a confusion about class among blacks.

Regarding our results for whites, they suggest that pluralist interpretations of social class contain an element of truth: confusion about class does

---

[3]Use of two weaker measures of class comprehension give parallel but weaker results. These measures come from interviewers' observations about whether respondents seemed to have any trouble understanding the class terms, and about how much they hesitated on the occupational sort-board task (see chapter 2). With the first measure, there is a moderate decline in the amount of variance the basic model explains for the 185 whites who have some apparent problem understanding the class terms (the R^2 drops from .28 to .24). Similarly, for the 60 whites who hesitated "a lot" on the sort-board task, the R^2 for the basic model is .19 (compared to .27 for the remaining white respondents).

lead to a poorer relationship between personal social standing and class identification. Our results also suggest, however, that the pluralists are critically wrong on two counts. First, minor or occasional inaccuracies in the class placement of occupations are not sufficient to weaken the basic relationship between social standing and class identification. Second, only a small minority are substantially confused about class.[4] While the basic model of class identification explains considerably less variance for this group of people, their numbers are too small to do more than introduce a minor amount of "noise" into the estimates for the whole sample (which is reflected in a reduction of about 3 percent in the amount of variance explained).

AFFECTIVE SIGNIFICANCE OF CLASS

How does variation in the strength of affective class bonds influence the accuracy with which people convert their objective status characteristics into a class identification? In chapter 3 we found significant evidence of affective class bonds, especially among people in lower classes. Now we assess the implications of those class bonds for our basic model of class identification.

Logically, one might expect that those who have more of an emotional investment in their class will pay sharper attention to the issue and will convert their own social standing more accurately into a subjective class. Whether this does occur, and the way in which it occurs, has important theoretical implications.

Pluralists have portrayed American social life as a web of overlapping group memberships and crosscutting cleavages. Based on an implicit assumption that people are equally committed to all groups to which they belong, pluralists posit that overlapping group memberships lead to split loyalties and hence to a muting of all social cleavages. Emotional ties to any one group are weakened by the fact that other group memberships also command the individual's attention and loyalty. This is exacerbated by the fact that someone's group affiliation on one dimension may be shared with people who occupy a different group membership on an-

---

[4]In this respect, it is noteworthy that nonconformity with modal responses on the sort board does not reflect an alternative conception of class that excludes occupation. Indeed, such nonconformity is not associated with any tendency to downgrade the importance of occupation for class. Those who depart from the modal class assignments of occupations are no different from others in the mix of criteria that they employ to define class. Thus, highly deviant responses on the sort board are most plausibly interpreted as evidence of confusion about class.

other status dimension. These factors are thought to contribute to the weakening of the relationship between objective status and class identification. Confusion about class stems not only from cognitive gaps but from the low emotional significance of class.

That people belong to more than one social group is undeniable. The critical issues are whether this arouses emotional conflicts, and how people resolve any such conflicts. Is it necessary for a social class to have overriding emotional significance before a person can identify with it? or is it rather the case that a person's orientation to social class is simply enhanced by having stronger bonds?

We have argued that people are more likely to give emotional precedence to those group memberships that lie at the subordinate rather than the dominant end of a relationship of inequality. This suggests that instead of being equally sensitive to all their group affiliations, people tend to care more about those that place them in a subordinate position. Our analyses in chapter 3 suggested that when people hold group memberships of incongruent status, they are less likely to divide their loyalties equally between the two than to opt emotionally for the lower status-group membership. Thus, middle-class blacks are emotionally preoccupied with race, and among poor whites class bonds prevail over race bonds. Logically, one might expect the former group to pay less attention to class cues than the latter group (in fact, we argued earlier that this phenomenon explains the weak fit between social standing and class identification among working- and middle-class blacks).

But what of the many people who express equal attachment to their race and class? Do such "split loyalties" weaken their reaction to class cues, as the pluralist position implies, or are people able to identify effectively with more than one group at a time? In other words, is an accurate conversion of objective status into subjective class possible only among those whose class feelings clearly prevail over their feelings for other groups to which they belong?

We assess the impact of class bonds on the social-standing/class- identification nexus in two different ways. First, we compare the basic model of class identification for two groups who vary in their emotional attachment to their own social class over other classes. Second, we compare the basic model for three groups who vary in the relative strength of their class and race bonds: those for whom class has more emotional significance than race, those for whom class and race have equal significance, and those for whom race is more salient than class. The first analysis addresses the fundamental issue of whether an increase in the emotional significance of class membership is associated with a more finely tuned response to class cues, as logic would lead us to expect. With this point established, we can turn to the question of how plural group memberships influence people's sensitivity to social class cues.

Recall from chapter 3 that respondents were asked "how warm or cold" and "how close" they felt to their own and other groups. Here, as in the earlier analysis, we are concerned with their feelings toward each of the five social classes (including their own) and, for comparative purposes, toward blacks and whites. To classify respondents according to the strength of their affective class bonds, we adopt the following procedure. For any respondent, there are four own/other class comparisons involving both warmth and closeness. Thus, for a working-class identifier there is the difference between degree of warmth felt toward the working class and toward the poor, and the differences between degree of warmth felt toward the working class and each of the other three classes. Four parallel difference scores are calculated for feelings of closeness. Each of these differences has a possible range of +8 (extreme own-class preference in feelings) through 0 (neutrality) to -8 (extreme other-class preference). For each respondent, we take the average (a) of the four warmth difference scores and (b) of the four closeness difference scores as providing two overall measures of the strength of that respondent's affective class bonds.[5] From this, in each case, we form two groups. Those with average scores greater than or equal to 1 are classified as either warmer toward or closer to their own class; those with scores less than 1 are counted as having neutral feelings or (more infrequently) an other-class preference.

It is clear that this classification is relatively stringent. To be scored as displaying an overall own-class preference, respondents are required to show that on the average they prefer their own class across *all four* different comparisons. In other words, neutral feelings toward any one other class must be outweighed by a higher degree of own-class preference on the remaining comparisons in order to get a positive score of 1 or higher. Despite this, a high proportion demonstrate own-class preference. Among whites as a whole, own-class preference is expressed by 32 percent on warmth and by 41 percent on closeness. Recall as well from chapter 3 that the proportion showing own-class preference is considerably higher among the poor and the working class. Of the remaining responses, the vast majority are neutral (less than 12 percent express other-class preference on either scale, and almost all of these have scores between 0 and 1). Given this distribution, we distinguish between those with a general own-class preference and all others, and we label the latter category "neutral."

---

[5]Note that these calculations are not made for upper-class identifiers but do include the feelings of others toward the upper class.

Two sets of estimates are reported in table 6.4. The first panel contains the figures for our basic model by degree of warmth toward one's own social class; the second panel has the corresponding figures for degree of closeness. The pattern of these estimates is straightforward. The principal effect of affective class bonds is to increase the fit of the model. For those who express own-class preference on warmth, the R^2 is .302, as opposed to .245 for those who are neutral. This is a drop of almost 20 percent. The fit of the model also drops when we compare people who feel closer to their own class with those who do not: the R^2 of .234 is almost 30 percent lower than .325. Apart from this, the coefficients for head of household's SEI and earned family income do not vary significantly by degree of own-class preference, although the coefficient for education is slightly smaller among those who are neutral.

It is interesting to note that we obtain a similar pattern of results when the sample is divided according to the intensity of their class identification (recall that this measure was discussed in chapter 2). For the 49 percent of the white sample who reported that they felt "very strongly" about their class identification, the basic model has an R^2 of .322. Among the 30 percent who reported feeling "somewhat strongly," this drops to .238, and among the remaining 21 percent of the sample who feel "not too strongly," the corresponding figure is .202. At the same time, as in table 6.4, the coefficients for the variables themselves do not vary noticeably across levels of intensity, with the partial exception of education (the coefficients for which follow the same pattern as in table 6.4).

In all, then, the patterns are consistent with our expectations. Those who express stronger emotional bonds to their class also translate their own social standing more accurately into a class identification. At the same time, strong class bonds are far from being essential. Among those who display a weaker attachment to their social class, the basic model takes the same form, and it still accounts for about one-quarter of the variance in class identification. Thus, people's orientation to social class is not completely dependent on the existence of strong class bonds, although it is certainly enhanced by them.

We now turn to the way that dual group memberships influence class identification. Here we focus on the performance of the basic model across groups that vary in the *relative* emotional significance they attach to their class versus their racial affiliation, using the variables that were introduced in chapter 3. Each respondent's warmth toward (closeness to) his subjective class was subtracted from his warmth toward (closeness to) his racial group. The resulting variables for warmth and closeness are categorized into three groups: those who feel warmer toward (closer to)

TABLE 6.4

EFFECTS OF EDUCATION, OCCUPATIONAL STATUS, AND FAMILY INCOME ON CLASS
IDENTIFICATION (BY DEGREE OF OWN-CLASS WARMTH AND CLOSENESS; WHITES ONLY)

Class Feelings	REduc	HHSEI	FamInc	Constant	R^2	N	Percentage of total N
Warmth							
Warmer toward	.056	.007	.014	1.348	.302	435	32.3
own class	(5.1)	(4.7)	(5.3)	(12.1)			
Neutral	.047	.006	.014	1.688	.245	911	67.7
	(6.2)	(6.2)	(7.5)	(20.6)			
Closeness							
Closer to	.057	.007	.014	1.373	.325	556	41.3
own class	(5.9)	(5.6)	(5.8)	(13.9)			
Neutral	.048	.006	.014	1.672	.234	789	58.7
	(5.7)	(5.9)	(6.8)	(18.7)			

NOTE: Main table entries are the metric regression coefficients; entries in parentheses are their t-ratios.

their subjective class than to their race, those who feel equally warm toward (close to) their class and race, and those who feel warmer toward (closer to) their race than to their class. The distributions on these variables were given by class and race in table 3.2.

Table 6.5 displays estimates for the basic model of class identification for three groups of whites on each measure of class versus race bonds. The first panel divides people according to their relative warmth toward the two groups; the second panel divides people according to their relative closeness to the two groups. In each panel, the first row is for those whose class feelings exceed their race feelings; the second is for those people whose feelings for their race and class are equal; the third row is for those who express stronger feelings for their race than for their class.

There are two main patterns evident in the estimates in table 6.5. First, the basic model of class identification is dramatically weaker for whites who feel warmer toward or closer to their racial group than to their subjective class. Second, however, the estimates for the basic model do not vary substantially between those who express stronger class feelings and those who feel equally strong about their class and race memberships. These patterns are revealed principally in the coefficients of determination. In the first panel of table 6.5, the R^2 drops slightly from .342, for

TABLE 6.5

EFFECTS OF EDUCATION, OCCUPATIONAL STATUS, AND FAMILY INCOME ON CLASS
IDENTIFICATION (BY RELATIVE STRENGTH OF CLASS VERSUS RACE FEELINGS; WHITES ONLY)

Class versus race feelings	REduc	HHSEI	FamInc	Constant	R^2	N	Percentage of total N
Warmth							
Class > Race	.072	.005	.019	1.218	.342	388	28.7
	(6.3)	(3.1)	(6.2)	(10.3)			
Class = Race	.048	.007	.013	1.590	.281	731	54.1
	(5.7)	(6.3)	(6.5)	(18.4)			
Class < Race	.015	.007	.011	2.150	.129	233	17.2
	(0.8)	(3.5)	(2.7)	(11.6)			
Closeness							
Class > Race	.068	.006	.013	1.317	.296	410	30.4
	(5.9)	(3.8)	(4.1)	(11.3)			
Class = Race	.051	.007	.015	1.531	.301	704	52.2
	(6.1)	(6.3)	(7.8)	(17.4)			
Class < Race	.017	.007	.012	2.108	.156	235	17.4
	(1.0)	(3.6)	(2.9)	(11.5)			

NOTE: Main table entries are the metric regression coefficients; entries in parentheses are their t-ratios.

those who feel warmer toward their class, to .281, for those who feel
equally warm toward their class and race; the R^2 then plunges to less than
half of the latter figure (.129) for those who feel warmer toward their race.
In the second panel, the R^2 does not vary across the first two groups (.296
versus .301), but it is again reduced by about half to .156 for those who feel
closer toward their race than toward their class. As in table 6.4, the
coefficients for head of household's SEI remain unaffected in both panels.
The coefficients for family income become smaller as we move down the
first panel; this is not, however, true for the second panel. Only the effects
of education change substantially: there is a small decrease in the coefficients for education from the first to the second row, whereas in the third
row there is a dramatic drop in both panels to a value that is statistically
insignificant at any meaningful test level.

These results indicate that for the small minority of white respondents
who are emotionally preoccupied with their racial-group affiliation, there

is clearly less sensitivity to class cues. At the same time, whites who have "split loyalties" between their subjective class and their racial-group membership relate to class cues in a way that is essentially similar to those whose race feelings are preempted by their subjective class. Except for the small minority of whites who express stronger bonds to their racial group than to their class, dual group memberships do not act to weaken sensitivity to social class cues.

We have interpreted the weak relationship between objective status and class identification among working-and middle-class blacks as reflecting their emotional preoccupation with their racial-group identity. We cannot test this interpretation directly among blacks, because the relative importance of class bonds is so strongly related to subjective class in this group. Only a small fraction of poor blacks are preoccupied with race, as compared to a clear majority of middle-class blacks. Aside from the problem of too few respondents, any attempt to categorize blacks as whites are categorized in table 6.5 would severely restrict within-group variance in class identification. The results in table 6.5 for whites, however, do reinforce our interpretation for blacks. If a larger proportion of whites were preoccupied with their racial identity, the basic model of class identification would have a much poorer fit among whites as well. As it happens, for more than 80 percent of whites, sensitivity to social class is not diminished by the fact of dual group membership. Given the weight typically attached to the race cleavage in the United States, it is especially significant that race generally fails to distract whites from class cues.

CONCLUSIONS

The analyses in this chapter suggest that people process social-class cues in a rational and consistent manner. Contrary to the common argument, Americans' sensitivity to class cues is not weakened by widespread confusion about and emotional detachment from social class. To be sure, some people are confused about class, and for these people, the basic model does not perform very well. The critical point, however, is that these individuals comprise a very small minority.

The way people define and feel about class bears directly on the way they convert their own social standing into a class identification. Thus, for example, the weights people attach to various criteria in defining social class bear directly on how sensitive they are to various personal characteristics in forming their own class identification. These results suggest that a person's reactions to social class do not occur in isolation from one

another. Instead, they imply that people's orientation to social class generally follows a coherent pattern.

Strong emotional attachments to class do sharpen the translation of
objective status characteristics into a class identification, but even those
with weaker class attachments interpret their objective social standing in
much the same way. Most important, dual group memberships do not
usually weaken sensitivity to social class. We have argued that many
working- and middle-class blacks display a weak fit between their objective status and their class identification because their racial identity outweighs their class identity. Very few whites, however, are distracted from
social class by race. Moreover, those who are drawn equally to their race
and class process class cues in much the same way as do those who attach
greater emotional significance to their class. Thus, dual group memberships do not automatically imply split loyalties, and, more importantly,
split loyalties do not translate neatly into weaker loyalties.

From the evidence here, then, it seems that dual group memberships
are unlikely to have the "ameliorative" function that pluralists have attributed to them. People's sensitivity to class cues is more likely to be
weakened by membership in alternative *subordinate* groups than alternative dominant groups. Thus, to the extent that multiple group memberships do have an effect, it seems that they are less likely to be salient as
alternative sources of reward than as alternative sources of grievance.

7

Family Influences on Subjective Class

Our approach to class identification assumes that the nuclear family is the primary unit of stratification. The nuclear family is the principal residential unit in the noninstitutionalized population–the pervasiveness of normative support for the family still far exceeds that for any other interpersonal living arrangement. The logical outcome of this is that when individuals establish a family, they cease to be independent status units and instead their status becomes bound up with that of their family. Our model treats education, which is generally acquired in a discrete period during childhood and early adulthood, as a uniquely personal attribute. Occupational status, however, is specified as emanating from the household head, and family income rather than personal income is used to reflect economic status.

These assumptions about the primacy of the nuclear family as a status unit conform with those generally made by students of stratification. They have, however, come under attack from two different sources. First, some have argued that the increasing entry of married women into the labor force may have undermined the status unity of the nuclear family, or at least changed the traditional way that family members estimate their status. This approach presupposes that when the wife takes up the role activity that has been traditionally in the husband's domain, there results a fundamental restructuring of traditional family relationships.

The significance of the nuclear family as a source of status has also been questioned from a very different perspective. Pluralist theory has emphasized that a person's family is but one of a number of overlapping ties and affiliations that work jointly to undermine any sharp status distinctions.

The competing source of status most immediately at hand is the individual's family of origin. Pluralists have argued that intergenerational social mobility gives people close personal ties to more than one status group and makes current status seem both less enduring and less significant.

In this chapter, we assess these different arguments by examining the constituent effects of present and origin family status. In the first section, we focus on the nuclear family (and hence on married respondents). What are the effects on class identification of the husband's and the wife's personal status characteristics, and what impact does the wife's labor force participation have on the calculation of her own and her husband's social standing? This is followed by an analysis of the influence of the family of origin. To what extent are people sensitive to their origin status, and does social mobility undercut the affective significance of class?

WIVES' AND HUSBANDS' CONTRIBUTIONS
TO CLASS IDENTIFICATION

Through the late 1960s, the family was commonly considered to be the basic unit in systems of stratification (e.g., Parsons 1942; Lenski 1966: 402). Further, as Acker (1973) has pointed out, most studies assumed (implicitly or explicitly) that the social standing of the family is generated by the social standing of the male head of household. Women determine their own social status only when they are not part of a family (i.e., when they are unattached to men). Thus, the social standing of the majority of women is determined by the males to whom they are attached. Phrased differently, it has been generally assumed that women borrow their social status from their husbands.

Until recently, these assumptions were seldom questioned or evaluated empirically. It is evident, however, that the "status-borrowing" model is not the only possibility. Indeed, as more women have entered the labor force, this model has come under increasing attack. Expectations were initially high: "Employment [of wives] increases the family level of living, the prestige of the mother, the appreciation of her by her husband, and the amount of democratic decision-making in the family" (Nye 1963:264). Minimally, Acker (1973) and Haug (1973), among others, have argued that it is unreasonable to suppose a priori that the employed wife disregards her own occupational standing in estimating her social status. Two alternative approaches have been suggested.

One obvious alternative to the asymmetric borrowing of status is a pattern of symmetric sharing of statuses, where each spouse influences the other's social standing. This model still conceives of the family as the basic unit, but family members are thought to derive their status from the characteristics of both the husband and wife, rather than just the husband. In a perfectly symmetrical case, the status characteristics of both husband and wife would contribute equally to the family's status, but it would not be inconsistent with the model for the husband and wife to make unequal contributions, so long as both affect the status estimates of individual family members. The second alternative involves an independent status model in which married women's status is influenced by their own occupation and income rather than that of their husbands (e.g., Felson and Knoke 1974). Here the family is no longer treated as the status unit–instead, the husband and wife respond separately to their individual status characteristics. Of course, unlike the status-borrowing model, the status-sharing model bears primarily on families in which both spouses are employed, and the independent-status model is intended to apply exclusively to such families.

The two key issues involved here are (a) whether the family or the individual is the basic unit of stratification, and (b) whether the derivation of family members' status is influenced by the increasing entry of women into the labor force. Our own working assumption has been that the family is the primary source of status (for people who live with their families). We distinguish, however, between those aspects of social standing that are currently conspicuous and those that have been attained in the past.[1] Thus, we have used the respondent's (rather than the head of household's) education, since people typically do not directly experience someone else's educational attainment. In contrast, both income and occupational status are currently visible elements of social standing, and these we regard as deriving from the family. Hence our use of family income, on the grounds that the family is the unit of consumption. For occupational status, we assume that all family members draw on the head of household's occupation. Recall, however, from chapter 4 that we did not simply assume the head of household to be male. Instead, those not living alone were asked, "Do you think of anyone here as the head of household?" Those who said that they did were free to name one or more individuals as the head.[2]

It is instructive to examine briefly the responses to this question. Table 7.1 cross-classifies those individuals selected as heads of households by

---

[1]Consistent with this, recall that in chapter 5 we restricted analyses to cases in which the respondent was the head of household when we examined the effects of occupational experiences (e.g., job authority and union membership) that are not directly felt by other family members.

[2]See chapter 4 for details on how information identifying the head of household was used in the construction of the measure of head of household's SEI.

TABLE 7.1
Sex of Household Head (by Sex of Respondent) and Employment Status of
Respondent and Spouse (for Married Whites)

| | Head of Household Identified As: | | | |
	Male	Female	Both/Neither	Base N
Male Respondents				
Only Male Employed	74.6%	1.7	23.7	236
Both Male and Female Employed	59.4%	2.5	38.1	197
Female Respondents				
Only Male Employed	81.5%	2.6	15.8	265
Both Male and Female Employed	78.2%	3.6	18.2	225

sex and by current employment status of both spouses, for white married respondents (excluded from the table are 16 employed women whose husbands were not employed, 17 unemployed men whose wives were employed, and 156 respondents who reported that neither they nor their spouses were employed). This table indicates that the clear majority of both husbands and wives regard the male as the head of household, and the employment status of the wife has only a negligible effect on this phenomenon. Among wives, about 80 percent name the male as the household head, whether or not they themselves are employed. Husbands appear slightly more sensitive to their wives' employment status: even so, about 60 percent of husbands whose wives are employed still identify themselves as the sole household head. Thus, the traditional assumption that the male is the household head appears to be valid in the majority of cases. At the same time, a significant minority of cases (about one-quarter) do not name the male as the head of household.

These data are perhaps not surprising in view of results that have been reported on the limited effects (at best) of wives' labor force participation on domestic roles. Traditional sex roles in domestic life appear quite resilient, even in the face of the wife assuming more responsibilities outside the home. It seems that the modal pattern when the wife joins the labor force is for her to retain the bulk of her traditional domestic responsibilities in addition to the responsibilities she acquires in the work place

(Duncan, Schuman, and Duncan 1973; Bahr 1974; Moore and Sawhill 1978).[3]

These considerations suggest that labor force participation of the wife may not have upset traditional domestic arrangements nearly to the extent that some have presumed. If so, the traditional assumption that it is the husband who determines the family's status may still be relatively accurate, even when the wife works. But the degree to which this pattern holds as more women enter the labor force remains an open question. Studies that have directly examined husbands' and wives' contributions to class identification have generally credited the wife with at least some effect, although the size and nature of that effect varies from one study to another.

Felson and Knoke (1974) report only limited effects of wives' status characteristics: the coefficients for education of husbands and wives were of equal size, but the effect of working wives' occupational status was much lower than that of their husbands. In a related study, Rossi et al. (1974:178) argued that wives contribute about half as much as their husbands to the family's social standing.

Other studies have argued that the wife's contribution is much larger. Three studies of the class identification of working wives conclude that the contribution of wives' social standing is roughly comparable to that of their husbands (Ritter and Hargens 1975; Hiller and Philliber 1978; Van Velsor and Beeghley 1979). These results are taken to support the status-sharing model, and the sharing is seen as approximately symmetrical. In a companion to one of these papers, however, Philliber and Hiller (1978) found that husbands with working wives are oblivious to their wives' status characteristics, which suggests that different family members use different rules in identifying with a class.

One difficulty in evaluating these results is that important variables are sometimes omitted. Ritter and Hargens, for example, do not consider the effects of education or income, and the two studies by Hiller and Philliber exclude education. The two analyses that do report relatively complete models draw conflicting conclusions about the relative effects of husbands' and wives' occupations. Felson and Knoke (using NORC Prestige Scale scores) report that wives' contributions are small (1974:521), but Van Velsor and Beeghley (using the blue-collar/white-collar distinction) report

---

[3]Interestingly, time-use studies suggest that when the wife is employed, the discrepancy between the amount of time she and her husband spend on housework is smaller than when the wife is not employed outside the home. This difference arises, however, because the employed wife spends less time on housework than the nonemployed wife. The amount of time a husband spends on housework is not affected by his wife's labor force participation (Meissner et al. 1975; Walker and Woods 1976; Pleck 1977; 1979; Robinson 1977:61-69).

that wives' contributions outweigh the contributions of husbands. It is difficult to assess these conflicting results, since the two studies use noncomparable measures of occupational standing. In addition, the former study pools the responses of both husbands and wives, while the latter study is confined to wives. In view of Hiller and Philliber's conflicting results for husbands and wives, this difference in research design is unfortunate.

Thus, while all of these studies suggest that wives' status characteristics have at least some impact, the size and nature of that impact remain unclear. Because several studies omit potentially relevant status characteristics of the husband and wife, we cannot estimate the relative importance of each of these factors for husbands and wives.

According to our own working assumptions about the derivation of individuals' socioeconomic status, we would anticipate that the wife's impact is limited. Unless she is a head of household (and she usually is not), the only aspect of her own status to which the wife is expected to be sensitive is her educational attainment. Education is in most cases completed before marriage, and so the education of one's spouse is a remote stimulus relative to one's own education. For other aspects of status that are currently more conspicuous, her family becomes the unit of stratification, and traditional domestic norms imply that her own contribution to her family's status will be minor.

Previous studies do not help us to resolve these issues. Such a resolution requires a model in which respondents' class identification is specified as a function of six factors: the education, occupational status, and income of the respondent and the spouse. Obviously, such a model can be estimated only for married respondents where both spouses are employed. In order to test for possible sex differences in the coefficients, it is also essential that we estimate the model for men and women separately. Once these basic comparisons are made, we can expand the focus to include people from more traditional families in which only the husband is employed.

Of the 1,130 married white respondents, 38 percent are from families in which both spouses are employed, and 45 percent are from families in which only the husband is employed. (Among the remaining 17 percent, 3 percent report family situations in which only the wife works, and 14 percent report that neither spouse works.) These proportions do not vary systematically by sex or with socioeconomic status.

Table 7.2 displays the estimated effects of respondents' and spouses' status characteristics on class identification for married whites in families where both spouses are employed. The first panel contains the figures for the full model estimated separately for men and women. All of the

TABLE 7.2
CONTRIBUTION OF HUSBAND'S AND WIFE'S STATUS CHARACTERISTICS TO CLASS
IDENTIFICATION (FOR MARRIED WHITES IN FAMILIES WHERE BOTH SPOUSES ARE EMPLOYED)

	REduc	SpEduc	RSEI	SpSEI	RInc	SpInc	Constant	R^2	N
Males	.057	−.009	.006	.001	.018	.009	1.466	.271	184
	(2.9)	(0.3)	(2.3)	(0.2)	(3.0)	(0.8)	(5.6)		
Females	.057	.014	.002	.004	.005	.018	1.317	.285	211
	(2.2)	(0.7)	(0.7)	(2.0)	(0.8)	(3.6)	(5.4)		
Males			.012	.002			2.011	.198	192
			(5.7)	(0.6)			(17.9)		
Females			.007	.009			2.086	.202	217
			(3.0)	(4.6)			(19.8)		
Males	.061	.001	.008	.000			1.477	.255	190
	(3.2)	(0.1)	(3.3)	(0.1)			(6.0)		
Females	.077	.008	.002	.007			1.285	.246	216
	(3.1)	(0.4)	(1.0)	(3.2)			(5.2)		

NOTE: Main table entries are the metric regression coefficients; entries in parentheses are their t-ratios.

variables are defined as in previous chapters, except that the Duncan SEI scores refer to the respondent and the spouse (instead of the head of household), and the income measures identify income solely from the main job of the respondent and of the spouse.

The figures in the first panel are unambiguous. Employed married women play a minor role in family social status compared to their husbands. From the first row, we see that the husbands of employed women rely exclusively on their own status characteristics–there is not even a hint of any "sharing" of the wife's status characteristics. From the second row, it is clear that husbands' status characteristics also dominate employed wives' class identifications, with one exception. Married employed women draw on their own, rather than their husbands', education. Apart from this, women borrow their status from their husbands. Thus, despite their labor force participation, the role of wives' status characteristics is a very limited one.

While this pattern is consistent with our own expectations, it clearly runs counter to the thrust of much of the recent research on this topic. Why should this be so? A major reason, we believe, is the omission of key

variables in previous studies. Consider the figures in the second panel of
the table, where education and income are excluded, and where we focus
solely on the effects of respondent's and spouse's SEI. Married men
continue to ignore their wives' status, but married women appear to rely
on both their own and their husbands' SEI, with only slightly more
emphasis on the latter. In other words, among women there is apparent
evidence of status sharing, just as Ritter and Hargens (1975) and Hiller
and Philliber (1978) concluded, although this is not reciprocated by men
(Philliber and Hiller 1978).

As we noted earlier, however, these studies failed to control for education. As the figures in the bottom panel of table 7.2 indicate, this omission
is unfortunate. While the control does not alter the basic pattern among
men, its effect among women is dramatic. The apparent sensitivity of
married women to their own SEI when we ignore other factors is spurious
and reflects a sensitivity to their educational rather than their occupational attainment. This means that the experience of current labor force
participation among married women does not affect their class identification. Rather, they continue to defer to the occupational status of their
husbands. This pattern might have become evident in earlier studies had
those studies considered the effects of education, an experience that most
spouses complete before marriage.

Our results to this point suggest that labor force participation by the
wife does not disrupt traditional notions about the sources of family
status. Should we therefore conclude that there is no distinction between
employed and nonemployed wives? Does the wife's employment increase her sensitivity at least to her own educational attainment?

To address this question, we compare the model of class identification
for married working women with the same model for married nonemployed women. Table 7.3 reports the effects of respondent's and
spouse's education, spouse's SEI, and spouse's income on class identification for these two groups of married women (the analysis remains restricted to whites). The two variables that had no effect for employed
wives in table 7.2 (respondent's SEI and respondent's income) are excluded from table 7.3. Of course, these two factors are not even potentially
relevant in the case of nonemployed wives.

The estimates in table 7.3 indicate that wife's employment has at most a
modest effect on the way she derives her class identification. Both groups
of women appear equally sensitive to husband's SEI and income. The
only distinction between the two groups is that whereas employed
women ignore their husbands' education and rely on their own, nonemployed women are less sensitive to their own education and more
sensitive to their husbands'. Even this distinction, however, is mini-

TABLE 7.3
Contribution of Husband's and Wife's Status Characteristics to Class
Identification (for Married White Women by Labor Force Participation)

	REduc	SpEduc	SpSEI	SpInc	Constant	R^2	N
Respondent and spouse employed	.070 (3.1)	.014 (0.7)	.005 (2.2)	.018 (3.6)	1.258 (5.3)	.277	212
Only spouse employed	.040 (1.9)	.031 (1.8)	.005 (2.8)	.015 (4.5)	1.443 (7.5)	.332	231

NOTE: Main table entries are the metric regression coefficients; entries in parentheses are their t-ratios.

mal—for nonemployed women, both the education coefficients are of borderline statistical significance ($p = .07$).

In all, these analyses suggest that the class identification of the husband is unaffected by his wife's employment, and even the wife is barely influenced by her own employment. So-called nontraditional marriages look much like traditional ones in the way the class identification of husbands and wives is derived. Why does the wife's labor force participation fail to bear on family social standing?

This phenomenon could result from one or both of two different processes. One possibility is that families seek to maximize their social status and thus ignore whichever spouse's status characteristics are lower. If wives generally have lower status attainment than their husbands, wives' characteristics could fail to influence class identification for this reason alone. Thus, while discriminatory forces outside the home may cause the wife to have lower status, within the family her contribution could be ignored solely because family members are attempting to maximize their social standing.

Appealing as this explanation may sound, there is very little evidence to favor it. Respondents do not systematically rely on the characteristics of the higher-status spouse. Consider education: both husbands and wives draw on their *own* educational attainment, and there is no systematic tendency for either husbands or wives to have the edge on educational attainment. Among respondents from couples in which both spouses are employed, there is an even breakdown between cases where husbands have the educational edge (34 percent), where wives have the edge (33 percent), and where both are equal (33 percent), and this breakdown does not vary with the sex of the respondent. For socioeconomic status, both spouses draw on the husband's SEI. Again, however, there is no tendency for the husband's SEI to exceed the wife's. As with education, the distribution of husband's and wife's relative SEI gives three groups of roughly equal size. In view of this distribution, if people were simply trying to maximize their status, we would expect the coefficients for husband's and wife's SEI to be of approximately the same magnitude. They are not, however. The only factor that fits the status-maximizing argument is income. Both husbands and wives draw solely on the husband's income, and for fully 80 percent of the respondents from couples in which both spouses are employed, wives indeed earn less than their husbands.[4]

That only one of the three status characteristics fits the expectations of a status-maximizing perspective clearly indicates that other factors are operative. In addition, even this scanty support is subject to an alternative interpretation. The lower earnings of employed married women are caused at least in part by their greater tendency to part-time employment and interrupted labor force participation (see, e.g., Mincer and Polacheck 1974, and the papers and comments on "economic dimensions of occupational segregation" in Blaxall and Reagan 1976). These factors, in turn, are heavily influenced by normative pressures on women to conform to the prescriptions of the wife-mother role (see, e.g., Rossi 1974). If the wife's lower income is partly due to domestic demands made on her by her family, her income cannot be treated as an independent stimulus to which the family merely responds in sex-neutral terms.

Indeed, this second line of reasoning suggests a more plausible interpretation of the results as a whole. Both the husband and the wife are trapped by general sex-role norms into discounting the wife's contribution to family status, regardless of whether her contribution might result in a lower or higher class identification. In other words, even when the wife is employed, entrenched cultural norms dictate that she continues to be seen by her family and by herself as primarily a housewife. The housewife's contribution to the family is expected to derive from her domestic functioning as a wife and mother (what Parsons and Bales [1960:22-26] label the "expressive role"), and it remains to the husband to fulfill the "instrumental role" that links the family to the outside status system. Thus, even when the wife works, her domestic role is not significantly altered—the working wife is more likely to worry guiltily about

---

[4]Another way to consider the status-maximizing argument involves comparing estimates from models as in table 7.3 for families in which the husband has higher status (say, SEI) with estimates for families in which the wife has higher status. We avoid this procedure here since it involves what is essentially a double control for status. It also introduces impossible collinearity between husbands' and wives' status characteristics.

whether she is maintaining her housewife role satisfactorily in the face of external pressures than she is to reject that role as inappropriate to her circumstances.

Such an interpretation is consistent with the pattern of results found for income, occupational status, and education. The only socioeconomic characteristic where the wife draws on her own achievements is the one that both she and her husband most likely attained prior to their marriage and which is no longer conspicuous–that is, education. Likewise, the husband also draws on his own education. Other achievements of the wife that take place within the constraints of family life are discounted in favor of the husband's, by both spouses.

The preoccupation of the family with the maintenance of traditionally prescribed domestic relationships is reflected in several aspects of the interplay between home life and work life. We have already alluded to some of these. There are two main ways that the wife's work life is affected: her greater tendency to work part time and to have an interrupted employment history. Two major aspects of family life that reflect traditional norms are the tendency for the wife to have major responsibility for household duties and for the husband to be considered head of the household. In families where the wife has an uninterrupted, full-time employment history, where the husband and wife share household duties equally, and where no one person is seen as head of the household, we might expect the wife's current status characteristics to contribute to the household's social standing. In other words, only when families have abandoned the traditional husband-wife relationship will they also abandon the husband's preeminence in the household's social standing. Such a desertion of sex-role prescriptions has only rarely taken place.

Let us consider in more detail the four factors we have just listed. Each is measured as follows. We define full-time employment as working at least thirty-five hours a week. To measure continuity of labor force participation, we estimate the proportion of adult life in which respondents have been employed (defining adult life as 21 to 64 years of age, inclusively) or the proportion of married life in which spouses of respondents have worked (this distinction is necessary because a spouse's employment prior to marriage is both less conspicuous and less salient to the respondent). The relative contribution of each spouse to the housework is derived from the following question:

> We're interested in knowing how much of the housework here is done by different people.
>
> How much of the housework do *you* do?

How much does your (*husband/wife*) do?[5]

Five response options were provided: "all," "most," "about half," "some," and "none or very little." A respondent and spouse are treated as participating equally in household chores if the respondent either gave the same response for both or gave responses in adjacent categories. This yields a generous measure of equality in household chores. Finally, the way heads of households were identified has already been described (see table 7.1).

Table 7.4 presents the distribution of these variables among married, white respondents who report that both they and their spouses are currently employed. Of the four factors, full-time employment is the only one found among a majority of employed wives, and even here, almost one-third are employed less than full time (the corresponding figure for their male counterparts is 6 percent). For each of the other three factors, only a minority can be described as nontraditional. Little more than one-third of the working wives have had an uninterrupted employment history. Barely one-quarter of these respondents report equal sharing of household chores, even by our generous definition. Only about one-quarter report that the husband is not the sole head of household. Taken together, these patterns suggest that married women's labor force participation has not undermined traditional family arrangements nearly as pervasively as some might have anticipated. In other words, wives' current labor force participation is not a good proxy for female emancipation.

We estimated models like those in table 7.2 for males and females who differed on each of the four classifications in table 7.4. The results of these analyses are not displayed here, but they provide no evidence of attention to wife's SEI or income for any of the groups. For example, married women who have worked their entire adult life were no more likely than others to contribute to their own or their husband's class identification. These analyses, however, hardly constitute a thorough test of the impact of sex-role prescriptions on the wife's minor part in family social standing.

One problem is that many of the subgroups are too small to permit reliable inferences. More important, each of these factors taken singly tells us about only one element of the family life we are trying to describe. Unless there is a great deal of overlap between one non-traditional category and the next, each component is only a partial indicator of the condition in which we are interested. It is instructive to see how little the

---

[5]Other responses were, of course, available to cover possible contributions by children, paid help, and the like. We ignore these here since we are concerned with the relative participation of each spouse.

TABLE 7.4
WIFE'S EMPLOYMENT CHARACTERISTICS AND STANDING IN THE HOUSEHOLD (FOR MARRIED
WHITE RESPONDENTS, BOTH SPOUSES EMPLOYED)

		Base N
Does wife work fulltime (i.e., at least thirty-five hours weekly)?		
Yes	No	
68.6%	31.4%	420
Has wife worked all her adult/married life?		
Yes	No	
37.1%	62.9%	399
Do husband and wife share housework equally?		
Yes	No	
23.8%	76.2%	420
Who is the head of household?		
Husband and wife,		
or nobody	Husband only	
28.4%	71.6%	409

four nontraditional categories do overlap. Among whites, there are only *10 cases* in which the wife has an uninterrupted employment history, works full time, shares housework equally with her husband, and has equal ranking with her husband as household head. This constitutes a tiny 2.3 percent of the 427 white respondents from couples in which both spouses are currently employed. Even if we relax the stipulation for uninterrupted labor force participation from 100 percent down to at least 75 percent of adult or married life, still only a total of 15, or 3.5 percent, can be described as nontraditional. The tiny size of this group underscores the intransigence of traditional sex-role arrangements, even in the face of wives' labor force participation.

Throughout this section, our results point to the nuclear family as the primary unit of stratification, and to the husband as the primary contributor to family status. The only exception to this pattern is the sensitivity of wives (especially those who are employed) to their own rather than their husbands' level of education. For the two aspects of status that are a current part of the family's experience (occupation and income), both the husband and the wife draw exclusively on the husband's achievements. In other words, we have found no evidence for the status-sharing model, and our only evidence for the independent-status model comes from education, which is generally acquired prior to marriage. Our results are best described by the traditional status-borrowing model–an outcome that remains unaffected by the wife's employment outside the home.

How do these results bear on our basic model of class identification? Our reliance on respondent's own education requires no further comment. At the same time, our use of head of household's occupational status and family income conforms with the empirical emphasis on family rather than individual status. Our results also suggest that family status is overwhelmingly determined by the husband. Indeed, empirically it is impossible to separate the effects either of head of household's SEI from husband's SEI or of family income from husband's income, even where both spouses are employed.[6] In our remaining analyses, however, we prefer on conceptual grounds to continue our focus on the head of household's SEI and family earnings. It is better to avoid measures that build in assumptions about the sex of the head of household, even though for most married respondents this individual is male. Similarly, our use of total family income provides a more complete picture, which incorporates any supplements to the husband's earnings that may be made by the wife. Nonetheless, it is important to remember that the same results would be obtained were we to restrict our attention (among married respondents) to the occupation and earnings of the male spouse. The common assumption that families are typically headed by the male "breadwinner" remains pervasively true.

FAMILY OF ORIGIN AND SUBJECTIVE CLASS

We now extend the analysis beyond the current nuclear family to include the family of origin. Specifically, we examine the way in which the occupational status and the class of family of origin influence current class identity.

The presence of social mobility requires such an analysis, because we cannot assume that everyone's family background characteristics correspond to his present circumstances. People's sensitivity to the status of their family of origin is important for two reasons. First, we need to assess the degree to which adults break away from their family of origin when they leave home. Do they begin to regard themselves as independent

---

[6]Among white married respondents where both spouses are employed, the correlations between husband's and head of household's SEI are .95 for men and .97 for women, and the correlations between husband's and family income are .87 for men and .82 for women. If for these same respondents we estimate class identification as a function of either (a) respondent's education, husband's SEI, and husband's income, or (b) respondent's education, head of household's SEI, and family income, we obtain the same results.

status units? or do they continue to draw on their family background to determine their class identification? Second, some have claimed a more pervasive effect of social mobility–that it weakens people's affective commitment to their social class. Affective bonds to parents (or children) who have a different status create crosscutting loyalties that undermine the development of class bonds. In addition, social mobility is thought to remove the sense of permanence of a particular class affiliation, and in so doing, makes it a less compelling affiliation.

Family of Origin and Class Identification

We begin with the basic issue: do the social standing and the class of family of origin bear on current class identification? As a first step in addressing this question, we simply add status of family of origin to current status characteristics in our model of class identification. The two aspects of family of origin that we consider are the respondent's father's occupational status (as reflected in a Duncan SEI score) and the respondent's estimate of the social class of her family of origin. For both variables respondents were asked to refer to the period when they were "about 16" years of age.[7]

Two assumptions govern the selection of these variables. First, we take the family as the status unit, and second, we take the father's occupational status as defining that of the family of origin. These two assumptions, of course, draw on the analyses of the last section. If the family currently is the unit of stratification, then it is logical to assume that this was also true one generation earlier. Likewise, if families now define their social standing primarily in terms of the male spouse's status, it is logical to assume that the same pattern held a generation ago, when married women's labor force participation was hardly the issue that it has since become.

Our use of father's occupational status to indicate his objective social standing reflects our emphasis on this factor in earlier chapters. For example, remember from chapter 2 that occupation was more likely to be rated "very important" than education or income as a criterion for class membership, and from chapter 6 that the effect of occupation on class

---

[7]To identify the father's occupation, respondents were asked "When you were about 16, was your father working, retired, unemployed, or what? . . . What was his main occupation? (What sort of work did he do?)" Those whose fathers were not working when they were 16 were asked to name their father's last occupation before he became unemployed, retired, became disabled, or died. Class of origin family was identified through the question: "Out of the same list of social classes [as in the main class identification question], which one would you say your family belonged to when you were about 16?" Note that these questions on the father's occupation and the origin family's class were asked at quite different points in the interview schedule.

identification is a robust one. Using father's occupation also has a practical advantage: the respondent is more likely to be able to recall accurately his father's occupation than either his father's educational attainment or the income of his family of origin. His father's education was certainly less visible than his father's occupation, and the problem with recalling origin-family income is even more severe. Even assuming that all respondents knew their family income when they were teenagers (a tall order in itself), the fact that they were teenagers at different times coupled with inflation would make their answers difficult to compare.

Since we do not wish to rely solely on an objective measure of the background family's status, we also employ the respondent's estimate of the background family's social class. As well as providing a subjective perspective on the origin family, this gives a more encompassing picture of the origin family than can be obtained with any single measure of objective status. Of course, we must approach this variable cautiously, because its subjective character may make it more liable to errors of recall. But its relatively global nature should protect this measure from the kinds of bias that might be expected with recall of more peripheral or detailed aspects of parents' lives. Remember, too, that the results in chapter 2 indicate that respondents have a clear conception of the class terms themselves.

While we cannot directly assess the amount of error in this variable, there are some logical checks that we can make. First, we compare the distribution of origin class with that of respondents' class identification. On the basis of changes in the occupational structure, there should be a greater proportion of origin families in lower classes. This is indeed the case. The distribution of responses on origin class is as follows (for the 1,909 people for whom we have data): poor = 16.4 percent; working class = 42.9 percent; middle class = 28.0 percent; upper-middle class = 7.8 percent; upper class = 1.7 percent. "Other" responses ("don't knows," etc.) were offered by 3.1 percent.

As a second check, we compare the relationship between father's SEI and class of origin with that between current head of household's SEI and respondent's class identification. We would expect the former relationship to be as strong as the latter if origin class and current class are being calculated according to the same rules. Again, these expectations are borne out. For the former pair of variables we get the following regression estimates for whites: origin class = 1.79 + .018 Father's SEI (r = .452). For the current pair of variables we obtain: class identification = 2.09 + .013 HHSEI (r = .416).[8] Since one might reasonably expect potential recall

---

[8]Naturally, these analyses exclude respondents who named a parent, uncle, aunt, or grandparent as the head of household.

problems to increase with the respondent's age (as distance from the stimulus increases), we also checked the same relationship for three age groups (less than 35, 35 to 54, and 55 or older). If recall problems increased with age, the relationship between father's SEI and class of origin would decline with age. We find, however, no evidence of this: both the regression and the correlation coefficients increase slightly for the middle age group and then decline slightly, but all the differences are small. In all, the results of these checks lend confidence to the measure of origin family class (and to father's SEI) as an independent assessment of the family of origin.

Table 7.5 displays the estimates obtained when our basic model of class identification is expanded. In the first row, father's SEI is added to the equation; in the second, class of origin family is added; and in the third row, both background factors are included. These estimates suggest that father's SEI has a modest effect on class identification over and above the effects of current social standing. The coefficient for father's SEI in the first row is about half the size of that for head of household's SEI and there is a mild increment to the R^2 over that from the basic three-variable model.[9] The figures in the second row indicate that the class of origin family has a more pronounced effect than father's SEI. Including this variable leads to a more substantial improvement in fit (the R^2 increases from .28 for the three-variable model to .34), and the coefficient is much more precise (its t-ratio is 11.1, compared to 3.1 for father's SEI). The only effect of including either background factor on the three coefficients for current status characteristics occurs with the education coefficient, which is lowered slightly (by 10 percent) with the introduction of father's SEI and lowered much more substantially (by over one-third) with the inclusion of origin class.

The last row of table 7.5 shows that when both origin factors are considered, the effect of origin class is dominant. The coefficient for father's SEI no longer attains statistical significance, while that for class of family is unaffected. This means that father's SEI has no direct effect on respondent's class identification—what small effect it does have is indirect and mediated by origin class. Again, of the three coefficients for the basic status variables, only that for respondent's education is reduced.

It is noteworthy that education is the only one of the current status characteristics to be affected by the introduction of class of origin family. This reflects the fact that despite our labeling of it as current in this section

[9]In this comparison, the estimates for the baseline three-variable model are calculated excluding those respondents with missing data on father's SEI, so that the two coefficients of determination are based on the identical N. The same procedure is employed in subsequent comparisons against the baseline model in this chapter.

TABLE 7.5
REGRESSIONS OF CLASS IDENTIFICATION ON SOCIAL STANDING OF CURRENT FAMILY,
FATHER'S SEI, AND CLASS OF FAMILY OF ORIGIN (FOR WHITES)

REduc	HHSEI	FamInc	FaSEI	ClassFam	Constant	R^2	N
.049	.006	.016	.003		1.495	.293	1262
(7.1)	(6.8)	(9.7)	(3.1)		(21.8)		
.036	.007	.015		.219	1.221	.343	1325
(5.5)	(7.8)	(9.9)		(11.1)	(17.7)		
.037	.007	.016	−.001	.217	1.223	.346	1253
(5.5)	(7.7)	(10.0)	(0.9)	(9.9)	(17.1)		

NOTE: Respondents living with the family of origin, as identified in note 8, are excluded. Main table entries are the metric regression coefficients; entries in parentheses are their t-ratios.

(since it is a characteristic of the respondent), education is a link between origin family and current status. For example, the vast majority of respondents were still receiving their education when they were "about 16." Besides, many of those who obtained more education (including college) were subsidized in whole or in part by their family of origin. Thus, the respondent's education is essentially a status characteristic conferred on him by his family of origin and it is more subject to the family's direct influence than either his own occupation or his own income (c.f., Blau and Duncan 1967:chap. 5).

That the size of the coefficient for education drops when we include class of origin means that part of the effect of education reflects background factors. This pattern is also consistent with our conclusion earlier in this chapter that education is less a current family characteristic and more an individual background characteristic.

Does the importance of family background characteristics vary by sex and age? There are reasons to expect differences across each of these characteristics. We begin with possible differences between men and women. It has long been maintained in the literature on kinship that adult women keep closer ties with their families of origin than do men (e.g., Robins and Tomanec 1962; Sweester, 1963; Udry, 1971:337). Because of this, we would expect origin-family characteristics to have a greater effect on women's class identification. Remember, too, (from chapter 4) that current socioeconomic status accounts for less variance in class identification among women than among men. This could reflect a greater sensitivity among women to origin-family status.

We estimated the models in table 7.5 separately for white women and white men. The results are not displayed here, since in general the differences are minor. Overall, women do appear to pay slightly more attention to family of origin: the coefficient for origin-family class is 15 percent higher among women than among men. Adding this variable to the basic three-variable model gives a net increase of .07 in the explained variance for women (the R^2 goes from .244 to .314), and the corresponding figure for men is .05 (the R^2 goes from .338 to .385). Since current status characteristics account for less variance among women, this means that the *proportional* contribution of origin family class is higher for women's class identification. Consistent with these patterns, the coefficient for education is more sensitive to the inclusion of origin-family class among women: this coefficient drops by 43 percent to .031 for women, and by 29 percent to .040 for men (for both sexes, the coefficients for head of household's SEI and family income are unaffected).[10] In all, then, the differences between men and women follow the anticipated pattern, although these differences remain minor.

The second factor that may influence the relative contribution of origin and current status characteristics to class identification is age. The argument here is straightforward: as the family of origin becomes a more temporally remote stimulus, people may be less influenced by it. Such a pattern would be evident if the size of the coefficients for origin-family status declined as we move from younger to older respondents.

To address this question, we estimated (for whites only) the models in table 7.5 separately for the three age groups identified in chapter 4 (see table 4.7): less than 35, 35 to 54, and 55 or older. Again, we do not display the estimates here, but we can report that the effects of origin-family status do not decrease with age. Instead, the results we observed in table 7.5 for all whites are essentially duplicated for each age group. Thus, father's SEI has no direct effect on class identification, the coefficients for origin-family class range from .221 to .231, and of the three basic variables, only the coefficient for education is reduced by the inclusion of origin-family class. The only hint of an aging effect occurs between the youngest and the remaining two age groups. For the youngest group, the addition of origin-family class to the model increases the R^2 by .08 to .305. For the other two groups, the increment is .055 (the R^2 for the 35 to 54 group is .430; for those 55 or older, the R^2 is .346). In all, these results suggest that the major break with family of origin is made in early adulthood, after

---

[10]A further minor distinction is that father's SEI has a significant effect among women, but not among men, when it alone is added to the basic three-variable model. When both the father's SEI and origin-family class are added to the model, the former effect no longer attains statistical significance for either group.

which time people's origin status has a fairly stable effect on their class identification which is small relative to the influence of their own achievements.[11]

Class Mobility and Class Bonds

The pluralist view of American society emphasizes overlapping group memberships and split, weakened loyalties to particular groups (e.g., Coser 1956:77; Hodge and Treiman 1968). As part of that view, intergenerational social mobility has been regarded as instrumental in weakening the salience and affective significance of social class (e.g., Lipset and Bendix 1959:64). Here we explore the validity of this argument.

According to the pluralist perspective, the principal effect of social mobility is to introduce overlapping loyalties to both origin-family class and current class. Because the socially mobile have experienced more than one class, they are less likely to interpret issues from the perspective of either class alone, and are less likely to feel intensely about their current class membership. Along with this, the socially mobile have family ties to people in a class different from their own, which is thought to inhibit any overriding sense of loyalty to their own class. Personal ties to the members of another class confound the development of feelings for one's own class. As a corollary, the socially mobile are likely to attach little significance to *any* divisions along class lines. A second posited effect of social mobility is that it undercuts the permanence of class affiliations and hence makes them more peripheral. While the existence of social mobility has often been seen as lending an ephemeral quality to class generally, this pattern should be particularly pronounced among those who have themselves experienced mobility.

The pluralists' interpretation of social mobility and class in advanced industrial societies must be considered within the context of their optimistic view that upward mobility and increasing middle-class affiliations are the order of the day. Hence the idea that everyone is becoming classless, or at least merging into one bland middle class. But the logic of their argument about the effects of social mobility applies no less to the downwardly mobile than to those who have moved upward.

If social mobility does undercut the affective significance of class, as the pluralists argue, the mobile should feel less involved with their current subjective class. This should be manifested in the following patterns.

---

[11]Centers (1949:179) reached a similar conclusion: "Where a man comes from is of some importance, but where he is now is a more significant index to his present states of mind and behavior, beyond a doubt."

First, the mobile should be less likely to draw distinctions in their feelings between their own and other classes. Thus, they should be less likely to distinguish in their feelings between their origin family class and their current class. At the same time, this ambivalence should have a more general expression, making the mobile less likely to draw affective distinctions between their own class and *any* other class. This more general tendency should, in turn, be reflected in a second pattern. The socially mobile should feel less intensely about their class identification, and they should display lower levels of affect for their current class.

We begin by addressing the issue of whether class mobility weakens the affective distinctions people make between classes. Our analysis draws on the measures of affective class bonds that we examined in chapter 3. (Recall that these measures reflect respondents' relative warmth toward and closeness to their own and each of the four other classes.) Our procedure is to compare the affective bonds of those who have experienced class mobility with the class bonds of the nonmobile. In these comparisons, we focus on two levels of affective distinctions: first, those drawn between origin class and current class by the socially mobile, and between the same two classes by their nonmobile class peers; and second, the distinctions drawn between current class and other classes.

This procedure requires a number of comparisons. Table 7.6 displays the percentages expressing greater warmth toward their own class in the four possible class contrasts, by origin class and current class. The main diagonal of the table contains the nonmobile, the cells below the diagonal contain those who have moved downward, and the cells above the diagonal contain the upwardly mobile. Within each cell, the four relevant class contrasts are presented, ordered from the contrast between own class and lowest other class to the contrast between own class and highest other class. Thus, for example, in the top left-hand cell (for the nonmobile poor), P-W identifies the percentage who feel warmer toward the poor than toward the working class, P-M identifies the percentage who prefer the poor to the middle class, and so on. In each cell for the mobile, the contrast between origin and current classes is italicized (e.g., in the cell for those who report a working-class identification and a poor family of origin, *W-P* is italicized). The corresponding table for feelings of closeness is not displayed here because it gives a similar pattern of results.[12]

The first point to note in table 7.6 is that half of the respondents are classified as nonmobile. As one might expect from the marginal distribu-

---

[12]A single summary measure of own-class preference (like that used in chapter 6) would permit a less cumbersome analysis than that presented in table 7.6, but it would also result in the loss of information that is vital to the substantive problem at hand.

TABLE 7.7

RESPONDENTS WHO FEEL VERY STRONGLY ABOUT THEIR CLASS IDENTIFICATION
AND VERY WARM TOWARD THEIR OWN CLASS (BY ORIGIN FAMILY AND
CURRENT CLASS; WHITES ONLY)

		Class Identification			
		Poor	Working	Middle	Upper-middle
	Percent with very strong class identification:				
Origin-Family Class	Poor	44.4% (36)	59.1% (110)	36.9% (65)	(13)
	Working	69.6 (23)	62.5 (339)	38.3 (282)	43.6% (39)
	Middle	(13)	51.9 (79)	37.4 (318)	48.6 (35)
	Upper-middle	(3)	60.0 (20)	36.7 (49)	42.0 (50)
	Percent with very warm feelings toward own class:				
Origin-Family Class	Poor	71.9% (32)	48.1% (108)	38.1% (63)	(13)
	Working	60.0 (20)	42.0 (331)	28.7 (275)	15.4% (39)
	Middle	(12)	25.6 (78)	26.2 (313)	16.7 (36)
	Upper-middle	(2)	31.6 (19)	9.8 (51)	21.6 (51)

NOTE: Respondents living with the family of origin, as identified in note 8, are excluded. Cell Ns are given in parentheses. The method for obtaining the percentage who feel very warm toward their own class is defined in note 13.

tions for origin family and respondent's class discussed in the last section, the socially mobile have overwhelmingly been upwardly mobile (by a factor of three to one). Along with this, it is clear that most mobility occurs over a short distance: 80 percent of the mobile have moved between contiguous classes. These patterns are broadly consistent with the results of the mobility literature (e.g., Blau and Duncan 1967), and that most class mobility is upward ties in with one of the broad themes of the pluralist argument. Note, however, that these three patterns also mean that some of the cells have precariously low Ns: three cells contain fewer than fifteen respondents and another two contain fewer than twenty-five. Indeed, only two of the cells for the downwardly mobile have more than twenty-five cases.

As we examine the figures in table 7.6, we should bear in mind the main patterns in class bonds that we reported in chapter 3. Stronger class bonds are expressed by lower classes than by higher ones, and class distinctions are more likely to be drawn between (a) one's own class and higher classes, and (b) one's own class and more distant classes. What do the figures in table 7.6 tell us about the impact of class mobility on these patterns?

To begin, we see that the main effect of current subjective class on strength of class bonds is maintained within categories of origin class. For example, own- versus upper-class distinctions decline somewhat as one reads across the table. At the same time, there is little evidence of a simple origin-class effect. Thus, there is little systematic variance in the percentage expressing affective preference for their own class over the upper class as one reads down each column in the table. These two patterns suggest that origin class is a more remote stimulus than current class in the development of affective class bonds. This preliminary evidence undermines the notion that the socially mobile have one foot planted firmly in each (their origin and current) class.

Beyond these main effects, the figures in table 7.6 indicate only limited effects of mobility per se. There is a weak tendency for the socially mobile to minimize affective distinctions between current class and origin class. This tendency, however, is neither consistent across all cells representing class mobility nor generalized to affective distinctions between current class and classes other than the origin class.

As we have already noted, most of the mobility occurs between adjacent classes. That small minority who report more extensive mobility, however, do not exhibit more extreme effects on their affective bonds to their current class. Indeed, the two most pronounced cases that suggest mobility effects occur with one instance of contiguous-class mobility (from the middle to the working class) and one instance of more extreme mobility (from the upper-middle to the working class). In the former case, 19.2 percent prefer the working over the middle class, as compared with 35.5 percent of their nonmobile working class peers. In the latter case, 31.6 percent prefer the working over the upper-middle class, in contrast to 54.4 percent of their nonmobile working class peers (although the number of cases is marginal in this downwardly mobile cell: N = 19). Apart from these two instances, there are only minor or nonexistent differences between the mobile and the nonmobile members of any class in their degree of preference for their current class over the class of origin of the mobile. These differences between the mobile and nonmobile range from 12.4 percent (30.2 minus 17.8 for the *W-P* contrast) to -3.5 percent (29.8 minus 33.3 for the *M-UM* contrast).

The significance of this modest mobility effect is further diminished when we consider the affective distinctions made by the mobile and the nonmobile when they are comparing their current class with classes other than the pertinent origin class. In these cases, there is not even a hint of a coherent pattern: the mobile alternately make slightly larger, smaller, or the same affective class distinctions as do their nonmobile peers. In short, there is no evidence for the pluralist argument that mobility results in a general dilution of class bonds.

Taken as a whole, then, the pattern of results in table 7.6 suggests that the effects of class mobility on the development of class bonds are limited to a mild tendency of the socially mobile to retain some loyalty to the specific class in which they were brought up. Recall, however, that most mobility is upward and occurs between contiguous classes, and that even the nonmobile make the smallest distinctions between their own class and the next class down. Thus, the only effect of mobility is to diminish slightly what is already the weakest manifestation of class bonds.

To explore further our argument that class mobility has no general implications for the salience of subjective class, we examine its effects on the intensity of class identification and on the absolute levels of affect expressed for one's class. If mobility does have the effects claimed by the pluralists, people who have experienced class mobility should feel less strongly about their class identification and should have lower absolute levels of affect for their class than do the nonmobile. Table 7.7 displays the effects of class mobility on these factors. The top part of the table presents the percentage who feel "very strongly" about their class identification, by current class and origin class, and the bottom part of the table has the corresponding array for the percentage who express strong feelings of warmth toward their class.[13] As before, the comparable figures for feelings of closeness are not presented since they provide the same results.

The figures in table 7.7 lend further support to our argument that class mobility does not disrupt class feelings. The strength of people's class identification declines somewhat with ascending current class, but is unrelated to origin-family class. Further, there is no evidence that mobi-

---

[13]The measure of intensity of class identification was discussed in chapter 2. Recall that there were three possible responses to this item: "very strongly," "somewhat strongly," and "not too strongly." Recall, too, from chapter 3 that the scales for warmth and closeness range from 1 ("very cold/not at all close") through 5 ("neither cold nor warm/neither one feeling nor the other") to 9 ("very warm/very close"). In table 7.7, respondents are classified as having very warm feelings for their class if they scored 8 or 9 on the scale.

TABLE 7.6

RESPONDENTS WHO FEEL WARMER TOWARD THEIR OWN CLASS THAN TOWARD EACH OF FOUR OTHER CLASSES (BY ORIGIN FAMILY AND CURRENT CLASS; WHITES ONLY)

		Class Identification							
		Poor		Working		Middle		Upper-middle	
Origin-Family Class	**Poor**	P-W	21.9%	W-P	17.8%	M-P	20.6%		
		P-M	43.8	W-M	40.6	M-W	12.7		
		P-UM	58.1	W-UM	56.6	M-UM	30.2		
		P-U	63.3	W-U	61.7	M-U	46.0		
			(30)		(106)		(63)		(13)
	Working	*P-W*	15.0	W-P	30.2	*M-P*	28.4	UM-P	28.2%
		P-M	45.0	W-M	35.5	*M-W*	10.6	*UM-W*	15.4
		P-UM	55.0	W-UM	54.4	M-UM	44.7	UM-M	15.4
		P-U	55.0	W-U	61.4	M-U	56.6	UM-U	38.5
			(20)		(329)		(273)		(39)
	Middle			W-P	30.8	M-P	29.3	UM-P	25.0
				W-M	19.2	M-W	15.7	UM-W	22.2
				W-UM	46.8	M-UM	29.8	*UM-M*	8.3
				W-U	55.8	M-U	42.9	UM-U	41.7
			(12)		(77)		(311)		(36)
	Upper-Middle			W-P	21.1	M-P	35.3	UM-P	34.0
				W-M	15.8	M-W	23.5	UM-W	23.5
				W-UM	31.6	*M-UM*	33.3	UM-M	15.7
				W-U	52.6	M-U	47.1	UM-U	29.4
			(2)		(19)		(51)		(50)

NOTE: Respondents living with the family of origin, as identified in note 8 are excluded. The base Ns vary slightly across the four comparisons in each cell; we report the lowest observed cell Ns in parentheses.

lity per se undermines the intensity of class affiliations. Within each current class, the mobile exhibit either the same or even slightly higher levels of intensity than do their nonmobile class peers.

The results are similar in the second panel of table 7.7. Here, both current and origin class are negatively related to the absolute level of warmth in people's current class attachments, although the effect of origin class is the weaker of the two. Beyond this, mobility itself has no effects. Indeed, the relationships in the second panel of the table result in the highest levels of warmth sometimes being expressed by the upwardly mobile members of a class. In all, then, the results in table 7.7 reinforce our conclusion from table 7.6 that class mobility has no dissipating effects on the affective significance of subjective class.

CONCLUSIONS

In this chapter, we have focused on the way in which people's subjective social class is influenced by their present families and their families of origin. The fundamental questions at issue are whether the nuclear family serves as the basic unit of stratification, which family members contribute to the family's social standing, and how information from the individual's family of origin is incorporated into an identification with a class.

Our results are straightforward. To begin, people seem to derive their class identification primarily from their present family's, rather than their personal, social standing. For currently conspicuous aspects of status (occupation and income), the family appears to be the unit of stratification. Within the family, the husband is the principal source of status, and this state of affairs is unaffected by the wife's labor force participation. The pervasive dominance of the male head in this matter underscores the resilience of traditional domestic relationships: married women's labor force participation does not in itself imply the adoption of egalitarian domestic arrangements.

The only aspect of objective standing to which people respond in terms of their personal attainment, rather than the male spouse's, is education. This status characteristic should be seen as more of a background factor, one that is usually attained prior to the establishment of the current family, and which serves to link people to their family of origin.

Family of origin also appears to influence class identification. Our analyses indicate that the origin-family class supplements the effects captured in our basic model. At the same time, part of the effect of education in our basic model reflects its direct link with origin-family class. The primary break with origin family seems to occur in early adulthood. After this time, people rely for the most part on their current characteristics, with some continued sensitivity to their class of origin. This pattern parallels the results discussed in chapter 2 concerning the criteria people use to define classes. There we found that "the kind of family the person comes from" was rated as less important than current attributes.

Beyond this uncomplicated influence of origin family, we find no evidence for the pluralist argument that mobility attenuates the affective significance of class. People who are socially mobile remain a little less likely to distinguish in their feelings between the two classes involved in their mobility than are their nonmobile class peers. In their broader affective reactions to subjective class, however, the mobile and the non-mobile are indistinguishable.

In all, the results in this chapter support the way we have specified our basic model of class identification. The nuclear family remains the basic unit of stratification, whose status and income is determined primarily by the male head of household. At the same time, respondent's education reflects part of the linkage between people and their family of origin. In the next chapter, we address ways in which the performance of our basic model is influenced by other social patterns emanating beyond the nuclear family.

8

Social Contacts and Subjective Class

In previous chapters, we have addressed the ways in which different cues may affect the conversion of social standing into a class identification. These cues range from capital holdings (chapter 5) to the status of the family of origin (chapter 7). We have argued that these cues do not introduce stimuli that undermine the social-standing/class-identification linkage, but instead serve primarily to reinforce that linkage. We now consider the role in this process of informal social contacts outside the family.

Of all the cues we have considered, it is these personal social contacts that have been regarded as most critical in confusing or fostering a sense of class identity. A person's friends and associates define his social milieu: their characteristics become part of his experience. While a person's family is narrowly predetermined by fate of birth, his friends and contacts reflect broader social forces. The significance of this broader network inheres in its potential either to diversify or to homogenize further a person's experience.

How much heterogeneity do our friends and associates introduce into our lives, and how influential are those contacts in reinforcing or confusing our identity? These issues are at the heart of two critical questions: how "open" is society? and to what extent are people influenced by the vicariously experienced characteristics of their associates versus their own directly experienced characteristics?

Two radically different answers have been offered to the first of these questions. Marxist and derivative views have of course emphasized the constrained nature of social networks as the hallmark of capitalism. In a less dramatic way, the interest-group approach to classes also implies relatively homogeneous friendship circles. Since social standing dictates the pattern of individuals' social lives, people mix primarily with others of the same socioeconomic status. In sharp contrast, the pluralists assume that in American society, other overlapping dimensions are just as salient as the socioeconomic one in activating the patterns of social life (e.g., Rosenberg 1953; Case 1955; Coser 1956:72-81; Wilensky 1966). Thus, an individual's friends and associates are likely to occupy an economic status different from his own, even while they share other memberships and affiliations.

This disagreement is especially significant because both perspectives agree that the individual's self-conception is highly vulnerable to the nature of his social contacts. Thus, in the Marxist approach, objective status is not sufficient in itself to produce an accurate conception of class. It is the sharing of a common experience with others that leads people to interpret their experience in group, rather than individual, terms. Marx's famous passage in *The Eighteenth Brumaire* underlines the importance he assigned to social relationships as a major intervening variable between objective position and class:

> The small-holding peasants form a vast mass, the members of which live in similar conditions but without entering into man-ifold relations with one another. Their mode of production iso-lates them from one another instead of bringing them into mutual intercourse. . . . Each individual peasant family is almost self-sufficient; it itself directly produces the major part of its consump-tion and thus acquires its means of life more through exchange with nature than in intercourse with society. . . . In this way, the great mass of the French nation is formed by simple addition of homologous magnitudes, much as potatoes in a sack form a sack of potatoes. In so far as millions of families live under economic conditions of existence that separate their mode of life, their interests and their culture from those of the other classes, and put them in hostile opposition to the latter, they form a class. In so far as there is merely a local interconnection among these small-holding peasants, and the identity of their interests begets no community, no national bond and no political organization among them, they do not form a class. [Marx 1963:123-124]

While this general perspective sees homogeneous social networks as a catalyst for class identity, pluralists emphasize the heterogeneity of social networks as a critical impediment. Because a person's social contacts are heterogeneous, and because her class identification draws as much on the status characteristics of her friends and associates as on her own status characteristics, her choice of subjective class will often differ from one based on her own status exclusively. Hodge and Treiman summarize the argument well:

> The major defect of the interest theory of classes . . . lies in its systematic neglect of the great range of between-class contacts which are open to many citizens. . . . Such interclass contact is one cornerstone of democracy, preventing the emergence of social issues which would pit group against group in class struggle. [1968:547]

Whatever their perspective, analysts have credited particular significance to two spheres of social interaction. These are patterns of informal interaction in the work place, and the composition of friendship circles. Let us consider each of these in turn.

A Marxist approach views informal interaction patterns at work as an expression of formal economic relations. Relations with one's employer are not worked out on a personal, individual (if paternalistic) basis, but rather are negotiated on a contractual, group basis. The capitalist mode of production results in large masses of the proletariat sharing the same formal contractual relationship with their employer–informal interactions are restricted to peers. Indeed, this feature of capitalism is seen as particularly conducive to working-class political organization. Derivative perspectives, such as the interest-group approach, have generalized that work settings in which informal interactions are restricted to peers are more conducive to the development of class awareness. As Portes suggests,

> factory and construction occupations, by providing a setting of repetitive interaction between individuals in similar structural positions, permit the circulation of class-relevant political ideologies to a far greater extent than isolated service occupations. The latter . . . isolate their occupants–maids, gardeners, shoe shiners, etc.–from their class peers while confronting them frequently with individuals of higher socioeconomic standing and their political views. [1971:830]

From the pluralist perspective, relations in the work place are not seen as so highly constrained. Instead, the work place simply introduces another setting that provides opportunities to form crosscutting social ties.

It is clear that the work place has often been regarded as critical. Marx saw position in the production process as providing the formative life experience (Marx and Engels, 1939). Weber argued that change in the meaning of work was central to modernization, as the medieval concept of a religious vocation was transformed into a concept of a secular vocation requiring complete commitment (Weber, 1958). Nonetheless, informal interactions in the work place have potential significance only for those who are employed, and even for the employed, these interactions are restricted to their work lives. Indeed, Dubin (1956) has argued that the significance of the work place may have been overemphasized. Even for industrial workers, central life interests do not always emanate from the work place.

These considerations suggest that we should go beyond the work setting to examine the composition of people's personal friendship circles. For both the employed and the nonemployed, this involves the makeup of the people who comprise their circle of social intimates. While these friends may include work associates, they are not restricted either to those associates or to work-life interactions. Whether people's friends mirror their own status characteristics or introduce independent stimuli into their experience has thus been regarded as especially revealing, for the reasons we have already discussed.

Despite the theoretical importance of these issues, there has been little empirical research addressing them directly, and what has been done is only partial in its coverage. Laumann and Guttman (1966:177) reported from a survey of Detroit males that the respondent's status was substantially related to the status of his three best friends. In a reanalysis of 1964 NORC data, we obtained parallel results (Jackman and Jackman 1973:574). The likelihood of naming any high status friends and neighbors increased considerably with respondent's education, occupation, and income ($R^2 =$ .29). We also found that, contrary to the pluralist argument, status of friends and neighbors did not account for additional variance in class identification beyond that attributable to respondent's social standing, but instead interpreted a small part of the effects of the latter variables.

While these results are suggestive, they leave many important questions unanswered. First, they do not address the way patterns of informal relations at work may influence class identity. This omission is unfortunate given the emphasis of many theorists on the organization of the work setting. Second, even the friendship data are quite limited. Laumann and Guttman were concerned only with the "three best friends," which gives an incomplete picture of most people's friendship circles. The NORC data we used simply asked whether the respondent had *any* friends in a given occupational category. This, of course, does not identify the *proportion* of friends of a given status, and thus gives no information on the overall socioeconomic composition of the friendship circle.

In addition to these issues, the impact of patterns of social affiliation on subjective class has received only minimal attention. Laumann and Guttman's analysis was not concerned with class identity, and we focused solely on the cognitive process of class identification. Yet it is clear that the theoretical arguments we have just reviewed have more far-reaching implications. The status composition of friends and associates is thought to influence not only class identification but also the emotional significance of class attachments. Beyond their capacity to weaken the relation between a person's own social standing and his class identification, heterogeneous social contacts are thought to break down people's affective commitment to their class.

Our analysis proceeds as follows. In the next section, we describe our measures of informal interaction in the work place and the status composition of friendship circles, and we assess the degree of heterogeneity in these two spheres. We then examine the ways that these forms of social interaction may influence class identification and class identity, more broadly conceived. Most of this analysis focuses on whites, but we also consider whether the status contacts of black Americans follow a parallel or divergent pattern.

HOW HETEROGENEOUS ARE SOCIAL CONTACTS?

Informal Contacts at Work

Two aspects of informal interaction patterns in the work place bear on our concerns. First is the *absolute* amount of interaction the individual has with coworkers who occupy the same position of responsibility as he does, those who occupy higher positions, and those who occupy lower positions. How much informal interaction is there in the work place? and how seriously is it constrained between different levels of authority in particular? Second, and of more interest, is the *relative* amount of interaction with coworkers at the same level of authority versus interaction with those at higher or lower levels. For example, in comparing interaction with coworkers at the same level of authority to that with people at higher levels, does the respondent interact more with those above him (the chauffeur model), does he interact more with those at the same level (the proletarian model), or does he have equal amounts of interaction with both levels (the pluralist model)? If interactions are unconstrained, most people should report equal amounts of contact (whether minimal or extended) with those at the same and higher levels of authority, and any remaining respondents should be just as likely to report more interaction with those above them as to report more interaction with those at the same level.

This still leaves the important question of what kinds of interaction should be considered. Obviously, we need to avoid task-related interaction. We would expect considerable interaction of this sort between authority levels, but it relates to the execution of work tasks, and as such, it serves to express and reinforce the *formal* chain of command. The kind of interaction that does bear on the theoretical issues at hand is the socializing that occurs over coffee breaks and lunch. Who spends their time with whom in these short breaks in the daily work schedule? Do the hierarchical divisions imposed by the organization of work carry over rigidly into these break periods, or do they dissolve easily?

Our measures of informal work contacts reflect these concerns. They are built on the items used to measure job authority that were discussed in chapter 5. Recall that employed respondents were asked, "Are there any people with *more [less/about the same]* responsible positions than you at the place where you work?" With each of these questions, a "yes" response prompted the follow-up:

Do you and any of these people ever have lunch together or talk informally over coffee about things not related to work?

[IF YES] How often do you do this—very often, sometimes, or not too often?

Two different kinds of measures are constructed from these items. The first reflects the absolute amount of informal contact the respondent has with those of higher, the same, and less authority, taken separately. For each level of authority, this produces a classification of employed respondents ranging from those with no coworkers in a given authority level to those reporting frequent contact with coworkers at that level. This first set of measures is displayed in the top panel of table 8.1.

The second set of measures identifies the *relative* amount of contact employed respondents have with their peers as opposed to those of higher authority and lower authority. These are constructed from cross-classifications of (a) the amount of contact with peers and with superiors, and (b) the amount of contact with peers and with subordinates. In each case, respondents in the main diagonal are coded as having equal contact with two levels (which can range from no contact with either level to

TABLE 8.1
Frequency of Informal Contact at Work with People of Own Level and
Other Levels of Authority (Whites Only)

		Frequency of contact				
	No such coworkers	None	Not too often	Sometimes	Very often	N
Contact at work with those of:						
higher authority	19.4%	12.1	19.5	9.3	39.7	933
same authority	20.0%	5.5	12.3	6.9	55.2	884
lower authority	22.1%	9.7	17.5	9.4	41.2	885

	More with other level	Equal contact	More with same level	N
Relative amount of contact with those of same authority and:				
higher authority	16.1%	52.2	31.7	774
lower authority	19.8%	46.0	34.2	807

frequent contact with both levels).[1] Those falling in cells off the main diagonal are classified as having more contact with one level than another. Thus, this measure reflects the relative degree of contact with two levels, and is of necessity insensitive to the absolute levels of contact involved. This second set of measures is shown in the bottom panel of table 8.1.

The distribution of white respondents on these two sets of measures provides qualified support for the pluralist argument that the work place offers an opportunity for crosscutting social contacts.[2] From the first panel, we see that there is a fairly high degree of informal interaction between workers of both the same level and different levels of responsibility. As long as respondents have coworkers in a given level, they almost always have at least some interaction with people from that level, and this interaction is more likely to be frequent than intermittent. The only inconsistency with the pluralist position is that respondents are more likely to report very frequent contact with their peers (55 percent) than with either their subordinates or superiors (40 percent). This difference, however, is not a major one.

---

[1]Respondents were excluded if (a) they reported no coworkers at both levels in the comparison, or (b) they reported no coworkers at one level and no informal contact at the other.

[2]Despite the small number of blacks with valid data on these variables, the distributions for black respondents are similar to those for whites in table 8.1.

The figures in the second panel of table 8.1 suggest a similar pattern. Approximately half of the respondents report an equal amount of contact with workers from their own level and other levels of responsibility, and more detailed breakdowns indicate that most of these cases (70 percent) involve frequent interaction with both levels. The remaining respondents, however, are about twice as likely to report more contact with their peers than with either their superiors or subordinates.

It is interesting to note that a clear majority of those reporting more contact with those from either a higher or lower level of responsibility than with their own level do so because they lack coworkers at their own level. If we restrict our attention to those who do have coworkers at both levels of authority in a given comparison, almost no one reports more interaction with their superiors (7.5 percent) or subordinates (6.3 percent) than with their peers. A majority (about two-thirds) report equal contact with both authority levels, and the bulk of the remainder interact more with their peers.

Overall, these figures provide some support for one part of the pluralist argument. There is a generally high degree of informal interaction in the work place, and divisions created by the work hierarchy appear to introduce only limited constraints on these interactions. We turn now to an examination of people's more intimate social contacts.

Status Composition of Friends

Our assessment of the status of friends draws on a set of questions asking respondents about their circle of friends. These questions were introduced as follows:

> I would like to ask you some questions about the people you consider your good friends–by good friends I mean adults you enjoy getting together with at least once a month or so and any other adults who live elsewhere that you try to keep in close touch with by calling or writing.

Respondents were handed a sheet on which they wrote information about each of their friends (those who claimed more than 14 friends were given a second sheet).[3] After entering the first name of each friend, respondents listed the sex, race, employment status, and occupation (along with other characteristics) of each friend. Where respondents

---

[3]Respondents could name relatives as friends, except for their own children, parents, or spouse.

named all friends of one sex, and where any of those friends were married, information was also gathered on the employment status and occupation of each married friend's spouse.

For the sample as a whole, 88 respondents (4.6 percent) said they had no friends. Among those who did name friends, the median number of friends was 6. Although respondents who filled up one sheet were offered a second sheet, only 19 were moved to do so, while 174 drew the line at 14. Exhaustion may have got the better of our most gregarious respondents, but in most cases we assume that we obtained data on people's complete circle of "good friends."

Information on the status of friends comes from each friend's occupation, as reported in response to the following question:

> In column 5, could you write in what kind of job each of your friends has. For friends who are *not* working now, write in what kind of job they *last* had. We mean things like secretary or dentist or plumber or factory worker or other jobs [Instruction to interviewer: Pause while R does this. Check to see that R answers for *all* friends.]

The data that this item elicited were sufficiently detailed to allow for the Survey Research Center (SRC) two-digit occupation code, which is an abbreviated version of the three-digit Bureau of the Census occupation code.[4] For each friend, we derived a Duncan SEI score by taking the weighted mean SEI of the three-digit census occupations that were included in each two-digit SRC occupation category.[5]

We draw on these data to construct two basic measures of the status composition of friends. The first of these is the mean socioeconomic status of friends, which reflects the overall social standing of the friends, taken by themselves. The second measure focuses on the extent to which friends resemble the respondent's social standing: it consists of the mean deviation of friends' socioeconomic status from that of the respondent.

---

[4]Friends' occupation data were not sufficiently detailed to permit unambiguous coding of the three-digit Bureau of the Census occupation code (as opposed to the occupational data for respondents, spouses and parents described in previous chapters). The Survey Research Center (SRC) two-digit occupation code is described in the codebook for the 1973 SRC Fall Omnibus Study, which is available from the Inter-University Consortium for Political and Social Research at the University of Michigan (study no. 3625).

[5]The weights come from the proportion of employed persons in each three-digit census occupational category, as displayed in table 1 of the Subject Report on 1970 Census Occupational Characteristics [U.S. Bureaus of the Census, PC(2)-7A]. Our use of a weighted mean SEI score rather than a direct SEI score doubtless introduces a minor but unavoidable amount of random error into the measure.

For both measures, the 88 respondents who had no friends are excluded from consideration. Individual friends are also excluded from our calculations if their occupational status was not ascertained, or if they were currently housewives. Where the respondents named all female friends, each friend's husband's occupation was included (in those cases where there was a husband).[6] Thus, the friends who are described by our measures are those who have valid data on occupational status and who are not housewives, along with any husbands of friends who come from all-female friendship circles.[7]

The mean socioeconomic status of each respondent's friendship circle was created by summing the SEI scores of friends who met these criteria, and then dividing this quantity by the number of friends involved (obviously, the number of friends varies among respondents). Our second measure takes the absolute value of the difference between each friend's SEI and that of the respondent (in line with our earlier analyses, the latter is defined by the head of household's SEI). As above, these absolute deviations are summed across and then divided by the eligible number of friends in each friendship circle. We employ both the mean SEI of friends and the mean deviation of friends' from respondent's SEI to gauge the extent to which people's friendship circles serve either to reinforce or to diversify their experience.

We begin by estimating the relationship between respondents' social standing and the mean SEI scores of their friends. The estimates for whites are displayed in table 8.2. It is clear from these figures that respondents' social standing is strongly related to the average status of their friends: together, respondent's education, head of household's SEI, and family income account for almost 40 percent of the variance in friends' status, a figure that is 10 percentage points higher than the one we obtained with the cruder measure of friends' status available in the 1964 NORC survey (Jackman and Jackman 1973). Incidentally, the R^2 of .378 in table 8.2 is attributable primarily to respondent's education and head of

---

[6]This procedure is consistent with the results in chapter 7 on husbands' versus wives' contributions to family social standing. In view of those results, we made no attempt to include the occupational status of any wives of friends from all-male friendship circles. The ideal procedure would be to substitute husbands' SEI scores for those of *all* married female friends. Such a procedure, however, is not possible here since we are able to identify the spouses of individual friends only in those cases where all friends are of one sex.

[7]We experimented with a variety of plausible alternative specifications that relaxed some or all of these conditions (ignoring husbands of friends from all-female circles, including the past occupation of housewife friends, and so on). Results obtained with these alternatives are very similar to those reported in this chapter, reflecting the fact that all the alternatives are highly intercorrelated (with correlations on the order of .95) and are hence empirically indistinguishable.

TABLE 8.2

REGRESSION OF FRIENDS' MEAN SEI ON RESPONDENT'S EDUCATION,
HEAD OF HOUSEHOLD'S SEI, AND FAMILY INCOME, AND CORRELATIONS AMONG
THE SAME VARIABLES (FOR WHITES; $N = 1,263$)

	REduc	HHSEI	FamInc	Constant	R^2
	1.757	.259	.075	10.508	.378
	(12.4)	(14.1)	(2.2)	(6.9)	
REduc	1.0				
HHSEI	.487	1.0			
FamInc	.311	.322	1.0		
Friends' SEI	.516	.541	.272	1.0	
	REduc	HHSEI	FamInc	Friends' SEI	

NOTE: Main table entries in the top panel are the metric regression coefficients; entries in parentheses are their t-ratios.

household's SEI–the status of friends is less heavily dependent on family earnings.

These figures undercut the pluralist argument that people move in socially heterogeneous friendship circles, and thus that those circles provide stimuli that crosscut people's own status. It is clear instead that one's own status has a good deal to do with that of one's close friends. Indeed, it is noteworthy that of the correlations displayed in the second panel of table 8.2, the highest are the two between (a) friends' SEI and (b) respondent's education and head of household's SEI, respectively. These two correlations are in fact marginally higher than that between respondent's education and head of household's SEI. Overall, the patterns in table 8.2 are much more consistent with the interest-group view than they are with the pluralist view.

Our second measure focuses more directly on the homogeneity of friendship circles, because it reflects the degree to which the status of people's friends deviates from their own status. This measure suggests that people's friendship circles introduce only a modest amount of diversity into their lives. Among whites, the mean absolute deviation of friends' from respondent's SEI ranges from 0 to 73.4, with a mean of 18.8 and a standard deviation of 11.2. A more detailed breakdown of the distribution is displayed in table 8.3 and indicates that over one-fifth of the respondents have friends' deviation scores no greater than 10. The 10 to 15 and 15 to 20 categories each contains another one-fifth of the respondents. Among the remaining 40 percent of the respondents, high deviation

TABLE 8.3

DISTRIBUTION OF MEAN ABSOLUTE DEVIATION OF FRIENDS' SEI FROM RESPONDENT'S SEI (WHITES ONLY; N = 1,355)

| | \multicolumn{8}{c}{Mean Deviation in SEI Points} |
	0–5	5.01–10	10.01–15	15.01–20	20.01–25	25.01–30	30.01–35	35.01–40	40.01–75
N	105	186	259	283	204	125	77	54	62
Percentage	7.7	13.7	19.1	20.9	15.1	9.2	5.7	4.0	4.6
Cumulative percentage	7.7	21.5	40.6	61.5	76.5	85.8	91.4	95.4	100.0

scores are rare: less than 5 percent have scores greater than 40. In all, the distribution on this variable is clearly skewed in favor of smaller deviation scores. For one-fifth of the respondents, their friends' status is very close to their own, and for most others, friends introduce at best a modest degree of status diversity into their experience.

That the data on friends suggest more homogeneous social circles than do the data on contacts at work probably reflects two factors. First, as we have already mentioned, contacts at work involve more superficial patterns of association. Intimate associations might be expected to be more sensitive to status distinctions. Second, our data on contacts at work are considerably cruder than our friendship data. The former distinguish only those with more, the same, or less responsibility than respondents, with no differentiation in terms of the *degree* to which work associates' authority differs from that of the respondent. A more detailed breakdown along these lines might well indicate similar patterns to those found among "good" friends.

SOCIAL CONTACTS AND CLASS IDENTIFICATION

How do people's patterns of association influence their class identification? Contrary to the pervasive assumption that social contacts play a vital role, we will show that their role is decidedly limited. Most people seem to rely primarily on their own status characteristics in forming their class identification. While social contacts may help to reinforce one's personal experience, they serve neither as a vital catalyst for the interpretation of one's own experience nor as a source of confusion. We discuss informal contacts at work and friendship circles in turn.

Informal Contacts at Work

We examine the effects of both absolute and relative levels of informal contact. Beginning with absolute levels of contact, we consider the proposition that frequent contact with people at higher (or lower) authority levels will raise (or lower) a person's class identification. To address this, we estimate the effects of frequency of informal contact with those in higher or lower authority levels on class identification, net of the effects of education, occupational status, and income. In each case, we employ a dummy variable classification reflecting the five levels of contact identified in the top panel of table 8.1 (with the second level–"no informal contact"–as the excluded category).

To conserve space, we do not display the results here, but they consistently suggest that the absolute frequency of contact with people in different levels of authority at work has no influence on people's class identification. We found no evidence of workers being led to identify with their superiors because of informal contact with them. Conversely, we found no evidence of informal contact causing people to identify with their subordinates.

Of more interest, perhaps, are the effects of the *relative* degree of cross-level informal contacts. Such patterns of contact allow us to examine more directly whether heterogeneous social contacts confuse people's class identification. To address this question, we estimated our basic three-variable model of class identification separately for subgroups defined in terms of their relative degree of cross-level contact at work. The subgroups are those defined in the second panel of table 8.1. Thus, comparing the relative amount of contact with people of the same and higher levels, there are three subgroups: respondents who have more contact with their superiors, those who report the same amount of contact with both superiors and peers, and those who have more contact with their peers. The bottom row of table 8.1 identifies the corresponding three subgroups for relative amounts of contact with people of the same level and lower levels of authority.

If heterogeneous contacts confuse and homogeneous contacts reinforce experiences based on personal status, we would expect the following pattern of results. Those who interact primarily with people from other levels should be least able to translate their own social standing into a class identification, so that the coefficients for social status and the overall fit of the basic three-variable model should be low for this group. These are the respondents who should be most prone to conflicting stimuli–those stimuli associated with their own and their associates' discrepant status. Exactly the opposite pattern should obtain for those who interact most with their peers, since their peers' status reinforces their own. Those who report equal contact with peers and with people from other levels should fall in between these two cases. Such people should be subject to considerable confusion, although one would expect this to be less extreme than in the first case.

Table 8.4 displays the relevant regression estimates. The top panel contains those for the three subgroups defined by relative degree of contact with those in one's own level and higher authority levels, and the second panel has the corresponding figures for relative degree of contact with one's own level and lower levels of authority.[8] The figures in the top

---

[8]Note that the subgroups are defined as in the second panel of table 8.1. If these subgroups are defined more restrictively to exclude those who do not have both relevant authority levels present, the Ns become dangerously small for two of the three categories. Nonetheless, regression estimates for these more restrictive groups lead to conclusions no different from those drawn below.

TABLE 8.4

REGRESSIONS OF CLASS IDENTIFICATION ON RESPONDENT'S EDUCATION, HEAD OF
HOUSEHOLD'S SEI, AND FAMILY INCOME (BY RELATIVE AMOUNT OF CONTACT WITH
THOSE OF THE SAME, HIGHER, AND LOWER LEVELS OF AUTHORITY; WHITES ONLY)

	REduc	HHSEI	FamInc	Constant	R^2	N	Percentage of total N
Relative contact with those in the same and higher levels							
More contact with a higher authority level	.068 (2.4)	.0054 (1.5)	.014 (2.0)	1.341 (4.2)	.186	118	16.6
Equal contact with both levels	.051 (4.1)	.0076 (4.8)	.016 (4.6)	1.451 (10.7)	.298	366	51.5
More contact with the same authority level	.077 (5.0)	.003 (1.4)	.023 (6.2)	1.187 (6.9)	.354	226	31.8
Relative contact with those in the same and lower levels							
More contact with a lower authority level	.051 (2.4)	.008 (2.5)	.019 (4.4)	1.361 (5.8)	.310	145	19.6
Equal contact with both levels	.039 (2.9)	.008 (4.7)	.021 (6.5)	1.508 (9.9)	.305	337	45.6
More contact with the same authority level	.083 (5.9)	.003 (1.4)	.017 (4.4)	1.244 (8.2)	.313	257	34.8

NOTE: Main table entries are the metric regression coefficients; entries in parentheses are their t-ratios.

panel provide some mixed support for the common argument. As that argument anticipates, the overall fit is poorest for those who have more contact with their superiors ($R^2 = .186$) and is best for those interacting more with their peers ($R^2 = .354$). In addition, the coefficient for family income is lowest in the former group and highest in the latter. The coefficients for education and head of household's SEI, however, do not follow *any* interpretable pattern across the three subgroups. Indeed, the coefficient for SEI, which ought to be most sensitive to differences in cross-level contacts, is *lowest* (and statistically insignificant) for those people who interact more with their peers. This is precisely the group for which the common argument would lead us to expect that occupational status should have its most pronounced effect. Thus, the estimates for the three subgroups in the top panel of table 8.4 do not consistently follow the predicted pattern. The strongest evidence for the common argument comes from the coefficients of determination. Even here, however, we should note that for those exhibiting the most common form of cross-level interaction (equal contact with two levels), the fit of the model is only slightly less than for those in the third row of the table. A substantial drop in the R^2 occurs only for those having more contact with their superiors, a relatively small group (16.6 percent of the total); even in this case the R^2 remains reasonably high.

If the evidence for the common argument in the top panel of table 8.4 is mixed, that in the second panel is not. Comparing the three subgroups representing relative degree of contact with those in one's own and in lower levels of authority, there is no hint of any form of cross-pressure. First, the overall fit of the model does not vary at all across the three subgroups (the lowest R^2 is .305; the highest is .313). Thus, those who report more informal contact with subordinates are no less likely to translate their own social standing accurately into a class identification than are others. Second, there is no meaningful pattern to any of the coefficients (even for income) across the three subgroups. Indeed, the coefficient for SEI is again lowest (and statistically insignificant) for those reporting more contact with peers–the group for whom this coefficient should be highest. A comparison of the coefficients for education (in the first column of the bottom panel) and income (in the third column) indicates no monotonic increase as we move from the first to the third row. Similarly, there is no clear pattern to the constant terms (just as there is not in the first panel): degree of cross-level contact does not even influence class identification in a simple additive manner.

In all, then, the figures in table 8.4 provide little support for the argument that people's class identification is confused by informal contacts at work across different levels of authority. Whether or not people experience such crosscutting interactions has little bearing on how they convert their own social standing into a class identification. As we shall show in the next section, a comparable conclusion is suggested when we consider the potential cross-pressures introduced by more intimate friendship circles.

Status Composition of Friends

In line with the distinctions we drew earlier in this chapter, we examine the effects of friendship circles in two ways. First, how does the average overall status of people's friends influence their class identification? Second, what kind of effect does the status homogeneity of their friendship circles have?

To address the first issue, we follow the procedure we used earlier (Jackman and Jackman 1973) and simply add the mean status of friends to our basic three-variable model of class identification. If the pluralist view is correct, adding this variable to the model should increase its overall fit considerably, reflecting the idea that people respond as much to their friends' status as to their own (Hodge and Treiman 1968:546-547). This, of course, presupposes that friends' status is substantially independent of respondent's status. While the figures in table 8.2 undermine that assumption, the fit between one's own status and friends' status ($R^2 = .378$) does not completely preclude an independent effect of friends' status on class identification. The interest-group view, in contrast, anticipates no such pattern. Instead, because friends' status reflects one's own, adding this variable to the model may help to elaborate the linkage between one's own status and class identification, but should have no independent effect beyond this.

Table 8.5 displays the appropriate estimates. From the first row, we see that the mean socioeconomic status of friends has a positive net effect on class identification. But comparing the coefficient of determination for this model with that for the basic three-variable model in the second row (which is estimated for the same cases) indicates that incorporating the mean SEI of friends does not increase the explanatory power of the model. Nor does the addition of this variable lead to a dramatic decrease in the size of the coefficients for personal social standing. Comparing the first two rows, the coefficients for education and head of household's SEI are each reduced by less than 20 percent, and the coefficient for family income is the same in each row. In addition, a comparison of the first and third rows indicates that the simple bivariate effect of friends' mean SEI is reduced by about 70 percent when we include the three basic variables in the model: the coefficient for friends' mean SEI drops from .0156 in the third row to .0048 in the first row.

These estimates suggest the following. First, contrary to pluralist expectations, the socioeconomic status of friends does not introduce an independent stimulus that influences class identification. Second, there is

TABLE 8.5

REGRESSIONS OF CLASS IDENTIFICATION ON RESPONDENT'S EDUCATION, HEAD OF HOUSE-
HOLD'S SEI, FAMILY INCOME, AND FRIENDS' MEAN SEI (WHITES ONLY; $N = 1,242$)

REduc	HHSEI	FamInc	Friends' mean SEI	Constant	R^2
.041	.0056	.014	.0048	1.540	.270
(5.8)	(6.0)	(8.8)	(3.7)	(21.1)	
.049	.0068	.014		1.590	.262
(7.3)	(7.9)	(9.0)		(22.0)	
			.0156	2.003	.133
			(13.8)	(37.7)	

NOTE: Main table entries are the metric regression coefficients; entries in parentheses are their t-ratios.

only modest support for the Marxist and interest-group emphasis on the importance of social contacts in consolidating social standing. A small part of the relation between social standing and class identification is interpreted by the status of one's friends. But most of the zero-order association between the latter variable and class identification is spurious, reflecting the dependence of both factors on people's own social standing.[9]

We now turn to our second way of evaluating the impact of the status composition of friends on class identification. Here we focus directly on the extent to which a person's friends mirror or diverge from his own social standing, and how this influences the way he converts his social standing into a class identification. As in the last section, common expectations suggest that this conversion is much looser among those with heterogeneous friendship circles.

To address this issue, we estimate our basic three-variable model of class identification for subgroups defined by the status heterogeneity of their friends (see table 8.3 for the distribution on this variable). The first subgroup is defined very stringently to include those respondents with friends who mirror their own occupational standing closely: only those with a friendship circle that has an average deviation from their own SEI of no more than 10 SEI points are included. The second group contains

[9]These reults are consistent with those of our earlier analysis (Jackman and Jackman 1973). While we emphasized the mediating role of friends' social standing in that article, most (about 60 percent) of the zero-order association between friends' status and class identification in the 1964 NORC study was also spurious.

TABLE 8.6

REGRESSIONS OF CLASS IDENTIFICATION ON RESPONDENTS' EDUCATION, HEAD
OF HOUSEHOLD'S SEI, AND FAMILY INCOME (BY STATUS HOMOGENEITY OF
FRIENDSHIP CIRCLES; WHITES ONLY)

Mean absolute deviation of friends' from respondent's SEI	REduc	HHSEI	FamInc	Constant	R^2	N	Percentage of total N
0–10	.045	.008	.013	1.596	.355	268	21.6
	(3.0)	(3.9)	(5.0)	(11.6)			
10.01–20	.040	.007	.016	1.691	.239	498	40.1
	(3.4)	(4.3)	(6.0)	(13.7)			
20.01–75	.057	.006	.012	1.511	.232	476	38.3
	(5.6)	(5.5)	(4.3)	(12.7)			

NOTE: Main table entries are the metric regression coefficients; entries in parentheses are their t-ratios.

respondents whose friends might be variously described as loosely similar to or moderately divergent from themselves. It consists of those with friendship circles that have a mean deviation from their own SEI of more than 10 but no more than 20 SEI points. The third group includes those who have a more clearly heterogeneous circle of friends. It contains those respondents whose friends' mean deviation is greater than 20 SEI points.

The regression estimates for these three subgroups are presented in table 8.6. The figures offer some support for the view that homogeneous friendship circles reinforce the interpretation of one's own experience, but such friendship circles appear far from critical. The clearest evidence for a friendship effect occurs in the coefficients of determination. Among those with very homogeneous friends, the R^2 is .355, which is considerably higher than the R^2s for the remaining two groups. It is important to emphasize, however, that the latter figures are themselves quite high, and are also of similar magnitude to each other (.239 and .232). This means that the only distinction that has any significance for class identification is the one between very homogeneous friends and all others. There is no further decline in goodness of fit as the status of friends becomes increasingly different from one's own. In addition, the fit of the model remains good even where friendship circles are very heterogeneous in terms of their status.

Beyond the issue of goodness of fit, there are no systematic differences across the three subgroups in the *form* of the relation between personal social standing and class identification. Whether people's friends closely mirror their own status or introduce diverse stimuli into their lives, the way in which personal social standing is converted into a class identification remains essentially the same. What minor differences do exist in the coefficients across subgroups follow no interpretable pattern.[10]

In summary, if we focus on informal contacts at work or on friends, we find only limited evidence that social contacts influence people's class identification. It appears that frequent interaction with his superiors on the job does not make the chauffeur middle class. Even in relation to their intimate associates, people appear to place considerably more weight on their own direct experience than on the more vicariously experienced status of their friends.

SOCIAL CONTACTS AND CLASS FEELINGS

Along with their effects on the cognitive process of class identification, crosscutting social ties are commonly thought to weaken class feelings. That the heterogeneity of one's social contacts has little bearing on the former process does not imply that contacts have no bearing on the affective significance that people attach to their identification. Specifically, while heterogeneous social contacts do not lead people to change their conception of which class they belong to, such contacts may erode their feelings of attachment to that class.

In the last chapter we probed the way that crosscutting family ties may influence people's affective reactions to class. Here we briefly address the same general issue, but with a specific focus on people's *chosen* associates: do their chosen associates have more influence than their family of origin on the formation of people's emotional ties to class and on their interpretation of class issues?

Having friends and associates whose experience reinforces one's own has been commonly regarded as critical to the development of a sense of group identity. From a Marxist perspective, this is a critical factor that

---

[10]Reestimation of the models in table 8.6 substituting the Stevens and Featherman (1981) male and total SEI scores for the Duncan SEI scores did not even reveal differences in goodness of fit across the three subgroups. We have more confidence, however, in the results displayed in table 8.6. Because lower-status occupations are more closely bunched together in the new SEI scales, and because head of household's SEI is related to the mean SEI of friends, head of household's SEI becomes positively associated with the status heterogeneity of friendship circles. In contrast, when the Duncan SEI scores are employed, head of household's SEI is uncorrelated with the status heterogeneity of friendship circles. Thus, when the Duncan scores are used (as in table 8.6), the effects of head of household's SEI and the status heterogeneity of friends are not mutually confounded.

distinguishes the feudal peasant from the industrial worker. The former is more likely to interpret his experience in individual terms because he is relatively isolated from other peasants in his work life while he has a personal relationship with his "boss." By contrast, the industrial worker is relatively isolated from his boss, and the organization of work brings him into close contact with his peers, making it easier for him to recognize their common fate. The pluralist position would anticipate a similar outcome, although the process involved is thought to be slightly different. Heterogeneous social contacts may not lead people to interpret their experience in individual terms, but such contacts do mean that people develop split and therefore weakened loyalties to a variety of groups.

To address this issue, we examine the extent to which homogeneous associates and friends influence people's class bonds and their interpretation of class issues. Here we employ the measures that were introduced in chapters 2, 3 and 6: intensity of class identification, affective class bonds, interpretations of class distinctions, and perceptions of class interests. According to the common expectations that we have outlined, people with homogeneous friends and associates should exhibit the following tendencies. First, their affective bonds to their class and the intensity of their class identification should be stronger. Second, they should be more likely to explain class distinctions in terms that reflect their own class interests. Those in lower classes should become more likely to attribute class differences to biased opportunities; those in higher classes should become more likely to attribute such differences to subcultural or genetic factors. Third, those with homogeneous social contacts should be more likely to perceive economic issues in class terms. Among lower classes, this would involve a greater tendency to see class interests as mutually opposed; among higher classes, this could involve either the perception of mutually opposed interests or the belief that the interests of their own class represent the general interest. Taken as a whole, such patterns would of course indicate more class consciousness among those with homogeneous social circles than among those with heterogeneous social circles.

The results of our analyses are not displayed here, but they uniformly indicate that people's class bonds and the degree to which their perspective is permeated by class interests are not affected by the homogeneity of their friends or work associates. Cross-level interaction in the work place (in terms of both absolute and relative levels) and the status homogeneity of friends were cross-tabulated with each of the measures of class feelings and beliefs (for whites as a whole and, where appropriate, by class). In no case was there any suggestion that people draw on their friends' experience either to reinforce or to modify their own. This pattern parallels that obtained in the last chapter, and suggests that associates generally (whether they are chosen or family associates) have little influence on people's class attachments.

STATUS HOMOGENEITY OF SOCIAL CONTACTS AMONG BLACKS

Our focus has been on the social contacts of whites, but it is useful to ask the same questions about black Americans. We have established that among blacks, personal social standing has little bearing on class identification beyond the poor/nonpoor distinction. We have also found that for many blacks, especially those identifying with the middle class, feelings of racial identity outweigh class feelings. Indeed, the class feelings of black middle-class identifiers suggest a greater affinity to the poor than to their own class. One interpretation of these patterns is that ghettoization has resulted in blacks forming social ties that are highly sensitive to racial boundaries but insensitive to socioeconomic distinctions. This argument implies that the existence of black ghettos makes it more difficult for blacks to restrict their interaction to people of similar socioeconomic standing. Blacks of higher socioeconomic achievement may therefore be more likely than comparable whites to have friendship ties with people from lower classes.

Plausible as this interpretation might seem, it flies in the face of Wilson's recent argument (1980) that socioeconomic distinctions are becoming more pervasive within the black community. It is also inconsistent with our own data, which show no major race differences either in the socioeconomic composition of friendship circles or in the capacity of friends' status to account for additional variation in class identification. First, education, occupational status, and income account for 30 percent of the variance in the mean status of friends of black respondents (which is only slightly lower than the R^2 of .378 reported for whites in table 8.2). Among blacks, the mean status of friends is more sensitive to income and less sensitive to occupational status than it is among whites, but these differences are not dramatic. Second, as was the case with informal contacts in the work place (see note 2 of this chapter), there are no race differences in the status homogeneity of friendship circles. The distribution on this variable for blacks is very similar to that for whites displayed in table 8.3. Third, when the mean status of friends is added to our basic three-variable model of class identification for blacks (as is done for whites in table 8.5), none of the coefficients (nor the overall equation) is statistically significant. In other words, the status of their friends does not help account for the class identification of blacks. Finally, the status composition of friends is no more relevant among blacks than it is among whites in accounting for feelings of class identity.

Given these patterns, it is evident that the race differences in class identity discussed earlier in chapters 3 and 4 do not reflect greater socioeconomic heterogeneity in friendship circles among blacks. Of course, in evaluating the parallel nature of black and white friendship patterns, it is important to recognize that they *are* parallel: segregation along racial lines far exceeds socioeconomic segregation. Of the 1,514 whites with data on friends, only 151 people (10 percent) have *any* black friends, and most of this select group (97 respondents) have only one black friend. Among the 157 blacks with data on friends, 35 percent have any white friends, and in over half of these cases only one white friend is involved.[11]

Thus, our data support Wilson's argument about the prevalence of status distinctions within the black community. At the same time, these status distinctions are most unlikely to cut across racial boundaries. The prominence of racial identity among blacks is better understood as deriving from a conspicuous restriction of contact with whites than from an unrestricted interaction with blacks of all socioeconomic levels.

CONCLUSIONS

Great significance has traditionally been attached to the influence of socioeconomic factors on patterns of informal association. These patterns are regarded as a reflection of the openness of society, which in turn has been treated as a critical force in the development of class identification and class feelings.

Our results indicate that patterns of association do follow socioeconomic lines. While informal interaction in the work place is less constrained by status distinctions, friendship circles that involve more intimate social ties are substantially determined by such distinctions. These patterns hold for both whites and blacks. At the same time, we find that these patterns of association have only a modest direct bearing on people's class identification and no bearing on their affective class bonds. Having heterogeneous social contacts does not appear to confuse people's interpretation of their own experience. Having homogeneous friends is

---

[11]That blacks are a little more likely to name white friends than vice versa reflects the small proportion of blacks in the population (about 12 percent). All other things equal, this proportion means that the probability of interracial contact is lower for whites than it is for blacks.

mildly reinforcing, but most of their effect is spurious and reflects instead people's own social standing. In short, people seem to draw primarily on their own personal experience rather than the experience of their social contacts.

These results challenge the almost universal assumption that it is critical to have social contacts who share one's own experience in order to interpret that experience in group terms. While there is little support for the pluralist conception of free and open interaction across socioeconomic levels, this outcome does not have the critical bearing on the subjective interpretation of socioeconomic status that both pluralists and Marxists have assumed. Neither the relatively strong evidence of class identification and class bonds among whites nor their relatively weak manifestation among blacks can be attributed to patterns of informal association.

Among blacks and whites, patterns of friendship serve as an expression of socioeconomic distinctions, albeit an imperfect expression. Racial boundaries are more sharply delineated in patterns of association, but socioeconomic status still exerts a powerful force on friendship within each racial community. While classes are not such mutually exclusive social groupings as those formed by the racially ascriptive black/white distinction, their social ramifications are similar. Both may be seen as status groups in the Weberian sense, since both serve to shape the pattern of informal association in society.

The boundaries of status groups can be rigidly enforced by ritual (as in a caste situation) or by law, but Weber argued that they are usually maintained by social convention alone. He did not see these groupings as typically being rigidly exclusive, suggesting instead that they are often "amorphous" communities. Of course, Weber prefaced his discussion of status groups with the statement, "*In contrast to classes*, status groups are normally communities [emphasis added]" (1946:186). But although his primary goal was to separate these two concepts, Weber did concede that classes can become social communities.

We conclude that socioeconomic distinctions do produce patterns of informal association that are aptly described as "amorphous communities." Because they have a clear socioeconomic foundation, one that is grounded in the person's own experience in the "market situation," these communities should be regarded as social classes. Social classes incorporate Weber's concepts of class and status group: they are loosely organized social groupings that have a socioeconomic basis.

9

Social and Political Implications of Class Identification

Our attention has been focused on the process of class identification: its intrinsic meaning and significance, and the experiential factors that contribute to its development. All of our analyses point to an interpretation of class as an important concept in the everyday existence of Americans. Social classes resemble status groups that are loosely bounded but coherently perceived. People convert their own social standing into a class affinity in a predictable and straightforward manner.

One critical question remains: how important is social class in shaping people's reactions to their wider environment? This question devolves into two issues. First, do socioeconomic distinctions in general affect the way people become oriented socially and politically? Second, does subjective class serve as a catalyst linking socioeconomic standing to social and political attitudes? We know that the class terms we have used in our analyses conjure up a sense of affiliation that involves both cognition and affect. We have yet to determine, however, whether these feelings themselves help us understand the formation of social and political orientations, or whether subjective class has no intrinsic effects beyond those of objective status alone.

There is an extensive literature on the general linkage between socioeconomic standing and social and political attitudes. While functionalists have stressed the consensual nature of such attitudes, the more common view is that those attitudes do vary with socioeconomic status. The strength of that influence and the kinds of factors that mitigate it are, however, less clear. Pluralists have emphasized the ameliorative effects of crosscutting cleavages and overlapping group memberships. Others assume that dominant groups always have the ideological advantage: their ideology permeates the major institutions of society, making radical challenge from subordinate groups unlikely. But since the dominant ideology does not satisfactorily portray the experiences of subordinate groups, these groups modify that ideology in a way that does incorporate their own interests. This typically involves an assertion of subordinate group rights to a larger share of the pie, but does not seriously challenge the nature of the pie itself. Such an interpretation of muted class conflict is reflected in Parkin's (1971:chap. 3) notion of the "subordinate" or "accommodative" value system, Huber and Form's (1973) treatment of "pragmatic egalitarianism," and, to a lesser extent, in Rodman's (1963) concept of the "lower-class value stretch."

Symptomatic of the hold that the dominant ideology has over the major institutions of society is the failure of the electoral system to provide a forum for debate about critical class issues. While some have assumed that the electoral system provides an unconstrained reflection of issues that concern the electorate, other analysts have pointed to powerful constraints that prevent threatening challenges from entering the public agenda and that minimize issue voting generally (Michels 1959; Bachrach and Baratz 1970). For political candidates, it is often rational to take ambiguous policy stands, emphasizing symbolic rather than tangible issues, and to minimize party differences (see, e.g., Downs 1957; Edelman 1964; Page 1978). Since class issues are seldom discussed in the electoral arena, voters may have little opportunity to vote on the basis of those issues. As V. O. Key (1966:2) put it, "The voice of the people is but an echo. The output of an echo chamber bears an inevitable and invariable relation to the input." Because class issues are rarely promoted by political candidates, there is little reason to expect class to have a sustained electoral expression in the United States (Converse 1958; Vanneman 1980).[1]

In spite of these considerations, most studies of the political impact of social class have focused primarily on voting patterns or party identification (e.g., Converse 1958; Guest 1974; Weatherford 1978; Vanneman 1980). It is more useful, however, to remove the analysis one step back from the electoral arena, and to consider instead people's social and policy predispositions. Even here we should not expect radical viewpoints to abound, since people's consciousness of class issues must be molded by

---

[1]Contrary to Guest's (1974:501) assertion, Converse posits a class-vote relationship that fluctuates (rather than declines) over time according to economic conditions, the themes offered by candidates for office, their personalities, and convergence versus divergence in party positions. Indirect evidence of such a pattern is found in Axelrod's analysis (1972; 1978) of the demographic sources of voting behavior in American presidential elections.

the themes assumed in public discussion of those issues. Nonetheless, we can learn more about the "grass-roots" impact of class if we focus directly on people's social and policy orientations: these are less tightly constrained by the electoral choices available than are partisan reactions.

What kinds of orientations are most relevant? First, we need to consider people's social predispositions. While the concept of "social distance" (Bogardus 1925) is a familiar one in studies of race attitudes, little attention has been given to it in empirical studies of class.[2] This is unfortunate, because the degree to which people express a desire to restrict social interaction to "their own kind" is a sensitive indicator of the stringency of group boundaries. Indeed, Weber's discussion of status groups emphasizes the exclusive proclivities of such groups. Do social classes exhibit such proclivities? Second, it is important to consider class-relevant policy orientations. Here we must assess orientations that range from broader ideological questions to specific single-issue applications, and from fundamental redistributive challenges to more moderate demands. What kinds of issues generate consensus across classes? and what kinds of issues are most prone to produce class division?

Apart from the general issue of whether socioeconomic distinctions have any social or political implications, there remains the question of what role, if any, is played by subjective social class. Do class differences in attitudes disappear once we consider more objective elements of social standing, or is class itself important in the formation of social and policy attitudes? This question goes to the heart of the issue of whether socioeconomic distinctions are most usefully seen as simple objective continua or whether they produce subjective groupings that have significance for the way people orient themselves to social and political life. This issue, however, has rarely been addressed. Centers's analysis (1949:chap. 8) suggested that class differences were more important than occupational standing for a number of political attitudes, but subsequent analyses have not pursued this issue.[3]

We address these questions by examining the effects of objective status characteristics and subjective class on social and political predispositions. Our analysis proceeds in two ways. First, we consider the extent to which various social and political predispositions vary as a function of objective status and class identification, with special attention to the question of

---

[2]One of the few scholars to have analyzed social distance outside the area of race and ethnic relations is Laumann (1966), who examined people's social predispositions toward seventeen different occupational categories. See also Laumann and Senter (1976).

[3]Guest (1974:508-509) reports that the relationships he found between class and political attitudes "hold up after introducing controls for objective socioeconomic measures." The details of these analyses are unclear, however.

whether class identification serves to mediate any observed relationships between objective standing and attitudes. Second, we pursue the significance of social class further by asking whether the emotional bonds that people feel to their class have an influence on the relations between social standing, class identification, and attitudes.

CLASS AND SOCIAL PREDISPOSITIONS

How does class influence the kinds of close social interactions people regard as desirable? Is there any evidence that people prefer to interact with those of their own class? To pursue this question, we need to examine preferred patterns of interaction in concrete settings (as opposed to general expressions of preference). Respondents were therefore asked to consider two central situations involving patterns of marriage and neighborhood preference, respectively, with the following questions:

> Would you personally prefer your children and other close relatives to marry people who are poor, working class, middle class, upper-middle class, or upper class?

> Would you personally prefer to live in a neighborhood with mostly poor people, working-class people, middle-class people, upper-middle-class people, or upper-class people?

The response options listed in the items were also listed on a show card for respondents, who could name any one or combination of the five classes (interviewers were instructed to mark *all* mentions).

While these two items do not exhaust possible areas of desired social interaction, they do reflect two critical ones.[4] Preferences about marriage indicate people's propensity to admit others from different backgrounds to their immediate family, and neighborhood preferences reflect the lifestyles to which people aspire. At the same time, the second item perhaps involves respondents more directly than the first because it concerns the neighborhood in which *they* would like to live. Although it also addresses a sensitive area, the first item is concerned with the preferred behavior of others (children and other close relatives), and respondents may see such behavior as beyond their own purview (properly or otherwise).

---

[4]Note that these items were administered after the basic class identification items in the questionnaire. Between the two sets of items were a series of questions on sex roles and on desirable income levels for different occupations.

The logic underlying the construction of our items is similar to that underlying standard social-distance scales, with two major differences. In their most common usage, standard social-distance items have been employed in studies of race and ethnic relations to identify the attitudes of dominant groups (typically whites) toward subordinate groups (typically blacks). In that context, social distance items are meant to reflect the degree to which dominant groups are willing to accept subordinate group members into their own social life. We generalize the concept of social distance, however, to reflect the exclusivity of any group. Indeed, this is intrinsic to Weber's notion of status groups. Second, the wording of our items places more emphasis on *preferences* than on mere willingness to interact with members of other groups: we regard people's "first choice" as a more sensitive indicator of group boundaries than is their bottom-line personal tolerance of other groups.

At the same time, the extension of social distance measures to all groups involved in a relationship raises another consideration. Dominant groups control a disproportionate share of rewards in society, and we should expect this to be a factor in the way members of all groups form their social predispositions toward one another. Thus, subordinate groups may express a desire for more interaction with dominant groups because this automatically implies more access to society's rewards. Concomitantly, dominant groups may wish to restrict their interaction with subordinate groups, at least partly to avoid devaluing their own position. Material acquisition and personal taste should both lead to exclusiveness among dominant groups, but for subordinate groups these two considerations may conflict. All other things being equal, then, we might expect dominant groups to display more exclusive proclivities than those in subordinate positions.

In terms of our two items, these considerations suggest that poor people and, to a lesser extent, working- and middle-class people, may want to live in higher-class neighborhoods and to have their children marry into higher classes for material reasons alone. After all, most people wish to optimize their material standard of living. This pattern should be especially evident with the item involving marriage preferences, to the extent that most people "want the best" for their children.

The distribution of responses to these two items among white respondents is presented in table 9.1.[5] Since respondents could nominate one or more classes, responses are arranged into groups that reflect the degree to which people prefer to restrict social interaction to their own

---

[5]Although we do not display them here, the distributions for black respondents are essentially the same as those for whites.

TABLE 9.1

SOCIAL PREDISPOSITIONS IN NEIGHBORHOOD AND MARRIAGE PREFERENCES
(BY CLASS; WHITES ONLY)

Class Preferences for Neighborhood				
	Poor	Working	Middle	Upper-middle
Own class exclusively	20.3%	52.5%	57.3%	40.5%
Own class and lower	—	1.0	7.7	12.2
Own class and higher	6.3	9.0	3.4	1.4
Own class and lower and higher	—	0.5	1.2	0.7
Lower class exclusively	—	1.7	12.0	33.8
Higher class exclusively	62.0	26.1	9.8	4.1
No preference, "Don't know"	11.4	9.0	8.5	7.4
	100.0%	99.8%	99.9%	100.1%
Base N	(79)	(587)	(762)	(148)

Class Preferences for Marriage of Children and Other Close Relatives				
	Poor	Working	Middle	Upper-middle
Own class exclusively	2.6%	24.3%	39.8%	37.8%
Own class and lower	—	—	3.9	10.8
Own class and higher	1.3	7.6	7.6	2.7
Own class and lower and higher	—	—	2.2	4.1
Lower class exclusively	—	0.3	5.0	18.9
Higher class exclusively	74.0	41.3	18.7	4.1
No preference, "Don't know"	22.1	26.5	22.7	21.6
	100.0%	100.0%	99.9%	100.0%
Base N	(77)	(589)	(761)	(148)

class, to include their own and other classes, or to avoid interaction with their own class. The last row in each panel displays responses indicating no preference, "don't know," or preference for *all* classes (the overwhelming majority of these are expressions of no preference).

The figures in table 9.1 suggest that there is a marked tendency toward preference for contact with one's own class. As anticipated, this pattern is more pronounced with neighborhood preferences. Here over half of the working- and middle-class identifiers and 40 percent of the upper-middle class are predisposed toward their own class exclusively. As with affective class bonds, people also readily distinguish among other social classes, with more inclusiveness toward adjacent classes than to those more distant. Thus, almost all of the people who nominate other classes are nominating a class adjacent to their own. In all, very few respondents express predispositions that could be characterized as unselective or even broadly inclusive, either by nominating several classes or by expressing uncertainty or no class preference. Marriage preferences follow the same pattern, although exclusive own-class preference is less frequent, and more inclusive predispositions occur with somewhat greater frequency.[6]

Degree of own-class preference varies somewhat by class, although not entirely as anticipated. The major distinction is between the poor and other classes. As expected, the poor are much less likely to nominate their own class exclusively and much more likely to nominate higher classes exclusively. They are also more likely than people from other classes to nominate nonadjacent classes (although about one-half of those preferring higher classes exclusively are, in fact, thinking of the working class). This pattern is noteworthy in view of the especially strong affective class bonds observed among the poor in chapter 3. As we pointed out, a subordinate group may desire social contact with more privileged groups for material reasons, despite their emotional affinity with their own group. In this vein, it is interesting that the same pattern obtains with blacks' social predispositions toward whites. For example, despite their strong emotional preference for blacks, only 24 percent of blacks say they would prefer to live in a neighborhood that is "all black" or "mostly black," while 50 percent would prefer a neighborhood that is half black and half white.

Among the nonpoor, the degree of own-class preference in social predispositions does not clearly follow the anticipated pattern. There is some increase from the working to the middle class, but the upper-middle class is not the most exclusive. This suggests that without pronounced material deprivation, material considerations provide a less compelling motivation. Nonetheless, we should bear in mind that while

---

[6]Two additional points deserve note. First, the proportions indicating no preference and "don't know" on the two items in table 9.1 are comparable to these expressions by blacks and whites on two items dealing with racial preferences for neighborhood and work place. Second, respondents frequently said that they felt "very strongly" about their class predispositions–58 percent of whites responded in this way with each item. The poor were especially likely to feel very strongly (over three-quarters of them reported such feelings, in contrast to about 56 percent of respondents from other classes).

material improvement may become less of a factor with ascending social class, feelings of own-class affinity also decline. Thus, among the poor, the conflict between emotional and material considerations appears to be generally resolved in favor of the latter. For the working class, this conflict is less readily resolved. In the upper-middle class, there appears to be neither a strong emotional nor a clear material basis for exclusivity, although it is important to understand that their inclusiveness seldom extends beyond the middle class. In this respect, the upper-middle class differs from whites, who have both emotional and material forces pushing them toward exclusiveness. For example, almost 80 percent of whites say they would prefer to live in a neighborhood that is "all white" or "mostly white."

The results in table 9.1 indicate that people's social predispositions favor their own or adjacent classes, especially in terms of their preferred neighborhood composition. Is this merely an association that spuriously reflects the influence of objective status characteristics, or does subjective class itself serve as a catalyst for social predispositions? To address this question, we rearrange the data on predispositions somewhat and regress people's preferred class(es) on class identification and the three components of their objective status.

Each of the items on social predispositions was recoded to form a new eight-category variable that orders single and multiple responses by the class(es) nominated. The eight categories are ordered as follows: 1 = poor or poor + working; 2 = working; . . . ; 4 = middle; . . . ; 6 = upper-middle; . . . ; 8 = upper. Codes 3, 5, and 7 are for multiple responses: 3 is for mentions of the middle class and at least one lower class; 5 and 7 are for comparable responses involving the upper-middle and upper classes, respectively. Respondents indicating no preference, and other variants, are excluded from this coding scheme.

Table 9.2 displays the regression estimates of the effects of class identification and objective status on the recoded measures of social predispositions. Overall, these estimates indicate that class identification does have a pronounced effect on social predispositions, net of the effects of objective status. Consistent with table 9.1, the estimates also indicate that people's neighborhood preferences are more bound by both their class and their objective status than are their marriage preferences for their children and other close relatives.

From the first row of table 9.2, we see that class and status account for 35 percent of the variance in neighborhood preference. Class identification has a highly significant t-ratio, and the effects of education and head of household's SEI are also significant. Only family income has no direct impact on neighborhood preference. Regressions not displayed here of

TABLE 9.2

EEFFECTS OF CLASS IDENTIFICATION AND OBJECTIVE STATUS ON SOCIAL PREDISPOSITIONS
(WHITES ONLY)

Dependent Variable	ClassID	REduc	HHSEI	FamInc	Constant	R^2	N
Neighborhood	.841	.069	.009	.001	.107	.351	1,272
preference	(16.0)	(5.3)	(5.2)	(0.4)	(0.7)		
Marriage	.493	.108	.003	.004	1.563	.153	1,064
preference	(6.7)	(5.7)	(1.3)	(0.8)	(7.0)		

NOTE: Main table entries are the metric regression coefficients; entries in parentheses are their t-ratios.

the effect of (a) the three socioeconomic status variables by themselves and (b) class identification by itself, indicate that class mediates much of the effect of objective status on neighborhood preference. Alone, class identification accounts for 30 percent of the variance; the corresponding figure for the three components of socioeconomic status is 22 percent. Along with this, only a small part of the class effect is a spurious reflection of objective status effects. The coefficient for class drops by only 22 percent when the objective status indicators are added to the model. In contrast, the addition of class to the model results in a drop of approximately 40 percent in the coefficients for education and head of household's SEI, and a precipitous drop (from .014 to .001) in the income coefficient.

The figures in the second row of table 9.2 for marriage preference indicate a moderated version of the same general pattern. The four variables together account for 15 percent of the variance, although only two coefficients (those for class identification and education) have significant t-ratios. Additional analyses not displayed here show that class identification mediates one-fifth of the effect of education and all of the effects of head of household's SEI and family income (the coefficients for the two latter variables are significant and over twice the size of those in table 9.2 when class identification is excluded from the model).

Taken together, then, these analyses indicate that social predispositions (especially those involving neighborhood preferences) are sensitive to both class identification and objective status. They also show that along with its independent effect, class identification mediates a good deal of the effects of objective status. Indeed, it mediates all of the effect of family income on both forms of social predispositions, and in the case of marriage preferences, it also mediates all of the effect of head of household's SEI.

To what extent are these patterns accentuated by one's affective class bonds? Those who feel warmer toward or closer to their own class should be more likely to express social predispositions that favor their own class. These, after all, are the people for whom class is most central. As we argued earlier, however, social predispositions should also be sensitive to material considerations, and the classes that express stronger class bonds are also more susceptible to upward-mobility aspirations. We have argued that the latter consideration applies particularly to people's marriage preferences for their children, while affective class bonds should play a more active role in people's preferences for their own neighborhood. Thus, the degree to which affective class bonds should determine social predispositions is not clear, especially with marriage preferences.

To address this question, we employ the classification of own-class affective preference introduced in chapter 6 (see table 6.4), which distinguishes those who feel warmer toward or closer to their own class than to other classes from those whose class bonds are weaker. As we noted in chapter 6, this is a relatively stringent classification, because to be coded as preferring one's own class, respondents are required to show that they prefer their own class on the average over *all four* remaining classes. Table 9.3 reports separate regression estimates of the effects of class identification and objective status on the two measures of social predispositions, by degree of own-class closeness. To avoid redundancy, we do not display the corresponding estimates by degree of own-class warmth, since these are very similar to those contained in table 9.3.

The figures in table 9.3 indicate that affective class bonds do accentuate the impact of subjective class on desired class composition of neighborhood, but they have little influence on preferred class of marriage partners for children and other close relatives. The top panel in table 9.3 shows that for whites with strong class bonds, class identification and objective status account for 44 percent of the variance in neighborhood preference, while the corresponding figure for those with weaker class bonds is 27 percent. The coefficient for class identification is also higher (by about 40 percent) among those with strong class bonds. Additional analyses not displayed in the table indicate that class also plays a more prominent mediating role between objective status and neighborhood preference among those with strong class bonds. For this group, the addition of class to the model results in a drop of over 60 percent in the education coefficient (which becomes statistically insignificant), and of about 40 percent in the SEI coefficient. The corresponding changes

TABLE 9.3
EFFECTS OF CLASS IDENTIFICATION AND OBJECTIVE STATUS ON SOCIAL PREDISPOSITIONS
(BY DEGREE OF OWN-CLASS CLOSENESS; WHITES ONLY)

	ClassID	REduc	HHSEI	FamInc	Constant	R²	N	Percentage of total N
Neighborhood preference								
Closer to	1.028	.032	.010	.003	−.054	.440	529	43.0
own class	(12.8)	(1.7)	(4.0)	(0.7)	(0.2)			
Neutral	.721	.089	.008	.000	.312	.268	700	57.0
	(9.5)	(4.9)	(3.3)	(0.1)	(1.3)			
Marriage preference								
Closer to	.563	.082	.003	.001	1.721	.133	449	43.5
own class	(4.4)	(2.7)	(0.7)	(0.1)	(5.0)			
Neutral	.509	.116	.003	.006	1.418	.159	583	56.5
	(5.1)	(4.6)	(1.0)	(1.1)	(4.5)			

NOTE: Main table entries are the metric regression coefficients; entries in parentheses are their t-ratios.

among the "neutrals" are less pronounced, although class mediates the effects of family income, whatever the strength of class bonds.

The bottom panel in table 9.3 shows that the impact of class bonds on marriage preference is considerably weaker. Among those with strong class bonds, the R^2 is actually slightly smaller, although the coefficient for class is a little larger than it is among those with weaker class bonds. Separate analyses indicate that class plays a more important mediating role between objective status and marriage preference among those with strong class bonds, but this pattern is less pronounced than it is for neighborhood preference.

The important role of class identification in the formulation of social predispositions is reflected in a marked own-class bias, even among those who do not express strong affective bonds to their own class. In general, our results suggest that own-class exclusiveness is blunted somewhat by a restricted degree of inclusiveness toward adjacent classes, and (especially for those in lower classes) by material aspirations. Marriage preferences for children and other close relatives appear to be more sensitive to these countervailing influences, presumably because people think they have less purview over others' personal choices and because most people "wish the best" for those close to them. Thus, marriage preference is relatively insensitive to the strength of affective class bonds, although it remains sensitive to class identification. The influence of class identification is more pronounced with neighborhood preference, and strong class bonds accentuate people's own-class bias in neighborhood preference even further.

CLASS AND POLITICAL ORIENTATION

What are the political implications of subjective class? That class is a tangible part of Americans' everyday social lives is clear, but does it translate into people's policy orientations, and if so, how? This question has generally been addressed in terms of partisan orientations in the electoral system. As we suggested above, however, such an approach presumes too much. We prefer to take the question to a more grass-roots level, and to focus on how people approach different kinds of economic policy issues.

We begin by considering their views on the role of the federal government in social welfare activities. The specific items were interspersed in a series of questions on the federal government's role in race relations, in policies that affect women, and in economic policies. The series was introduced as follows:

> People have different opinions about how much the federal government is doing about various things. People also differ about how much they think the federal government *should* be doing about these things. (Instruction to interviewer: Make sure R understands distinction between "is" and "should be" questions.)

> How much do you think the federal government *is* doing to make sure that everyone who wants a job can get one?

> How much do you think it *should be* doing about this?

> How much do you think the federal government *is* doing to make sure that everyone has at least a minimum income?

> How much do you think it *should be* doing about this?

Respondents were asked to give a response from a card containing the following options: a lot, quite a bit, a little, nothing.

These items seek to identify support for economic liberalism, as associated with the New Deal and the Great Society. Thus, they assess support for an activist federal role in establishing and maintaining minimum economic standards. Within this area, the construction of each pair of items is designed to gauge satisfaction with government performance by evaluating both how much people think the government is doing and how much they would like to see done. In this way, the first item in each pair serves to anchor the second. By subtracting people's responses to one item from their responses to the other in each pair, we generate a seven-point scale ranging from -3 (government *is* doing nothing and *should* be doing a lot) to $+3$ (government *is* doing a lot and *should* be doing nothing).[7]

Table 9.4 reports the percentage distribution of whites on each item-pair, by class. For ease of presentation, each distribution is collapsed into four groups: those who think the government should be doing a lot more than it is (scores of -3 and -2), those who think it should be doing a little more (-1), those who are satisfied (0), and those who think the government should be doing less ($+1$ to $+3$).

From this table, it is clear that opinions about federal government intervention in social welfare activities vary with class. It is also evident that among the nonpoor, there is somewhat more support for guaranteed employment than for a guaranteed minimum income. Thus, class differences are slightly higher on the latter issue than on the former. This doubtless reflects the fact that minimum-income proposals are more clearly redistributive than are proposals for full employment. Nonetheless, both issues fall in the same general domain of minimal redistributive policies, and the correlation between the two difference scores is .46[8]

The figures in table 9.4 also show that people rarely endorse the sentiment that the government should be doing less than it is. While such endorsements increase with class, they remain a distinct minority, even among the upper-middle class. Most of the variation occurs between those who are satisfied with the status quo and those who support, in varying degrees, more government intervention. Here the class differences are quite pronounced. The poor are twice as likely as the upper-

---

[7]Observations with missing data or "don't know" responses on either item in a given pair are naturally excluded from these calculations.

[8]Along with this evidence of convergent validity, these items also show discriminant validity in relation to the other items in this series on the preferred role of the federal government in race relations and in policies that affect women. Among other things, this indicates that people are responding in terms of the substantive content of each of the items rather than in terms of their general attitude toward the federal government itself (for fuller discussion of this issue, see Jackman, 1981a; 1981b).

TABLE 9.4

OPINIONS ON THE ROLE OF THE FEDERAL GOVERNMENT IN SOCIAL WELFARE ACTIVITIES
(BY CLASS; WHITES ONLY)

	Poor	Working	Middle	Upper-middle
Job guarantees				
Government should do lot more	48.5%	42.6%	33.6%	23.6%
Government should do some more	22.7	26.8	29.5	32.1
Government is doing about right	24.2	23.0	27.5	30.0
Government should do less	4.5	7.6	9.4	14.3
	99.9%	100.0%	100.0%	100.0%
Base N	(66)	(530)	(695)	(140)
Minimum income				
Government should do lot more	50.8%	32.0%	18.6%	18.2%
Government should do some more	22.8	26.3	28.9	24.1
Government is doing about right	24.6	31.0	35.3	39.4
Government should do less	1.8	10.8	17.2	18.2
	100.0%	100.1%	100.0%	99.9%
Base N	(57)	(510)	(679)	(137)

middle class to think that the government should be doing a lot more to guarantee full employment (a 25-percentage-point difference), and they are more than twice as likely to express the same view about minimum income (a 33-percentage-point difference).[9]

To what extent does the association in table 9.4 indicate a genuine class effect? In examining this question, we form a new variable that is the mean of the two difference scores just discussed, which, like its components, ranges from -3 (government should do much more) to $+3$ (government should do much less). This variable is regressed on class identification and the three standard components of objective status. The resulting estimates are displayed in the first row of table 9.5, and they show that all of the variables except education have significant net effects on these policy views.[10] Separate analyses show that the net effect of class identification in this model is about 40 percent lower than its bivariate effect. At the

---

[9]Comparable figures for blacks are not displayed here. They show that blacks in the poor, the working class, and the middle class have a considerably higher level of support for government intervention in these issues than do their white class peers.

[10]Similar results are obtained if, instead of using the combined index, we focus on each of its components separately. We also experimented (and obtained similar results) with different versions of an expanded index including two additional items on the federal government role in providing welfare benefits and day-care services (all four items cluster together, but those employed in tables 9.4 and 9.5 have the highest intercorrelations).

TABLE 9.5

EFFECTS OF CLASS IDENTIFICATION AND OBJECTIVE STATUS ON OPINIONS ABOUT THE ROLE OF THE FEDERAL GOVERNMENT IN SOCIAL WELFARE ACTIVITIES (FOR ALL WHITES, BY DEGREE OF OWN-CLASS CLOSENESS)

	ClassID	REduc	HHSEI	FamInc	Constant	R^2	N
All whites	.143	.007	.003	.007	−1.507	.040	1,170
	(3.0)	(0.6)	(2.0)	(2.4)	(10.5)		
Closer to	.220	.009	.006	.012	−1.931	.106	487
own class	(2.7)	(0.5)	(2.2)	(2.7)	(8.5)		
Neutral	.084	.005	.001	.003	−1.165	.010	653
	(1.3)	(0.3)	(0.5)	(0.9)	(5.9)		

NOTE: Main table entries are the metric regression coefficients; entries in parentheses are their t-ratios.

same time, the estimates for head of household's SEI and family income are each decreased by about one-quarter when class identification is included in the model (the coefficient for education is statistically insignificant whether or not class is included in the model). Thus, while some of the bivariate effect of subjective class is a spurious reflection of objective status, class also serves to mediate a small part of the association between objective status and policy opinions. Finally, the model has only limited success in accounting for variance in this scale. As we noted from table 9.4, class differences on these policy opinions do not form a sharp rift between the advocacy of more government action and less action, but instead follow a relatively moderate pattern of disagreement.

The second panel of table 9.5 contains estimates for the same model, for two separate groups: those who express strong affective class bonds and those with weaker class feelings. As with social predispositions, this analysis is designed to assess whether the emotional significance of class influences the linkage between class identification and opinions on government intervention in the social welfare area. Class feelings in table 9.5 refer to own-class closeness, but similar results are obtained when the analysis is cast in terms of own-class warmth.

Again, the estimates show that strong emotional class bonds play an important role in accentuating the effect of subjective class. Indeed, their role is critical in conditioning the political implications of class. For those with relatively weak class bonds, neither class identification nor any element of objective status influences support for welfare policies, and the F-ratio for the overall equation is insignificant. By contrast, for those with stronger class bonds, all of the coefficients except that for education are significant, and the model accounts for 11 percent of the variance in welfare opinions.

The percentage distributions underscore the changes that strong class bonds introduce in the relation between class identification and welfare opinions. For whites lacking strong class bonds, the percentage consistently saying that the government should do a lot more does not vary systematically by class. Among those who do have strong class bonds, however, the relationship is pronounced: 48 percent of the poor consistently say that the government should be doing a lot more, compared with 28 percent of the working class, 14 percent of the middle class, and 2 percent of the upper-middle class.

In all, these results suggest that strong emotional bonds to one's class are not only important in accentuating the social implications of class and objective status but they have a more far-reaching political significance. Indeed, such bonds are a necessary condition for the translation of one's status experience into a distinctive political viewpoint.

In general, class identification appears as a more powerful determinant of social predispositions, especially of neighborhood preferences. Such preferences are heavily influenced by class, even among those without strong emotional bonds to their class. In contrast, political orientations do not seem to flow quite as easily from one's own status experience. Here the relationship with class and even objective status is nonexistent unless people feel a strong emotional attachment to their class. Political life is one step removed from people's everyday experience, and orientation toward policy issues requires the integration of relatively abstract ideas with one's own experience. Social predispositions flow more effortlessly from one's affiliative proclivities. Thus, while strong class bonds accentuate the effect of class identification on people's social predispositions, they play an even more vital role in the political arena by providing the impetus to link one's own experience with a political perspective.

As we have already noted, the policy items we have been examining thus far bear on minimal forms of redistribution. Such policies do not challenge the basic structure of existing economic arrangements, but instead they seek to establish a "safety net" within that structure. These are the kinds of policies that have had an airing in the American political arena, under the aegis of New Deal Democrats and their successors. But public discussion of even these policies has never been extended or thorough: sporadic debate over the desirability of such programs has been the pattern, rather than detailed discussion of alternative ways of structuring those programs. Meanwhile, more fundamentally redistributive proposals have been absent altogether from the public agenda.

Thus, the public has received only a restricted education from organized partisan politics in issues of economic equality. We now explore the limits of that education in two ways. First, we gauge people's views on the broad issue of economic (in)equality itself by asking them about preferred income distributions. Second, we assess their understanding of alternative forms of taxation and the degree to which they view taxes as a potential vehicle for income redistribution. For each of these areas, we are able to draw on people's responses to both structured and open-ended questions.

We have two measures of opinions about income inequality that come from structured items. The first of these comes from a global item on preferred degree of income inequality:

> Thinking about the amount of money people in different occupations earn, do you think there *should be* a great deal of difference, some difference, or almost no difference in how much people in different occupations earn?

The second measure is a preferred income ratio that is constructed from the last four of the following five items:

> We're interested in getting people's opinions about how much money people in different occupations should make. Please look at these occupations and tell me how much money you think people in each one *should* make, regardless of how much they *do* make. Just tell me what you think would be best.
>
> Now, how about a schoolteacher? How much money do you think an *average schoolteacher should* make in a year?
>
> How much money do you think an *average assembly-line factory worker should* make in a year?
>
> How much money do you think an *average doctor should* make in a year?
>
> How much money do you think an *average business executive should* make in a year?
>
> How much money do you think an *average janitor should* make in a year?

This second set of items actually preceded the global item in the interview schedule, and the items on class social predispositions were administered between the two.

The specific occupations included in the second set of items were chosen to include two high-level occupations (one professional and one business) and two low-level occupations involving unskilled labor. The schoolteacher item represents the middle range of occupations. As with the occupation-class sort board introduced in chapter 2, our concern was to include a range of readily recognizable occupational titles. At the same time, we sought to restrict that range to exclude the highest and lowest extremes (e.g., corporation presidents or migrant farm workers), which are beyond the mainstream of common experience. These items were used to calculate a preferred income ratio for each respondent, which is the mean of four individual ratios: janitor to executive, janitor to doctor, factory worker to executive, and factory worker to doctor.[11] A low ratio score thus reflects support for a wider income gap.

To what extent do egalitarian opinions vary with class? Table 9.6 presents the distribution of responses to the global inequality item, by class, for whites.[12] The prevailing feature of this table is the singular lack of support for income equality in any class. Such support is most prevalent among the poor, but even here it attracts only 16 percent. Most people believe there should be *some* income inequality, and the bulk of the disagreement is between this opinion and the view that there should be a great deal of inequality. Class differences are modest. Among the poor, the working class, and the middle class, opinion favors some inequality over a great deal of inequality by a margin of about two to one. Only in the upper-middle class is this pattern reversed: here preference for a great deal of inequality has a slight edge.

The results with the mean income ratio follow a similar pattern. Fully 92 percent of whites have scores between .12 and .77, and 45 percent fall between .23 and .43. As with the global question, people's notions of the

---

[11]In constructing the individual ratios, we excluded observations with missing data (either where the data were not ascertained or where the respondent said "don't know"), along with three cases where the respondent used inconsistent units (e.g., hourly wages for some occupations and annual salaries for others) and five cases with extreme values on any variable included in the ratio. Observations with missing data on two or more individual ratios were excluded from the calculation of the overall mean ratio. (An alternative formulation that excludes observations with missing data on one or more individual ratios gives the same pattern of results.)

[12]Although not displayed here, the distribution on this item by class for blacks is similar to the figures for whites in table 9.6. This is also the case for all the remaining variables and patterns that are discussed in this chapter.

TABLE 9.6
OPINIONS ABOUT DESIRABLE LEVELS OF INCOME INEQUALITY
(BY CLASS IDENTIFICATION; WHITES ONLY)

	Poor	Working	Middle	Upper-middle
Desirable income differences among occupations				
Great deal of difference	24.0%	26.2%	32.0%	49.0%
Some difference	48.0	59.2	58.2	42.3
Almost no difference	16.0	10.9	7.5	7.4
Don't know	12.0	3.7	2.2	1.3
Base N	75	588	759	149

appropriate degree of inequality in specific salaries vary for the most part within a range from a great deal of inequality to a somewhat narrower income gap. The distribution of scores shifts slightly from one class to the next, which is reflected in the mean scores that range from .51 for the poor, to .45 for the working class, to .41 for the middle class, to .34 for the upper-middle class. Thus, the concept of complete or even near equality is rarely endorsed in any class, although lower classes tend to favor a somewhat smaller income gap than do higher classes.

To examine the nature of these modest class differences more systematically, we estimated the effects of class identification on each of these two measures, net of the effects of education, head of household's SEI, and family income. Paralleling the analyses in table 9.5, we also estimated this model by strength of own-class bonds (defined in terms of warmth and closeness). We do not display the figures here, but the results are readily summarized. In each case, the amount of explained variance is small: .031 for the global inequality item and .045 for the mean income ratio. In the former case, the coefficient for class has the expected sign but a low t-ratio (1.3), and only the coefficient for head of household's SEI is significant (with a t-ratio of 3.3). For the mean income ratio, only class and head of household's SEI have statistically significant coefficients (with t-ratios of 3.6 and 3.3, respectively). No consistent pattern emerges from the more detailed regressions by class feelings: strength of own-class affective bonds does not influence the modest relation between class and either the global inequality item or the mean income ratio.

Why does the fundamental endorsement of income inequality vary so modestly by class? To address this issue, we examine people's responses to an open-ended probe that followed the global inequality item: "Why do you think there should be (a great deal/some/almost no) difference?" We have coded responses to this probe into three broad categories, which we label *achievement*, *ability*, and *equality*.

Achievement responses are those arguing that people should be rewarded in accordance with their personal investment, either in terms of their preparation for a job or in terms of the demands of the job itself. Such responses include mentions of education, training, job experience, job responsibility, and the economic or social value of the job. Unequal rewards as a function of such achievement factors were justified either as intrinsically equitable or as an incentive. Responses that are coded in the ability category justify higher rewards for those with greater innate talent and ability. It is, of course, difficult to separate entirely mentions of ability from mentions of achievement, and some people specifically mentioned both factors. For those who did not, the ability category was reserved for responses that emphasized differences in innate abilities, while the achievement category was used for responses that emphasized acquired skills. The equality category was reserved for egalitarian arguments that mentioned such things as equality in people's needs (e.g., "everyone has the same needs to meet") or in their work effort (e.g., "when a person works as hard as others, he should earn as much as others do," and "all occupations are equally important").

These three categories capture three different kinds of norms. References to ability tie in with a Social Darwinistic line of reasoning that all people are not equal and that inequality thus reflects a "natural" order. References to achievement have more universalistic connotations, and for this reason they provide a justification of inequality that is singularly appropriate for capitalist democracies. Such an ideology directs attention toward meritocratic equality of opportunity rather than to equality per se. Egalitarian norms are more directly challenging to the status quo.

Responses to the open-ended question using these codes are displayed by class for whites in table 9.7. The outstanding feature of these distributions is the pervasive acceptance of the norm of achievement-based rewards. About two-thirds of each class justify inequality in terms of achievement. An additional 17 percent of whites justify inequality in terms of both achievement and ability. Thus, about 85 percent in all mention achievement-related factors as grounds for inequality. References to either innate ability or egalitarian norms take a very clear second place. This pattern is duplicated in each class with only minor variations. Lower classes have a slight tendency to be more egalitarian and to be even less disposed to mentions of ability (alone or in conjunction with achievement).

TABLE 9.7
REASONS OFFERED FOR PREFERRED AMOUNT OF INCOME INEQUALITY
(BY CLASS IDENTIFICATION; WHITES ONLY)

	Poor	Working	Middle	Upper-middle
Reason(s) offered				
Achievement	64.4%	70.4%	69.7%	62.2%
Ability	10.2	5.4	3.8	6.3
Equality	15.3	9.5	5.9	6.3
Achievement and ability	5.1	13.0	18.7	23.1
All other combinations of responses	5.1	1.7	1.8	2.1
Base N	59	537	707	143

Thus, while Social Darwinistic views are in a clear minority, so are outright egalitarian views. People in all social classes heavily endorse the norm of unequal rewards based on personal achievement.[13] Of course, people in lower social classes think the reward for achievement should be smaller than do those in the upper-middle class: they are more likely to say there should be "some" rather than a "great deal" of difference in incomes. Those in lower classes are also more likely to regard equality of opportunity as an unrealized goal (see chapter 3; also Huber and Form 1973). Consequently, lower-class support for achievement-based inequality does not imply acceptance of the full achievement ideology. A discrepancy still exists between the norm of rewards based on achievement and the perceived lack of equality in opportunities for that achievement. Nonetheless, the dominant achievement ideology permeates Americans' way of thinking sufficiently to submerge the issue of equality itself and to rephrase the political debate more in terms of equality of opportunity.

Beyond the ideological hurdle that is created by this shift in emphasis away from equality per se to equality of opportunity, there is a more practical difficulty. The way people orient themselves toward particular economic policies lacks an informed understanding of their redistributive implications. A pertinent example of this is provided by responses to two

---

[13]Despite the fact that we employ quite different analytic procedures, this parallels the conclusions reached by Jasso and Rossi (1977). Drawing on a survey of Baltimore, they found a consensus across demographic groups that differences in income should be based primarily on achievement factors.

structured questions and one open-ended probe on various forms of taxation:

Now please look at the three statements on this card and tell me which you agree with most.

1. People with higher incomes should pay the same fraction of their income in taxes as people with lower incomes.

2. People with higher incomes should pay a bigger fraction of their income in taxes.

3. People with higher incomes should pay a smaller fraction of their income in taxes.

If your federal, state, and local taxes were all paid with one type of tax, which of these types would you prefer–an income tax, a property tax, or a sales tax? (PROBE: But if you had to choose, which of these types of tax would you prefer?)

Why do you prefer this type of tax?

Responses to the two structured items can be easily summarized, and we shall not display the tables here. The main result is that in neither case does class have a sustained effect on tax preferences. On the first item, 53 percent of whites prefer a progressive tax and 44 percent prefer a flat rate (there is virtually no support for a regressive tax). The *only* deviation from this pattern occurs with the poor, who are slightly more likely to favor a progressive tax (62 percent) and slightly less likely to favor a flat-rate tax (32 percent). More complete regression and probit analyses indicate that preference for progressive taxes is unrelated to both class and objective status, and this is the case whether or not people have strong class bonds.

Preferred form of taxation also bears little relationship to class. For whites as a whole, income tax is most likely to be preferred (58 percent), followed by sales tax (24 percent), with property tax being the least popular (7 percent). The remaining responses are split almost evenly between those with no preference and "don't knows." Again, the only deviation from these figures is among the poor, who are slightly *less* likely to favor the income tax (47 percent) and slightly *more* likely to favor the property tax (15 percent), or to say "don't know" (15 percent).

In general, these results indicate that only a bare majority favors a progressive tax structure, and a similarly narrow majority favors an income tax. This weak public support for more redistributive forms of taxation stems from a lack of understanding about the redistributive implications of different forms of taxation. This is demonstrated in two ways. First, there is no connection between the degree of income inequality that people favor and the kind of tax they prefer. Opinions about whether the tax rate should be progressive or flat, or whether taxes should be based on income, property, or sales, bear no relation to people's overall position on the degree of social inequality that is desirable.[14] Thus, what limited challenge exists to economic inequality per se does not have systematic carry-over into the highly pertinent policy area of taxation. Second, within the taxation area itself, there is no carry-over from preference for a particular *rate* of taxation to preference for a particular *type* of taxation. Most significantly, preference for a progressive tax in no way alters the odds of someone choosing an income tax or even a property tax over a sales tax. In both cases, this lack of carry-over is apparent in all classes.

These patterns are underscored in people's responses to the open-ended probe on their reasons for preferring an income, property, or sales tax. The reasons people offered fall into six main categories: *universal burden* (everyone has to pay; no loopholes), *equal burden* (everyone pays the same rate), *proportional burden* (the more you make/own/buy, the more you pay), *equitable burden* (it's fairer, but not specified why), *convenient to pay* (automatically taken out of your check or added to your purchase; I'm used to it), and *less expensive* (you get a rebate; you can control the amount you pay by buying less or by owning less property). About 75 percent offered one of these reasons, and most of the remainder offered some combination of them.

The two most commonly offered reasons for preferring any type of tax are proportionality (24 percent of whites) and convenience (18 percent). Proportionality responses do not necessarily imply progressivity as a criterion, but this category is the one that comes closest to that kind of thinking. It is revealing that proportionality is equally likely to be offered as a criterion for choosing any type of tax, and it is equally likely to be mentioned by any class. The convenience factor does vary somewhat by type of tax preferred: the income tax is more likely than other taxes to be chosen on grounds of convenience. Use of this criterion also varies by class: lower classes mention it more often than higher classes.

The percentage of whites offering each of the other four single reasons is as follows: equitable = 13 percent; universal burden = 10 percent; equal

---

[14]This nonrelationship holds whether preferred degree of social inequality is defined in terms of the global inequality item or the income ratios.

burden = 5 percent; and less expensive = 7 percent. Equity is somewhat more likely to be mentioned in support of the income tax than other taxes, and reference to equity also increases with ascending social class. Concern with the universality or equality of the tax burden varies only slightly across classes, but these criteria are more likely to be used with reference to the sales tax than other taxes. The sales tax is also more likely to be preferred on the grounds that it is less expensive, and the poor are more susceptible than others to the use of this criterion.

In general, these data show that people's reasons for choosing a particular tax vary only slightly across the three types of taxes: each tax has a very similar profile of explanations offered in its favor. There is no common agreement or understanding about which taxes offer which advantages. Additionally, although just over half the whites prefer a progressive over a flat-rate tax, only about one-quarter are moved to select any tax on the grounds that it requires a contribution that is in proportion to a person's means. Use of this criterion does not vary by class, and indeed, classes do not vary much at all in their motivating concerns about taxation. Of the few class differences that are present, the relative preoccupation of lower classes with the convenience of tax payment is especially revealing. Amid all the ignorance about the redistributive ramifications of alternative taxation schemes, the poor and the working class are slightly more likely to choose a tax for its presumed convenience than because they think it creates a proportional burden. Thus, in the majority of cases overall, the wrong tax is chosen for the wrong reasons, and this collective ignorance is one commodity that is shared almost equally among the social classes.

IMPLICATIONS

The analyses of this chapter demonstrate that subjective class has clear outcomes for people's social predispositions and a more qualified impact on their political orientation. For both social predispositions and political views on social welfare issues, affective class bonds play an important role in crystallizing class consciousness. Affective class bonds accentuate the already strong impact of class and objective standing on social predispositions. They play an even more important role with opinions on welfare issues, where strong class bonds become a necessary condition for the emergence of opinions consistent with one's class and objective standing.

As we showed in the last chapter, this sense of emotional attachment to one's class does not derive from personal friendship ties that reinforce one's own experience. In further analyses that we have not displayed here, we found that reinforcing friendship ties also have no bearing on social or political predispositions. This suggests that people's world view is not conditioned by their personal friendship ties so much as it is conditioned by their own experience and their own interpretation of that experience. When people identify with a class not only cognitively but emotionally as well, class begins to shape their perspective beyond the social sphere and into the political arena. Thus, affective class bonds do not simply reflect a feeling of social attachment—they also sharpen the political connotations of class.

Whereas people's social predispositions seem to flow relatively effortlessly from their class membership, the linkage between class and political opinions is more difficult. Class is clearly a salient stimulus. Yet the impact of class on social welfare opinions is not automatic: it requires strong class bonds. Further, this political expression of class interests does not spill over effectively into either more fundamentally egalitarian issues or into a comprehension of specific redistributive strategies. Why, then, is the political impact of class so qualified? We cannot answer this question without returning to the considerations that we raised at the outset of this chapter.

Organized political life in the United States does not present the electorate with a cogent debate about the full range of class and redistributive issues. Instead, public discussion of these issues has centered on the themes of New Deal and Great Society liberalism and the conservative responses to them. These themes address minimal "safety-net" issues without challenging the general economic fabric of society, and in this way they voice more concern with equality of opportunity than with equality in the distribution of rewards. While this issue is less threatening than the more basic one of economic inequality, it has been sufficiently challenging to make even its discussion sporadic and unsustained. Thus, public discussion of class issues not only tends to bypass the fundamental area of social inequality—it also gives very limited treatment even to "safety-net" and equality-of-opportunity issues. For these reasons, public discussion of class issues lacks both breadth and depth. Class issues emerge sporadically, and single issues are not followed through with persistence and specificity. Public awareness focuses at the relatively low level of whether or not there should be a particular social welfare program rather than on the more sophisticated question of the optimal way to structure that program.

The tendency of the parliamentary left to focus on less threatening safety-net issues has often been observed for other Western democracies (e.g., Michels 1959; Miliband 1969; Parkin 1971; Mandel 1973; Jackman 1980). In the United States, this problem is compounded by a party system that reflects relatively loose coalitions that incorporate a variety of often inconsistent policy goals. As is well known, American political parties are not disciplined, programmatic organizations. Hence, what limited grass-roots awareness exists on economic welfare issues is not readily translated into electoral terms. In view of this, it is hardly surprising that class has little influence on partisan predispositions.[15] Beyond the failure of the American party system to provide a clear electoral outlet for distinctive class views, there is a feedback effect. Without a standing organization to represent consistently a particular political viewpoint, the electorate is not offered a coherent ideological context within which specific policies might be evaluated.

Given all these factors, organized political life provides the electorate with only a sparse education in class issues. People are loosely familiar with the general parameters of social welfare issues, but they have not been educated in either the more fundamental issue of social inequality or in the specific redistributive implications of alternative economic policies. In all, the potential political impact of class remains limited because an established counter ideology from which people might readily draw is not available.

---

[15]In analyses not displayed here of the effects of class and objective status on party identification, neither had a pronounced effect on partisanship, regardless of the strength of affective class bonds.

10
Social Class: Conclusions

We have pursued a variety of analyses in order to assess the significance and form of subjective class in American social life. Our approach takes as its basis the class terms that are commonly found in popular discourse, and then explores the meaning attached to those terms. We began with the fundamental issue of whether class exists at all in the public awareness, and, if so, how it is perceived. Beyond this, we examined, in turn, the importance of class as a source of emotional identity and perceived interests, the experiential factors on which people's class identification is based, and the social and political implications of subjective class.

As we have made abundantly clear, our results offer no support for the often-heard claim that the United States is a classless society. Nor do we find evidence that America is a society where class conflict is undermined by crosscutting affiliations and loyalties. On the other hand, the structure of subjective class does not conform to the dominant analytic formulations of class. Subjective classes do not capture a single distinction between owners and workers, between those with and those without authority, or between manual and white-collar workers.

In place of the traditional conceptions of class or classlessness that have defined the terms of debate, we have pursued an alternative conception of class that incorporates the complexity of socioeconomic standing without rejecting its significance as a source of group identity and conflict. Our approach owes more to the work of Richard Centers on the *psychology* of social class than it does to conceptions of class that are based on abstract analyses of the social structure. Evidence throughout the book supports our view that social life is organized into a graded series of groups that

behave like Weberian status groups but which have their basis in configurations of socioeconomic criteria. These groups we call social classes.

At their basis, classes take shape in the public awareness as clusters of
people with similar socioeconomic standing. This is evident in the way
people assign occupations to classes. Without difficulty and with considerable consensus, occupations are allocated in a manner that suggests a
clustered ranking based on several interrelated characteristics: prestige,
education, skill, income, job authority, task discretion. Similarly, personal
identification with a class is grounded solidly in overall socioeconomic
standing. Here, too, people are sensitive to several interrelated factors,
although a basic model of class identification that includes education,
occupational status, and earned income captures the essence of the distinctions that people find most important.

In calculating their socioeconomic standing, people take their current
nuclear family as the unit of reference, and within the family, domestic
roles dictate that it is the husband who dominates the family's status, even
when the wife is currently employed. This pattern holds for both men and
women. In general, women's participation in the stratification process is
not as active or sustained as men's. Yet traditional sex-role norms appear
to make it an effortless exercise for women to draw on the male head of
household's socioeconomic status almost as surely as if it reflected their
personal achievement.

The socioeconomic experiences of contacts outside the nuclear family
(extended family members, friends, and work associates) are considerably less salient than those of the nuclear family itself. To be sure, where a
person's friends duplicate his own social standing closely, they do reinforce and intensify his interpretation of his own experience. Having
heterogeneous friends, however, does not undermine his class identification. In view of the emphasis on individualism in American culture, this is
perhaps not surprising, but we may also infer that direct experiences are
more compelling than vicarious ones. In any event, this works to simplify
the individual's calculation of his socioeconomic standing and his social
class.

While socioeconomic distinctions provide the basis for class identification, it is also clear that class incorporates more than this. When asked
what factors define class membership, most people name cultural factors,
such as life-style and beliefs and feelings, as well as socioeconomic factors. When they assemble these various criteria to define their class,
people do not always assign the same weights to each one, and those
weights provide the implicit guidelines that they employ in forming their
own class identification. Thus, in the popular view, classes are social

communities that take shape from configurations of economic and cultural criteria.

The encompassing effect of class on social life becomes even clearer when we consider the significance of class as a source of emotional identity. Affective bonds are as integral to class identification as they are to racial identification, and a comparison of these two group identities is instructive. In general, people express greater emotional distance from classes higher than their own than from classes lower than their own. Among whites, these feelings are at least as strong as their racial feelings, and among those in lower classes, class feelings outweigh race feelings. Among blacks, class bonds are weaker than race bonds, except among the poor. These patterns suggest that subordinate statuses are more personally compelling than dominant ones. For blacks, this means that their subordinate racial status outweighs their sense of class unless they identify with the lowest class: the poor. Among the black poor (who have two clearly subordinate statuses), class and race bonds are equally strong. This is mirrored in the process of class identification itself among blacks. In this group, low socioeconomic status is translated relatively accurately into an identification with the poor, but subsequent distinctions among higher classes bear no systematic relation to personal socioeconomic standing. For whites, their dominant racial status does not create such a significant distraction from class, although with ascending social class, whites' class feelings lessen sufficiently to be on a par with their race feelings.

These considerations underscore three important points. First, class elicits strong feelings of emotional identity. Second, people do not weight all their group memberships equally, as is implied in many discussions of crosscutting group ties, but are instead more sensitive to group memberships that bring them subordinate status. Third, the racial division, which constitutes the primary alternative source of cleavage in American society, does not serve to undercut the class feelings of those in the dominant racial group. People are considerably more likely to be diverted by an alternative source of grievance than by an alternative source of reward.

Beyond this, the pattern of emotional differentiation among classes indicates that people do not make a categorical "us versus them" distinction, but instead react to classes as a graded series of groups. People express successively greater emotional distance from classes as they become less proximate to their own, and as we have already noted, people react differently to lower classes than they do to higher ones.

The sense of shared fate that is generated by class reinforces what we learn from class bonds. Class differences in the interpretation of the social structure suggest an experiential rift that rivals the one between races, although class differences take a gradational rather than a dichotomous form. With descending social class, there is an increasing sensitivity to biases in the opportunity structure, along with an increasing propensity to see classes as having opposed interests.

Cognitive and emotional identification are essential ingredients for any status group. There is, however, one further requirement: is the group associated with patterns of social interaction? On this count, too, classes fit the description of status groups. The socioeconomic distinctions that give rise to classes also constrain patterns of social interaction. Indeed, the association between the status of one's friends and one's own status is as strong as the associations among one's own status components themselves. This strong tendency for the status of people's friends to resemble their own status conforms to a pattern that suggests loosely bounded social communities. It is noteworthy that this holds for blacks as well as whites: status distinctions mold social interaction within each racial group. But because the racial boundary remains firmly in place, this produces two parallel (rather than overlapping) sets of social communities.

The pronounced influence of subjective class on social predispositions (especially those involving neighborhood preferences) underscores the social significance of class. In spite of the undoubted confounding of associational preferences with material aspirations, there is a marked preference for association with one's own class exclusively among all classes except the poor. When social preferences do extend across class boundaries, they seldom extend beyond adjacent classes, suggesting again a gradational conception of class.

The strong social expression of class in the United States has carried over only weakly into the political arena. Among those who have strong emotional identification with their class, there are pronounced class differences in support for social welfare policies. These differences, however, do not spill over effectively either into issues that are more fundamentally redistributive or into issues that require a more detailed understanding of specific redistributive polices. This reflects the fact that organized political life does little to provide a forum for the debate of class issues. As a result, there is no ready way that class issues can be given unambiguous electoral expression, and the public is left largely untutored in the politics of class.

In all, the evidence from our analyses sustains our view of classes as a graded series of status groups that are assembled from configurations of socioeconomic criteria. While these groups are not rigidly bounded, they do represent visible social communities that command emotional allegiance and affiliative ties. Weber, of course, sought to separate the idea of classes from that of social communities, but the basis of classes in a structural relationship of inequality gives them a compelling impetus for the development of social communities that is not always found with groups whose definition relies more on cultural factors. Intrinsic to inequality is one group's gain founded on another group's loss, and this relationship routinely produces social distinctions that are readily visible and keenly experienced. That social classes are status groups based on economic interests also gives them an inherent political potential that Weber was reluctant to accord to either classes or status groups. The American political system has worked to restrain that potential, but American society has not proved immune to the social pressures of inequality. Thus, while class finds only limited articulation in political life, it is pervasively expressed in the cohesive social communities that are found at the grass roots of American social life.

Bibliography

Abramson, Paul R. 1975 *Generational Change in American Politics*. Lexington, Mass.: D. C. Heath.

Acker, Joan. 1973 "Women and social stratification: a case of intellectual sexism." *American Journal of Sociology* 78 (January):936-945.

Alwin, Duane F., and Robert M. Hauser. 1975 "The decomposition of effects in path analysis." *American Sociological Review* 40 (February):37-47.

Axelrod, Robert. 1972 "Where the votes come from: an analysis of electoral coalitions, 1952-1968." *American Political Science Review* 66 (March):11-20.

————. 1978 "Communications: 1976 update." *American Political Science Review* 72 (June):622-624.

Bachrach, Peter, and Morton S. Baratz. 1970 *Power and Poverty: Theory and Practice*. New York: Oxford University Press.

Bahr, Stephen. 1974 "Effects on power and division of labor in the family." Pp. 167-185 in Lois W. Hoffman and F. Ivan Nye, eds. *Working Mothers*. San Francisco: Jossey-Bass.

Bell, Daniel. 1973 *The Coming of Post-Industrial Society*. New York: Basic Books.

Bell, Wendell, and Robert V. Robinson. 1980 "Cognitive maps of class and racial inequalities in England and the United States." *American Journal of Sociology* 86 (September):320-349.

Blalock, Hubert M., Jr. 1967 *Toward a Theory of Minority-Group Relations*. New York: John Wiley.

Blau, Peter M., and Otis Dudley Duncan. 1967 *The American Occupational Structure*. New York: John Wiley.

Blaxall, Martha, and Barbara Reagan, eds. 1976 *Women and the Workplace: The Implications of Occupational Segregation*. Chicago: University of Chicago Press.

Bogardus, Emory S. 1925 "Measuring social distance." *Journal of Applied Sociology* 9 (January-February):299-308.

Bohrnstedt, George W. 1970 "Reliability and validity assessment in attitude measurement." Pp. 80-99 in Gene F. Summers, ed. *Attitude Measurement*. Chicago: Rand McNally.

Bryce, James. 1899 *The American Commonwealth*. 3d ed. New York: MacMillan.

Butler, David, and Donald Stokes. 1974 *Political Change in Britain*. 2d ed. New York: St. Martin's.

Case, Herman M. 1955 "Marxian implications of Centers' interest group theory: a critical appraisal." *Social Forces* 33 (March):254-258.

Centers, Richard. 1949 *The Psychology of Social Classes*. Princeton, N.J.: Princeton University Press.

————. 1950 "Nominal variation and class identification: the working and laboring classes." *Journal of Abnormal and Social Psychology* 45 (April):195-215.

————. 1956 "The intensity dimension of class consciousness and some social and psychological correlates." *Journal of Social Psychology* 44 (August):101-114.

Coleman, Richard P., and Lee Rainwater. 1978 *Social Standing in America: New Dimensions of Class*. New York: Basic Books.

Converse, Phillip E. 1958 "The shifting role of class in political attitudes and behavior." In Eleanor E. Maccoby, Theodore M. Newcomb, and Eugene L. Hartley, eds. *Readings in Social Psychology*. New York: Holt, Rinehart and Winston.

Coser, Lewis A. 1956 *The Functions of Social Conflict*. Glencoe, Ill.: Free Press.

Dahrendorf, Ralf. 1959 *Class and Class Conflict in Industrial Society*. Stanford, Calif.: Stanford University Press.

Dalia, Joan T., and Avery M. Guest. 1975 "Embourgeoisement among blue-collar workers?" *Sociological Quarterly* 16 (Summer):291-304.

Davis, Kingsley, and Wilbert E. Moore. 1945 "Some principles of stratification." *American Sociological Review* 10 (April):242-249.

Downs, Anthony. 1957 *An Economic Theory of Democracy*. New York: Harper and Row.

Dubin, Robert. 1956 "Industrial workers' worlds: a study of the 'central life interests' of industrial workers." *Social Problems* 3 (January):131-142.

Duncan, Otis Dudley. 1961 "A socioeconomic index for all occupations" and "Properties and characteristics of the socioeconomic index." Pp. 109-161 in Albert J. Reiss et al. *Occupations and Social Status*. New York: Free Press.

————. 1966 "Methodological issues in the analysis of social mobility." Pp. 51-97 in Neil J. Smelser and Seymour Martin Lipset, eds. *Social Structure and Mobility in Economic Development*. Chicago: Aldine.

————. 1969 "Contingencies in constructing causal models." Pp. 71-112 in Edgar F. Borgatta, ed. *Sociological Methodology 1969*. San Francisco: Jossey-Bass.

Duncan, Otis D., Howard Schuman, and Beverly Duncan. 1973 *Social Change in a Metropolitan Community*. New York: Russell Sage Foundation.

Edelman, Murray. 1964 *The Symbolic Uses of Politics* Urbana: University of Illinois Press.

Evers, Mark. 1975 "Gender, race, and the influence of socioeconomic status on the change in subjective class identification." Paper read at the American Sociological Association annual meeting, San Francisco.

Feagin, Joe R. 1975 *Subordinating the Poor: Welfare and American Beliefs*. Englewood Cliffs, N.J.: Prentice-Hall.

Featherman, David L., and Robert M. Hauser. 1976 "Prestige or socioeconomic scales in the study of occupational achievement?" *Sociological Methods and Research* 4 (May):403-423.

Felson, Marcus, and David Knoke. 1974 "Social status and the married woman." *Journal of Marriage and the Family* 36 (August):516-521.

Gagliani, Giorgio. 1981 "How many working classes?" *American Journal of Sociology* 87 (September):259-285.

Gamson, Willian A. 1968 *Power and Discontent*. Homewood, Ill.: Dorsey Press.

Gans, Herbert J. 1974 *More Equality*. New York: Vintage Books.

Giddens, Anthony. 1973 *The Class Structure of the Advanced Societies*. New York: Harper and Row.

Glenn, Evelyn N., and Roslyn C. Feldberg. 1977 "Degraded and deskilled: the proletarianization of clerical work." *Social Problems* 25 (October):52-64.

Goldthorpe, John H., David Lockwood, Frank Bechhofer, and Jennifer Platt. 1969 *The Affluent Worker in the Class Structure*. London: Cambridge University Press.

Gross, Neal. 1953 "Social class identification in the urban community." *American Sociological Review* 18 (August):398-404.

Guest, Avery. 1974 "Class consciousness and American political attitudes." *Social Forces* 52 (June):496-510.

Haer, John L. 1957 "An empirical study of social class awareness." *Social Forces* 36 (September):117-121.

Hamilton, Richard. 1972 *Class and Politics in the United States*. New York: John Wiley.

Hancock, M. Donald. 1971 "The United States, Europe, and postindustrial society." *Comparative Politics* 4 (October):133-146.

Hartmann, George W., and Theodore Newcomb, eds. 1939 *Industrial Conflict: A Psychological Interpretation*. New York: Gordon Co.

Haug, Marie R. 1973 "Social class measurement and women's occupational roles." *Social Forces* 52 (September):85-98.

Hauser, Robert M., and David L. Featherman. 1973 "Trends in the occupational mobility of U.S. men, 1962-1970." *American Sociological Review* 38 (June):302-310.

————. 1977 *The Process of Stratification: Trends and Analyses*. New York: Academic Press.

Henretta, John C. 1979 "Race differences in middle class lifestyle: the role of home ownership." *Social Science Research* 8 (March):63-78.

Henretta, John C., and Richard T. Campbell. 1978 "Net worth as an aspect of status." *American Journal of Sociology* 83 (March):1204-1223.

Hiller, Dana V., and William W. Philliber. 1978 "The derivation of status benefits from occupational attainments of working wives." *Journal of Marriage and the Family* 40 (February):63-69.

Hodge, Robert W., and Donald J. Treiman. 1968 "Class identification in the United States." *American Journal of Sociology* 73 (March):535-547.

Huber, Joan, and William H. Form. 1973 *Income and Ideology: An Analysis of the American Political Formula*. New York: Free Press.

Jackman, Mary R. 1981a "Education and policy commitment to racial integration." *American Journal of Political Science* 25 (May):256-269.

————. 1981b "Issues in the measurement of commitment to racial integration." *Political Methodology* 7 (nos. 3 and 4):160-172.

Jackman, Mary R., and Robert W. Jackman. 1973 "An interpretation of the relation between objective and subjective social status." *American Sociological Review* 38 (October):569-582.

————. 1980 "Racial inequalities in home ownership." *Social Forces* 58 (June):1221-1234.

Jackman, Robert W. 1980 "Socialist parties and income inequality in Western industrial societies." *Journal of Politics* 42 (February):135-149.

Jasso, Guillermina, and Peter H. Rossi. 1977 "Distributive justice and earned income." *American Sociological Review* 42 (August):639-651.

Jencks, Christopher (and associates). 1972 *Inequality: A Reassessment of the Effect of Family and Schooling in America*. New York: Basic Books.

Jensen, Arthur R. 1969 "How much can we boost IQ and scholastic achievement?" *Harvard Educational Review* 39 (Winter):1-132.

Kain, John F., and John M. Quigley. 1975 *Housing Markets and Racial Discrimination: A Microeconomic Analysis*. New York: National Bureau for Economic Research.

Kalleberg, Arne L., and Larry J. Griffin. 1980 "Class, occupation, and inequality in job rewards." *American Journal of Sociology* 85 (January):731-768.

Key, V. O., Jr. 1966 *The Responsible Electorate: Rationality in Presidential Voting, 1936-1960*. Cambridge, Mass.: Harvard University Press.

Klugel, James R., Royce Singleton, Jr., and Charles E. Starnes. 1977 "Subjective class identification: a multiple indicator approach." *American Sociological Review* 42 (August):599-611.

Lane, Robert E. 1962 *Political Ideology*. New York: Free Press.

Laumann, Edward O. 1966 *Prestige and Association in an Urban Community*. New York: Bobbs-Merrill.

Laumann, Edward O., and Louis Guttman. 1966 "The relative associational contiguity of occupations in an urban setting." *American Sociological Review* 31 (April):169-178.

Laumann, Edward O., and James S. House. 1970 "Living room styles and social attributes: the patterning of material artifacts in a modern urban community." *Sociology and Social Research* 54 (April):321-342.

Laumann, Edward O., and Richard Senter. 1976 "Subjective social distance, occupational stratification, and forms of status and class consciousness: a cross-national replication and extension." *American Journal of Sociology* 81 (May):1304-1339.

Lenski, Gerhard. 1966 *Power and Privilege: A Theory of Social Stratification*. New York: McGraw-Hill.

Lewis, Oscar. 1966 "The culture of poverty." *Scientific American* 215 (October):19-25.

Lipset, Seymour Martin. 1960 *Political Man*. London: Heinemann.

Lipset, Seymour Martin, and Reinhard Bendix. 1959 *Social Mobility in Industrial Society*. Berkeley and Los Angeles: University of California Press.

Lopreato, Joseph. 1968 "Authority relations and class conflict." *Social Forces* 47 (September):70-79.

McClosky, Herbert. 1958 "Conservatism and personality." *American Political Science Review* 52 (March):27-45.

Mandel, Ernest. 1973 *An Introduction to Marxist Economic Theory*. New York: Pathfinder Press.

Mannheim, Karl. 1936 *Ideology and Utopia*. New York: Harcourt Brace.

Marx, Karl. 1963 *The Eighteenth Brumaire of Louis Bonaparte*. New York: International Publishers.

————. 1964 *Selected Writings in Sociology and Social Philosophy*. T. B. Bottomore and Maximilien Rubel, eds. New York: McGraw-Hill.

Marx, Karl, and Frederick Engels. 1939 *The German Ideology*. New York: International Publishers.

————. 1961 *The Civil War in the United States* New York: International Publishers.

Meissner, Martin, Elizabeth W. Humphreys, Scott M. Meis, and William J. Scheu. 1975 "No exit for wives: sexual division of labor and the cumulation of household demands." *Canadian Review of Sociology and Anthropology* 12:424-439.

Michels, Robert. 1959 *Political Parties: A Sociological Study of the Oligarchical Tendencies of Modern Democracy*. New York: Dover Books.

Miliband, Ralph. 1969 *The State in Capitalist Society*. New York: Basic Books.

Miller, S. M. 1964 "The 'new' working class." Pp. 2-9 in Arthur B. Shostak and William Gomberg, eds., *Blue-Collar World: Studies of the American Worker*. Englewood Cliffs, NJ: Prentice-Hall.

Mills, C. Wright. 1956 *White Collar: The American Middle Classes*. New York: Oxford University Press.

Mincer, Jacob. 1974 *Schooling Experience and Earnings*. New York: National Bureau of Economic Research.

Mincer, Jacob, and Solomon Polacheck. 1974 "Family investments in human capital: earnings of women." *Journal of Political Economy* 82 (March-April):76-111.

Moore, Kristin A., and Isabel V. Sawhill. 1978 "Implications of women's employment for home and family life." Pp. 201-225 in Ann H. Stromberg and Shirley Harkess, eds. *Women Working*. Palo Alto, Calif.: Mayfield Publishing Co.

Nisbet, Robert A. 1970 "The decline and fall of social class." Pp. 570-574 in Edward O. Laumann, Paul M. Siegel, and Robert W. Hodge, eds. *The Logic of Social Hierarchies*. Chicago: Markham.

Nye, F. Ivan. 1963 "The adjustment of adolescent children." In F. Ivan Nye and Lois W. Hoffman, eds. *The Employed Mother in America*. Chicago: Rand McNally.

Ossowski, Stanislaw. 1963 *Class Structure in the Social Consciousness*. London: Routledge and Kegan Paul.

Page, Benjamin I. 1978 *Choices and Echoes in Presidential Elections: Rational Man and Electoral Democracy*. Chicago: University of Chicago Press.

Parkin, Frank. 1971 *Class Inequality and Political Order*. New York: Praeger.

———. 1979 *Marxism and Class Theory: A Bourgeois Critique*. New York: Columbia University Press.

Parsons, Talcott. 1942 "Age and sex in the social structure of the United States." *American Sociological Review* 7 (October):604-616.

———. 1970 "Equality and inequality in modern society, or social stratification revisited." Pp. 13-72 in Edward O. Laumann, ed. *Social Stratification: Research and Theory for the 1970s*. Indianapolis: Bobbs-Merrill.

Parsons, Talcott, and Robert F. Bales. 1960 *Family, Socialization and Interaction Process*. Glencoe, Ill.: Free Press.

Philliber, William W., and Dana V. Hiller. 1978 "The implications of wife's occupational attainment for husband's class identification." *Sociological Quarterly* 19 (Summer):450-458.

Pleck, Joseph H. 1977 "The work-family role system." *Social Problems* 24 (April):417-427.

———. 1979 "Men's family work: three perspectives and some new data." *The Family Coordinator* 28 (October):481-488.

Polsby, Nelson W. 1980 *Community Power and Political Theory*. 2d ed. New Haven, Conn.: Yale University Press.

Portes, Alejandro. 1971 "Political primitivism, differential socialization and lower class leftist radicalism." *American Sociological Review* 36 (October):820-835.

Ritter, Kathleen V., and Lowell L. Hargens. 1975 "Occupational positions and class identifications: a test of the asymmetry hypothesis." *American Journal of Sociology* 80 (January):934-948.

Robins, Lee, and Miroda Tomanec. 1962 "Closeness to blood relatives outside the immediate family." *Marriage and Family Living* 24 (November):340-346.

Robinson, John P. 1977 *How Americans Use Time: A Social Psychological Analysis of Everyday Behaviour*. New York: Praeger.

Robinson, John P., Jerrold G. Rusk, and Kendra B. Head. 1968 *Measures of Political Attitudes*. Ann Arbor, Mich.: Institute for Social Research.

Robinson, Robert V., and Jonathan Kelley. 1979 "Class as conceived by Marx and Dahrendorf: effects on income inequality, class consciousness, and class conflict in the United States and Great Britain." *American Sociological Review* 44 (February):38-58.

Rodman, Hyman. 1963 "The lower-class value stretch." *Social Forces* 42 (December):205-215.

Rosenberg, Morris. 1953 "Perceptual obstacles to class consciousness." *Social Forces* 32 (September):22-27.

Rossi, Alice S. 1974 "Sex equality: the beginning of an ideology." Pp. 260-268 in Lee Rainwater, ed. *Social Problems and Public Policy: Inequality and Justice*. Chicago: Aldine.

Rossi, Peter H., W. A. Sampson, C. E. Bose, G. Jasso, and J. Passel. 1974 "Measuring household social standing." *Social Science Research* 3 (September):169-190.

Rugg, Donald, and Hadley Cantril. 1944 "The wording of questions." Pp. 23-50 in Hadley Cantril, ed. *Gauging Public Opinion.* Princeton, N.J.: Princeton University Press.

Schuman, Howard. 1966 "The random probe: a technique for evaluating the validity of closed questions." *American Sociological Review* 31 (April):218-222.

Schuman, Howard, and Stanley Presser. 1979 "The open and closed question." *American Sociological Review* 44 (October):692-712.

———. 1981 *Questions and Answers in Attitude Surveys.* New York: Academic Press.

Siegel, Paul M. 1971 "Prestige in the American occupational structure." Ph.D. dissertation, University of Chicago.

Stevens, Gillian, and David L. Featherman. 1981 "A revised socioeconomic index of occupational status." *Social Science Research* 10 (December):364-395.

Straussman, Jeffrey. 1975 "What did tomorrow's future look like yesterday?" *Comparative Politics* 8 (October):166-182.

Sullivan, John L., James E. Piereson, and George E. Marcus. 1978 "Ideological constraint in the mass public: a methodological critique and some new findings." *American Journal of Political Science* 22 (May):233-249.

Sumner, William G. 1883 *What Social Classes Owe to Each Other.* New York: Harper and Brothers.

Sweester, Dorian Apple. 1963 "Asymmetry in intergenerational family relationships." *Social Forces* 41 (May):346-352.

Tocqueville, Alexis de. 1969 *Democracy in America.* New York: Anchor Books.

Udry, J. Richard. 1971 *The Social Context of Marriage.* 2d ed. Philadelphia: J. B. Lippincott Co.

Vanneman, Reeve. 1980 "U.S. and British perceptions of class." *American Journal of Sociology* 85 (January):769-790.

Vanneman, Reeve, and Fred C. Pampel. 1977 "The American perception of class and status." *American Sociological Review* 42 (June):422-437.

Van Velsor, Ellen, and Leonard Beeghley. 1979 "The process of class identification among employed married women: a replication and reanalysis." *Journal of Marriage and the Family* 41 (November):771-779.

Walker, Kathryn, and Margaret Woods. 1976 *Time Use: A Measure of Household Production of Family Goods and Services.* Washington, D.C.: American Home Economics Association, Center for the Family.

Weatherford, M. Stephen. 1978 "Economic conditions and electoral outcomes: class differences in the political response to recession." *American Journal of Political Science* 22 (November):917-938.

Weber, Max. 1946 "Class, status, party." Pp. 180-195 in H. H. Gerth and C. Wright Mills, eds. *From Max Weber: Essays in Sociology.* New York: Oxford University Press.

———. 1958 *The Protestant Ethic and the Spirit of Capitalism.* New York: Charles Scribner's.

Westergaard, John, and Henrietta Resler. 1975 *Class in a Capitalist Society: A Study of Contemporary Britain.* New York: Basic Books.

Wilensky, Harold L. 1966 "Class, class consciousness, and American workers." Pp. 12-28 in William Haber, ed. *Labor in a Changing America.* New York: Basic Books.

Wilson, William J. 1980 *The Declining Significance of Race.* 2d ed. Chicago: University of Chicago Press.

Wright, Erik Olin. 1979 *Class Structure and Income Determination.* New York: Academic Press.

Wright, Erik Olin, and Luca Perrone. 1977 "Marxist class categories and income inequality." *American Sociological Review* 42 (February):32-55.

Index

Compositor/Text:	Expertel, Inc.
Compositor/Tables:	TriStar Graphics
Text/Display:	Linotron 202 Palatino
Printer:	Braun-Brumfield, Inc.
Binder:	Braun-Brumfield, Inc.